OWNED

In this compelling examination of the intersection of smart technology and the law, Joshua Fairfield explains the crisis of digital ownership – how and why we no longer control our smartphones or software-enabled devices, which are effectively owned by software and content companies. In two years, we will not own our "smart" televisions, which will also be used by advertisers to listen in to our living rooms. In the coming decade, if we do not take back our ownership rights, the same will be said of our self-driving cars and software-enabled homes. We risk becoming digital peasants, owned by software and advertising companies, not to mention overreaching governments. *Owned* should be read by anyone wanting to know more about the loss of our property rights, the implications for our privacy rights, and how we can regain control of both.

Joshua A. T. Fairfield is a Professor of Law at Washington and Lee University. He is an internationally recognized law and technology scholar of digital property, electronic contract, big data privacy, and virtual communities. He has published articles in top law journals, and his work has appeared in the *New York Times*, *Forbes*, and the *Financial Times*. He is a Fulbright grant recipient and member of the American Law Institute.

Owned

PROPERTY, PRIVACY, AND THE
NEW DIGITAL SERFDOM

JOSHUA A. T. FAIRFIELD
Washington and Lee University School of Law

CAMBRIDGE
UNIVERSITY PRESS

University Printing House, Cambridge CB2 8BS, United Kingdom

One Liberty Plaza, 20th Floor, New York, NY 10006, USA

477 Williamstown Road, Port Melbourne, VIC 3207, Australia

314-321, 3rd Floor, Plot 3, Splendor Forum, Jasola District Centre, New Delhi - 110025, India

79 Anson Road, #06-04/06, Singapore 079906

Cambridge University Press is part of the University of Cambridge.

It furthers the University's mission by disseminating knowledge in the pursuit of
education, learning and research at the highest international levels of excellence.

www.cambridge.org
Information on this title: www.cambridge.org/9781107159358
DOI: 10.1017/9781316671467

First published 2017
Reprinted 2017

Printed in the United Kingdom by Clays, St Ives plc

A catalogue record for this publication is available from the British Library

ISBN 978-1-107-15935-8 Hardback
ISBN 978-1-316-61220-0 Paperback

Cambridge University Press has no responsibility for the persistence or accuracy
of URLs for external or third-party internet websites referred to in this publication,
and does not guarantee that any content on such websites is, or will remain,
accurate or appropriate.

To Christine, Mary, Maggie, Hannah, and Grace

Contents

Acknowledgments

This book is the result of many productive conversations over several years. I particularly appreciate the editorial guidance of Matt Gallaway and Sara Versluis. I am also deeply indebted to those who helped me with drafts, including but not limited to: Elliot Alderman, Samuel Arbesman, Jane Bambauer, Kiel Brennan-Marquez, Christopher Bruner, Ryan Calo, Ted Castronova, Catherine Christopher, Bryan Choi, Danielle Citron, Brett Frischmann, James Grimmelmann, Woodrow Hartzog, Chris Jay Hoofnagle, Gus Hurwitz, Margaret Hu, Timothy Jost, Margot Kaminsky, Tim MacDonnell, William McGeveran, Michael Madison, Juliet Moringiello, Christina Mulligan, Helen Nissenbaum, Christopher Odinet, Aaron Perzanowski, Jason Rantanen, Joel Reidenberg, Doug Rendleman, Matthew Sag, Andrew Selbst, Jason Schultz, Kristian Stout, Katherine Strandberg, David Thaw, and Ari Waldman. I am also indebted to the participants and discussants at many conferences and events, including Internet Works in Progress, the ILI / ISP Joint Conference at the Intersection of Privacy and Property, the University of Minnesota Faculty Workshop Series, Privacy Law Scholars, and the Telecommunications Research Policy Conference. Finally, I owe a debt of gratitude to my research assistants Daniel Martin and Paul Keith for their tireless research and support in the preparation of the manuscript, and Jacob Lester for copyediting suggestions. I appreciate financial support from the Frances Lewis Law Center at Washington and Lee University School of Law.

1

Introduction

There is a myth – perhaps you saw a version of it in the movie *Braveheart* – told about the abuses of feudal lords, about the *droit du seigneur* or *ius primae noctis*: the "right of the lord" or the "right of the first night." A feudal lord supposedly had the right to sexual relations with the bride of a newly married peasant couple. The lord's power over the land on which his tenants lived and worked extended, in this story, to the power to interfere in even the most intimate and personal moments of a couple's lives. The story is just a myth – there is no record of the *ius primae noctis* being exercised in medieval times. It seems to have developed later as a popular and salacious description of the boundless arrogance and power of feudal lords over every detail of the lives of those who lived on their land.

But *this* is no myth: on September 13, 2016, as I was finishing this book, the *Chicago Tribune* reported that a class action lawsuit had been filed on behalf of tens of thousands of people against the makers of WeVibe, a popular couples' erotic massage device.[1] WeVibe was discovered to have been extracting the most intimate data possible from the device: date and time of each use, level of vibration intensity, vibration mode or pattern selection, even the temperature of the device and the email address of the user. The data were apparently collected for purposes of market research. The manufacturer of WeVibe – a company called Standard Innovation – was able to do this as a technical matter because the device was web-enabled, controlled wirelessly by a smartphone application, called We-Connect. Standard Innovation buried software in the device that communicated the intimate details to We-Connect, and We-Connect then secretly forwarded the details to SI's own servers. SI claimed the

---

[1] *See* Robert Channick, *Lawsuit Claims Smartphone-Enabled Massage Device Violated Privacy*, CHI. TRIB. (Sept. 13, 2016, 1:41 PM), http://www.chicagotribune.com/business/ct-vibrator-app-lawsuit-0914-biz-20160913-story.html.

legal right to do this because of terms hidden deep within the app's software license. Never mind that no one reads such terms, or that no one could understand them even if they did. Standard Innovation believed that merely by installing and using its app, users agreed to permit the company to intrude and spy on communications between themselves and their lovers.

This is digital *ius primae noctis*. With all of the brazen arrogance of a digital feudal lord toward his peasantry, SI felt justified in conducting the most gross invasions of privacy and property, in surveilling the most intimate moments between its customers, merely because of the power it holds as the owner of the intellectual property embedded in the device, and as the drafter of clauses buried deep within its license agreement.

Despite the surface flash of a life enhanced by new technologies, the laws and logic that undergird it are made of old and problematic material drawn from a time when many owned little and a few controlled much. The digital and smart devices that surround us are legion, but we do not truly own or control them; the companies that wrote the software inside do.[2] Intellectual property and contract law have crowded out everyday property ownership.

As I describe in this book, with every new push of software into everyday life, the owners of intellectual property assert more control over the daily lives of people who use their products.[3] Smart televisions report on the conversations of people who are merely standing within earshot.[4] Smartphones report the real-world location of users to manufacturers, operating system designers, and app providers.[5] The supposed owner often has less say in what a device or product is doing than does its manufacturer. The "owner" is a source of data to be harvested. As one commentator put it, many social networks and

[2] *See, e.g., PLAYSTATION®4 SYSTEM SOFTWARE LICENSE AGREEMENT (Version 1.1)*, Sony Comput. Ent. Inc. (2015), http://www.scei.co.jp/ps4-eula/ps4_eula_en.html ("All rights to use [the PS4] System Software are granted by license only, and you are not granted any ownership rights or interests in System Software."). The PS4 agreement further provides: "If SCE determines that you have violated this Agreement's terms, SCE may itself or may procure the taking of any action to protect its interests such as disabling access to or use of some or all System Software . . . or reliance on any other remedial efforts as reasonably necessary to prevent the use of modified or unpermitted use of System Software." *Id.*

[3] *See generally* Joshua A.T. Fairfield, *Mixed Reality: How the Laws of Virtual Worlds Govern Everyday Life*, 27 Berkeley Tech. L.J. 55 (2012).

[4] *See* Dave Lewis, *Is Your TV Spying on You?*, Forbes (Feb. 10, 2015), http://www.forbes.com/sites/davelewis/2015/02/10/is-your-tv-spying-on-you (noting that Samsung's privacy policy provides that "when you watch a video or access applications or content provided by a third-party, that provider may collect or receive information about your SmartTV . . . and your use of the application or service," and that "Samsung is not responsible").

[5] *See* J.D. Harrison, *Companies Know Where You Went Online. Now, They Can Follow You Around in Real Life*, Wash. Post (Apr. 10, 2015), https://www.washingtonpost.com/news/on-small-business/wp/2015/04/10/companies-know-where-you-went-online-now-they-can-follow-you-around-in-real-life-too (discussing businesses' use of location-based data analytics).

search engines "have turned into nothing more than the 21st century's mining companies, constantly mining for the next nugget of gold."[6]

We own and control fewer and fewer of the products that we must use to function in modern society. Many computing devices (iPads, for instance) run only those programs approved by the device seller. We cannot even tell our devices not to reveal our personal data.[7] The only guaranteed way to stop a smartphone from reporting on our web searches, web traffic, real-world location, texts, and surrounding ambient sounds and sights is to pull out its battery or not to carry one. This is an untenable position in an information-age society. In the United States alone, two-thirds of Americans own a smartphone and use it as "a key entry point to the online world."[8]

To be clear, I am no Luddite. Technology itself is not the problem. The problem is when our devices serve the companies who made them rather than the people who purchased them. And as our bridges and our bodies, our school buses and our supermarkets, our keychains and our grills become colonized with digital connections and capabilities – an infrastructure of networked sensors, software, electronics, and apps otherwise known as the Internet of Things – the question of control becomes only more significant.

To fix this, we must re-establish control of our digital and smart property at the most basic level. We must restore everyday property ownership. If we do not take back our ownership rights from software companies and overreaching governments, we will become digital peasants, only able to use our smart devices, our homes, our cars, and even our own software-enabled medical implants purely at the whim of others. Like the serfs of feudal Europe who lacked rights in the land they worked, without digital property rights, we aren't owners – we're owned.

The act of owning works considerable social magic. Private property performs an important role in balancing the parts that citizen, corporation, and state play in relation to one another in modern society.[9] Well-defined property rights spur investment. By controlling resources, owners may control their

---

[6] Henk Campher, *Data Mining: The Consumer Becoming the Consumed*, HUFFINGTON POST (Oct. 8, 2014), http://www.huffingtonpost.com/henk-campher/data-mining-the-consumer-_b_5949580.html.

[7] *See* Scott Thurm & Yukari Iwatani Kane, *Your Apps Are Watching You*, WALL STREET J. (Dec. 17, 2010), http://www.wsj.com/articles/SB10001424052748704694004576020083703574602 (noting that an investigation "showed that 56 [apps] transmitted the phone's unique device ID to other companies without users' awareness or consent").

[8] *See* Aaron Smith, *U.S. Smartphone Use in 2015*, PEW RES. CTR. (Apr. 1, 2015), http://www.pewinternet.org/2015/04/01/us-smartphone-use-in-2015.

[9] *See, e.g.*, Benjamin Powell, *Private Property Rights, Economic Freedom, and Well Being* 1 (Mercatus Ctr. at George Mason Univ., Working Paper No. 19, 2003), http://mercatus.org/sites/default/files/Private-Property-Rights-Economic-Freedom-and-Well-Being.pdf ("Observation of the countries around the world also indicates that those countries with an institutional

own destinies (or at least attempt to do so). Furthermore, owners can order their surroundings to their liking by modifying their property. An owner might repaint the walls of her room bright neon green. She might soup up the engine of her truck to make it less fuel-efficient but more powerful. She might plant a vegetable garden on her land, if she desires carrots, or plant flowers, if she decides otherwise. In other words, the control over surroundings that basic ownership supplies is linked to the democratic value of self-determination. There are other ways to provide this self-determination and control, to be sure – for example, with a focus on human rights.[10] But those systems cannot entirely replace simple, robust, old-fashioned ownership.

Property also works economic magic. Purchasing property is in many cases like taking money out of one's left pocket only to have it reappear in the right. Consider the act of buying and owning a house: the purchaser pays a monthly mortgage payment but, ideally, also builds equity in the house, which can be drawn upon in time of need. Yet new forms of property, such as Kindle e-books, come in forms that do not build or retain wealth; they cannot be resold.[11] Worse still, once consumers have built up libraries of Kindle e-books, they are subject to lock-in effects: if consumers shift to another device or service, they cannot take their library with them.[12]

These may seem like trivial things – who really counts the value of her book collection in her overall wealth anyway? – but software governance and the intellectual property rules that accompany them are infiltrating more economically important purchases, like houses, cars, and industrial equipment.[13] If those assets cannot be owned, the primary forms of wealth held by a large

environment of secure property rights and high degrees of economic freedom have achieved higher levels of the various measures of human well being.").

[10] *See* G.A. Res. 1514 (XV) (Dec. 14, 1960) ("All peoples have the right to self-determination; by virtue of that right they freely determine their political status and freely pursue their economic, social and cultural development.").

[11] *See, e.g., Kindle Store Terms of Use*, AMAZON (last updated Mar. 15, 2016), http://www.amazon .com/gp/help/customer/display.html?nodeId=201014950 ("Unless specifically indicated otherwise, you may not sell, rent, lease, distribute, broadcast, sublicense, or otherwise assign any rights to the Kindle Content or any portion of it to any third party, and you may not remove or modify any proprietary notices or labels on the Kindle Content.").

[12] In other words, those who invest in their Kindle e-book library are stuck using Kindle, even if at some later date they would prefer to use another e-book management system. *See* Dan Costa, *Nook, Kindle and the Perils of Lock-in*, PC MAG. (June 1, 2011), http://www.pcmag.com/ article2/0,2817,2386266,00.asp (noting that lock-in "makes a customer dependent on a vendor for products and services, unable to use another vendor without substantial switching costs.").

[13] One notable example, explored further in later chapters, is tractors, which "are increasingly run by computer software." Laura Sydell, *DIY Tractor Repair Runs Afoul of Copyright Law*, NPR (Aug. 17, 2015), http://www.npr.org/sections/alltechconsidered/2015/08/17/ 432601480/diy-tractor-repair-runs-afoul-of-copyright-law.

section of the population will simply vanish. What would happen if the rules that govern a smartphone (for example, you cannot modify the phone's software without hacking it; cannot effectively block surveillance; and must submit to having your information given to hundreds of advertisers) become the rules that govern your software-enhanced self-driving car or smart house?

The future of basic ownership rights in digital and smart property is uncertain and precarious because of two historical developments. First, internet technologies created an unprecedented ability to copy intellectual property – file sharing services spread pirated music like wildfire and fueled the music industry's fears for its own future[14] – before they created the ability to track and verify individual copies of electronic information.[15] In the absence of a company's ability to ascertain that Book A is actually John's book, and not merely a book that John has instantly and cheaply copied from Mary, intellectual property owners instituted a range of command-and-control powers in their software. Thanks to subsequent federal legislation, those controls came to be backed by a host of incredibly strong legal powers.[16]

This gave rise to both opportunism and missed opportunities. Companies opportunistically used these powers not just to fight piracy but also to lock owners out of their own property. Meanwhile, courts missed the opportunity to adapt the law of traditional ownership – property law – to new digital assets and smart property. The reasons for this are complex, but one consistent issue is that courts have struggled to define traditional property interests in intangibles – things that you cannot touch, weigh, or feel – while also honoring intellectual property concerns. This left a void in the law, a void filled by overextended intellectual property law, which further strengthened the power of companies to control consumers' property. What is needed – and what I attempt to provide in this book – is not merely an argument for reining in overreaching intellectual property law, but the development of a real alternative: a convincing theory of intangible property that courts can use to support consumers' claims of ownership.

The second development affecting the future of ownership rights was similar but distinct. Initially, consumers were not used to paying for internet-based

[14] *See* Eduardo Porter, *The Perpetual War: Pirates and Creators*, N.Y. TIMES (Feb. 4, 2012), http://www.nytimes.com/2012/02/05/opinion/sunday/perpetual-war-digital-pirates-and-creators.html.

[15] *See generally* Bill D. Herman, *A Political History of DRM and Related Copyright Debates, 1987–2012*, 14 YALE J. L. & TECH. 162 (2012) (providing a history of DRM and copyright).

[16] *See, e.g.*, *The Pros, Cons, and Future of DRM*, CBC NEWS (Aug. 7, 2009), http://www.cbc.ca/news/technology/the-pros-cons-and-future-of-drm-1.785237 (noting an incident where "Amazon used its DRM technology to remotely delete copies of George Orwell's 1984 and Animal Farm novels from users' Kindle e-book readers without their knowledge or consent").

services.[17] Business models of all kinds had to adapt to find new income streams. Newspapers were forced to rethink their operations and revenue structures because online users were used to getting content for free.[18] Likewise, software providers needed a revenue model that circumvented internet users' refusal to pay for content that they could obtain – usually illegally, but with some degree of safety – for nothing.[19] So software providers monetized information about their consumers by surreptitiously monitoring everything their users typed, clicked, or did, and selling that information to advertisers, who could use it to extract more and often costlier deals from their customers.

Information about consumers became the currency of the internet, and commercial surveillance became its funding model.[20] User information was increasingly gathered by software embedded first in internet websites,[21] and later into the very devices that consumers purchased to access and use internet technologies.[22] That information could then be monetized through targeted behavioral advertising.[23] By watching everything a consumer did, an advertiser could make enough enhanced revenue through targeted sales that it was willing to provide the relevant software (say, the operating system for a mobile smartphone) at a steep discount – or subsidize it for software companies. This is how Facebook monetized its services.[24] By knowing everything about the consumer, companies could charge consumers more if they were likely to pay more (Mac users pay more for hotel rooms booked online[25]), or offer

[17] *See* Bruce Schneier, Data and Goliath: The Hidden Battles to Collect Your Data and Control Your World 50 (W.W. Norton and Company 2015) ("Before 1993, the Internet was entirely noncommercial, and free became the online norm.").

[18] *See* Rachel Smolkin, *Adapt or Die*, Am. Journalism Rev. (June 2006), http://www.ajrarchive .org/Article.asp?id=4111 (discussing the trend of newspapers transforming "from newspaper companies to information companies" in the mid-2000s due to more prevalent internet usage).

[19] *See, e.g.,* Schneier, *supra* note 17, at 48 (noting that even the free game Angry Birds "collected location data").

[20] *See id.* at 49 (describing "[s]urveillance" as "the business model of the Internet").

[21] *See id.* at 48–49 (discussing the history of "third-party cookie[s] . . . tracking web users across many different sites" and noting that, based on 2010 data, even "a seemingly innocuous site like Dictionary.com installed over 200 tracking cookies on your browser when you visited").

[22] *See id.* at 59 (discussing "the rise of user devices that are managed closely by their vendors").

[23] *See id.* at 53–56 (discussing the use of "commercial surveillance data" in targeted advertising).

[24] *See* Geoffrey A. Fowler, *What You Can Do About Facebook Tracking*, Wall Street J. (Aug. 25, 2014), http://www.wsj.com/articles/what-you-can-do-about-facebook-tracking-1407263246 ("[Facebook's] main business is selling marketers access to you, but it does this without telling them who you are.").

[25] *See* Dana Mattioli, *On Orbitz, Mac Users Steered to Pricier Hotels*, Wall Street J. (Aug. 23, 2012), http://www.wsj.com/articles/SB10001424052702304458604577488822667325882 ("Orbitz Worldwide Inc. has found that people who use Apple Inc.'s Mac computers spend as much as 30% more a night on hotels, so the online travel agency is starting to show them different, and sometimes costlier, travel options than Windows visitors see.").

consumers deals that they would be unlikely to resist (comparison shoppers pay more for airfare because their browser histories indicate they are very interested in certain flights[26]). The consumer therefore does not pay directly for use of internet technologies, but pays by being surveilled to such an extent that she may engage in an increased number of costlier deals than would have been the case had she not been subject to surveillance by her own devices.

What began as simple exchange – information for valuable goods and services – has escalated to exploitation. A 2014 Pew survey indicates that 91 percent of respondents felt that they have lost control over what information is gathered, how it is gathered, to whom that information is revealed, how long that information may be used, and how far the information can travel.[27] The combination of loss of control over our devices and exploitation of the data our devices gather about us could yield a grim future, one in which there is no escape from the many devices that each person carries with them, or that other people carry, or that lie in wait wherever we go in an increasingly ubiquitous computing environment.

Escaping a network of integrated things designed from the ground up to leak information about their supposed owners will not be easy. Steering the Internet of Things away from its anticipated near-future as a distributed, mobile, and pervasive surveillance network will take some doing. But, as I argue in this book, escape is possible. Technologists have created tools to help handle the twin problems of piracy and payment that have caused intellectual property owners to assert such control over networked devices.[28] It is now possible to have a reasonable economy not predominantly based on exploitation of consumer information.

There is a narrow temporal window that is rapidly closing. Privacy is a scarce and precious social value. As our personal information becomes increasingly digitized, there is a growing concern not just about who collects our data, but what they collect.[29] We are learning helplessness in the face of rampant spying

---

[26] *See* Annie Lowrey, *How Online Retailers Stay a Step Ahead of Comparison Shoppers*, WASH. POST (Dec. 11, 2010, 5:32 PM), http://www.washingtonpost.com/wp-dyn/content/article/2010/12/11/AR2010121102435.html (explaining the process behind the "experience of buying a plane ticket through a portal such as Kayak, then seeing the final price jump $10 or $40 at check out").

[27] Mary Madden, *Public Perceptions of Privacy and Security in the Post-Snowden Era*, PEW RES. CTR. (Nov. 12, 2014), http://www.pewinternet.org/2014/11/12/public-privacy-perceptions.

[28] Cryptographic ledgers, for example, make it possible to transfer a specific single copy of digital property. This recording system will be further explained in Chapter 7.

[29] *See* Mary Madden & Lee Raine, *Americans' Attitudes About Privacy, Security and Surveillance*, PEW RES. CTR. (May 20, 2015), http://www.pewinternet.org/2015/05/20/americans-attitudes-about-privacy-security-and-surveillance ("90% of adults say that controlling what information

by the devices that surround us. We value privacy highly – in a recent survey, 93 percent of adults said that being in control of who can get information about them is important.[30] But as we realize our efforts to procure privacy are costly and fruitless, we may learn to stop trying.[31] This will cause further erosion – not of our desire for privacy, but of our efforts to obtain it or pay for it. If society truly teaches its citizens that the devices they own will inevitably be controlled not by them, but by corporations and government, then citizens will stop investing in the few technologies, devices, and services that attempt to provide even some small amount of control.

What is needed is an escape mechanism – a way out of the trap of device-based surveillance. This book proposes that such an escape would have four necessary components. They are simple extensions of the property rights that people have traditionally enjoyed over their possessions. First, people have the right to modify their own property.[32] Second, they can sell it to others, free and clear, when they are done with it. Third, they can use it and enjoy it free from the interference of others.[33] Fourth, they can exclude others from using it without their consent.[34] These four basic rights that all of us have over our ordinary property – the right to modify, the right to sell, the right to use, and the right to exclude others – are the foundation of this book's attempt to create a metaphorical escape button for an Internet of Things that overrides personal control and ownership.

In the online and digital landscape – a terrain increasingly synonymous with the "real" one – these traditional rights of ownership translate into the rights to hack, sell, run, and ban. Briefly, people must first be able to control, modify, and reprogram their devices: a "right to hack." People must be legally and technologically enabled to modify, destroy, reprogram, rework, upgrade, and change their devices to fit their own needs. There is growing support for this right: "jailbreaking" your iPhone or rooting your smartphone are necessary and popular actions. In fact, in 2015 the U.S. government granted consumers

---

is collected about them is important; 65% think it is 'very important,' while only 25% say it is 'somewhat important.'").

[30] *See id.* ("93% of adults say that being in control of who can get information about them is important; 74% feel this is 'very important,' while 19% say it is 'somewhat important.'").

[31] *See* SCHNEIER, *supra* note 17, at 59–61 (discussing the inability of consumers to resist the privacy-invading rules set by technology vendors).

[32] *See* 63C AM. JUR. 2D PROP. § 1 (2008) ("Ownership of property implies the right of possession and control.").

[33] *See id.* ("Generally, the common law concept of 'property' refers to the right and interest that a person has in an object, which extends beyond ownership and possession to include the lawful, unrestricted right of use, enjoyment, and disposal of the object.").

[34] *See id.* (noting that "the right to exclude persons is a fundamental aspect of private property ownership").

the right to jailbreak their smartphones, despite Apple's disapproval of the practice.[35] Intellectual property interests that obstruct the right to hack must give way. People must be able to modify their devices to stop them from leaking data to every app and service provider, should they wish to do so. Companies' promises about how they use our data are intentionally vague and filled with weasel words. The only way to ensure data security is to block the data flows at our end, on our own devices.

Second, I propose a "right to sell." A primary characteristic of property is that it can be sold to someone else. Copyright holders and digital service providers want to destroy markets for used goods so that they can make more sales. If Apple were to get rid of CDs on eBay, it could sell more music. Amazon does not want you selling your used Audible recordings or e-books when you are done with them: that is a sale it does not get. But secondary markets are good for consumers, and are well-established mechanisms for the turnover of property. We buy used goods on eBay because prices are lower. And, of course, consumers benefit doubly from consumer-to-consumer sales, because one consumer is happy to get rid of her old junk, and another is happy to get a great deal on something that is (to her) new and perhaps unavailable elsewhere.

Letting consumers sell their digital assets also impedes the lock-in effect. If you don't like one service, you should be able to sell your account and go elsewhere, just as if you sold your house in a gated community with an overly intrusive homeowners' association. You do not have to burn down your house to move; even the most meddlesome HOA does not have the capacity to forbid the sale of the property you own under its umbrella. In the same way, you should not have to delete your account, Audible downloads, MP3s, software, or e-books, or consign them to the digital dustbin; you could simply get some of your money back out by selling them to someone else. The right to sell protects consumers from attractive-looking offers that turn out poorly, or lets them free up money from things they no longer need.

Third, we must have the right to use our own property as we see fit, to run whatever code we like: a "right to run." Apple controls which software can run on its devices.[36] Often this protects customers from threats – invasive third

---

[35] *See* Andrea Peterson, *New iOS Malware Should Make You Think Twice About Jailbreaking Your iPhone*, WASH. POST (Sept. 1, 2015), http://www.washingtonpost.com/news/the-switch/wp/2015/09/01/new-ios-malware-should-make-you-think-twice-about-jailbreaking-your-iphone (noting that "the Librarian of Congress . . . approved an exception to the Digital Millennium Copyright Act, allowing consumers to jailbreak their smartphones," but that "Apple discourages the practice").

[36] *See id.* ("Apple keeps tight control over what apps are allowed on iPhones, running basic security tests before allowing them to be downloaded.").

parties, for example[37] – but just as often it locks the customer into running only programs approved by Apple, created by vendors who give Apple a cut and do not compete with Apple in its core business interests.[38] Citizens must have rights in software-enhanced and digital property that do not vanish at the sole discretion of intellectual property rightsholders.

Fourth and finally, we must be able to exclude intruding data collectors from our property.[39] An endless string of user agreements, intentionally complicated privacy controls, privacy policies that do not protect privacy, and, above all, devices that have been designed to leak information about the user at every level – hardware, firmware, operating system, user interface, and over-the-wire communication – make it infeasible for users to exercise their basic option to exclude. Yet the right to exclude is the most basic property right of all.[40] It is the right to stop other people from using property against the owner's wishes, or in the case of smart property, against the owner herself. I propose a "right to ban," to give full force and effect to users' rights to exclude companies who would subvert users' property to their own purposes. By giving users the legally enforceable right to say no to intrusion, law would effectively give them the right to exclude.

Sir William Blackstone, the giant of the common law, wrote: "There is nothing which so generally strikes the imagination, and engages the affections of mankind, as the right of property; or that sole and despotic dominion which one man claims and exercises over the external things of the world, in total exclusion of the right of any other individual in the universe."[41] I have always thought the second part of that quote got too much play. Our property is not ours to do with as we absolutely please. I cannot erect a

---

[37] *See* David Goldman, *Apple Bans Hundreds of iPhone Apps That Secretly Gathered Personal Info*, CNN (Oct. 19, 2015), http://money.cnn.com/2015/10/19/technology/apple-app-store (noting that Apple removed from its app store a number of apps which "gathered information about the people who downloaded the apps, including their email addresses and iPhone serial numbers").

[38] *See* Kushal Dave, *Apple's App Store Review Process Is Hurting Users, but We're Not Allowed to Talk About It*, Bus. Insider (Apr. 12, 2015), http://www.businessinsider.com/apples-app-store-review-process-is-hurting-users-but-were-not-allowed-to-talk-about-it-2015-4 ("Apple prohibits in-app purchases it can't get its 30% cut of, leading to a situation where users cannot buy books in their Kindle app or videos in their YouTube app or comics in their comics app, even though they can on Android. In the early days of the app store, Apple rejected apps just for competing with their own built-in apps.").

[39] *See* Schneier, *supra* note 17, at 59–61 (discussing the difficulty of preventing unwanted data collection).

[40] *See* 63C Am. Jur. 2d Prop. § 1 (2008) ("The right to exclude others, as well as their property, is one of the most essential sticks in the bundle of rights that are commonly characterized as property.").

[41] 2 William Blackstone, Commentaries *2.

hot pink three-story monument to poor taste on my land without the home-owners' association coming knocking. But the first part of the quote is very important. Property fires our imaginations. When people take it away, we react badly. We recognize instinctively that property represents our ability to control the world around us. As cyberlaw expert and professor Bryan Choi once remarked to me at a conference: "Property is an intuition. It is an emotion."

This book is an attempt to tap the emotion of property, and to then channel that emotion through careful analysis of the current legal state of affairs surrounding the Internet of Things. Its goal is to engage our imaginations, and to explain how we are losing control over the world around us as our property interests are eroded. In a sense, the failure of property online is a failure of the legal imagination. Courts have failed to imagine how we can own Bitcoins, magic swords, MP3s, smartphones, autonomous cars, or drones the same way that we own land, houses, or the money in our wallets. By tapping the intuitions of property we can help courts broaden their imaginations, and we can also see more clearly what is happening to us as our right to control our own smart devices and digital property fades.

By no means are property rules a magic cure. Property is not good or desirable in and of itself. Good property rules let humans work together; they make cooperation easier. Bad property rules reduce people to the level of commodities and prepare resources for easy theft by the powerful and unscrupulous. So here is the guiding principle for this exploration of property rules in a digital age: property rules should be measured by a human yardstick. Where they do not make human lives better, where they do not expand the range of possibilities for what humans can perform, they should be reformed. Property rules are a concession to essential human individuality, a method for tricking groups into working together by securing participants some part in the fruits of collaboration. That human individualism can bleed over into selfishness, and the stain of that selfishness can tarnish property discussions. Selfishness is the obstacle property helps to circumnavigate, not the end goal of its efforts. This book is not a paean to property; it is an attempt to reform property rules so that they better serve human interests in the era of the Internet of Things.

Life in the digital age does not require a regression into a time when individuals – we the people – have little or no control of the resources around them. The laws currently governing smartphones do not have to become the laws governing drones and voice-reading television sets. It is not set in stone that companies and governments will invade our devices at their whim. It is possible to avoid a future in which we are digital serfs, owning no digital property and using our devices only as long as we follow others' rules. We can return to normalcy, where we have the right to do as we wish with what is ours and to keep others from spying on us by using our own property against us. But if we don't want to get owned, we are going to have to do something about it.

2

The Death of Property

Property means different things to different people, but in a very brief sense, it is a way of allocating scarce resources, to help us avoid (some, though not nearly enough) fights over who owns what. This is my cookie, that is yours. Property also gives us resources and tools to do what we want to do in the world: survive, thrive, build homes, create, innovate, live in community, and find space to be alone. Property has been traditionally honored because it helps us maintain independence, build general welfare, and construct a home, a context, an identity.

But in the digital world, this understanding of property is unraveling. Something happened when traditional property ownership encountered the intangibility and centralization of the internet and digital and information technologies. Property ownership as we know it is under attack and fading fast.

The problem is, property rules guide the flow of power over tools and resources. They can create a world in which a few people own everything and use that ownership to control everyone else, or they can create a world in which many of us can do a whole lot with the plentiful tools and resources we own. One system is feudal: the king owns everything, a few dukes and barons manage big chunks of the king's land, and everyone else is an underling at best, a serf at worst. The other system is free: individuals can, within reasonable restraints, do as they wish with their own resources and tools. The feudal system is centralized. The free system is decentralized. The feudal system relies on a few rich and many poor. The free system relies on many people having enough. The feudal system relies on command and control. The free system relies on, well, freedom, backed by good rules and reasonable legal limits to handle disputes between neighbors.

If you take nothing else from this chapter – or even this book – take this: the Internet of Things and digital property ownership systems are being built on the old feudal model. The free model is in serious trouble. To get a handle on the current crisis in ownership, we will need to dig into what property has traditionally meant, what went wrong when property went digital, and why it is such a problem that software and content firms now rule the digital landscape like feudal lords.

WHAT IS PROPERTY?

Before we can understand the threats to traditional property ownership, it is helpful to have an understanding of property and property law. Property law is an evolving concept, although there are some common understandings of property both historically and today. This section first defines property as it is understood today and then examines different approaches we have used to understand property law. I then turn to the specific kinds of new property – digital and smart products – discussed in this book, and examine how property law develops alongside technology.

A Property Primer

Property law is a system for allocating resources. It has two dimensions. One is vertical, concerning relations between citizen, municipality, and state, and one is horizontal, dealing with questions between people. The question of who gets to decide whether I can build a shed on my land is vertical, in that my local homeowners' association, township, state, or even federal regulation decides what I can build. The question of who can trespass on my land is horizontal, in that my neighbors and I need to work out if their sheep can graze on my lawn.

The vertical axis of property is coercive. If the township says I cannot build my thirty-foot statue of Darth Vader in my backyard, then I cannot. The horizontal axis of property is generally not coercive. If my neighbor wants to block me from building my statue, he must buy my property from me, or buy one portion of the rights to develop the land from me and record that right with my deed. He may not act unilaterally and take my property. Thus, scholars call a rule a "property rule" when the law requires parties to come to agreement over how the resource should be used, and a "liability rule" when one party can just act first and beg forgiveness (or pay compensation) later.[1] Patents provide a good example to illustrate this distinction. Consider two companies, Aperture Science and Black Mesa. Aperture Science holds a

---

[1] *See* Guido Calabresi & A. Douglas Melamed, *Property Rules, Liability Rules, and Inalienability: One View of the Cathedral*, 85 HARV. L. REV. 1089, 1092 (1972) (discussing how entitlements are protected by property rules and liability rules).

patent. Black Mesa is infringing that patent. If Aperture Science sues Black Mesa, the "property rule" outcome is for the court to order Black Mesa to stop. Black Mesa must figure out some sort of agreement with Aperture Science if it wants to use the patent. On the other hand, the "liability rule" outcome is for the court to order Black Mesa to pay Aperture compensation.[2] In that sense, Black Mesa gets to use Aperture's patent, as long as Black Mesa is willing to pay the damages. It's a court-ordered forced license of Aperture's patent.

Property rules determine the allocation of resources not just between A and B, but everyone else as well. If you and I sign a contract, nobody else is involved. But if I sell you land, everyone else must abide by that decision. Our private deal controls the rights of everyone else. If you sell me a popular swimming hole, and I post a no-trespassing sign, the people you have always let swim there must now stay out.

Owners have traditionally had certain rights over their property, a group of rights sometimes called the "bundle of sticks."[3] Imagine that you buy a house. You have the right to control who makes use of the land, to exclude others, to use and occupy it, to sell it, and even to destroy it.[4] Historically, the power to exclude has been the most well-developed of these rights.[5] Several of the other powers derive from it. For example, the power to destroy can be described as the ultimate exclusion: excluding everyone from enjoying the property, including the owner. When we use the words *control, exclude, use, enjoy, modify, sell, destroy*, we are not just using regular verbs but describing core functions of property that have been long associated with the powers of ownership.

Out of this bundle of sticks, I will focus on the owner's power of control. Our control of our own devices and smart property is particularly under assault. We cannot control the software that manufacturers load onto our devices; we cannot control our own smart property (for example, a networked car can be

---

[2] *See, e.g.,* Ebay, Inc. v. MercExchange, L.L.C., 547 U.S. 388, 391 (2006) ("According to well-established principles of equity, a plaintiff seeking a permanent injunction must satisfy [among other things] . . . that remedies available at law, such as monetary damages, are inadequate to compensate for that injury.")

[3] *See, e.g.,* United States v. Craft, 535 U.S. 274, 278–84 (2002) (explaining the "bundle of sticks" metaphor for property rights).

[4] *See, e.g.,* Eyerman v. Mercantile Trust Co., N.A., 524 S.W.2d 210, 217–18 (Mo. Ct. App. 1975) (declining to uphold a provision in a will directing the executor to destroy the testator's house); *see generally* Lior Strahilevitz, *The Right to Destroy*, 114 YALE L.J. 781 (2005) (providing an overview of the right to destroy).

[5] *See* Dolan v. City of Tigard, 512 U.S. 374, 393 (1994) (observing that the "right to exclude others is 'one of the most essential sticks in the bundle of rights that are commonly characterized as property'" (quoting Kaiser Aetna v. United States, 444 U.S. 164, 176 (1979))).

remotely shut down without the owner's consent); we cannot control who or what extracts our personal information from our devices; we cannot control where our digital property is stored, or whether our e-books will even continue to exist if Amazon decides to delete them. Part of control is a negative right. The ability to control what goes on in and on and through our property is a function of our ability to exclude others. If they do not do what we want, we kick them out. But there is more to it than that. We do not buy property just to kick others off it. We buy it so we can control it – protect it from others, use it ourselves, and, if we permit them to, determine how others use it. So control has a positive aspect as well: if we own land, we want to control what is planted on it. If we own a house, we want to control what color it is painted. If we own a car, we want to control when the brakes are serviced, and who does the servicing. And when we own smart devices, we want to control who does what on them.

Defining Smart, Digital, and Traditional Property

Smart property is software-enhanced real property (land, houses) or personal property (cars, smartphones). The tension between ownership of the device and the residual power of the creator of the software embedded in the device spawns most of the conflicts we will discuss. Consumers own their devices, but they do not own the software inside them. That creates a conflict of ownership between the owner of the device and the owner of the software. It is as if the dealer sold you a car, but retained ownership of the motor. This overlap between property rights causes a conflict because you, as owner of the device, may wish to do something that the manufacturer, as owner of the intellectual property inside it, wishes to prevent you from doing. Or, worse, the manufacturer may wish to use its power over software embedded in your device to make it do things against your will. It is as if your car had a built-in backseat driver, one that constantly pulled you off the road to go to McDonald's, or drove you to WalMart instead of Target when you were not looking.[6]

Digital property is slightly different. Digital property refers to your ownership rights (which are admittedly small) in digital objects, like the game, movie,

---

[6] *See, e.g.*, Kushal Dave, *Apple's App Store Review Process Is Hurting Users, but We're Not Allowed to Talk About It*, Bus. Insider (Apr. 12, 2015), http://www.businessinsider.com/apples-app-store-review-process-is-hurting-users-but-were-not-allowed-to-talk-about-it-2015-4 ("Imagine buying a car that refused to drive to strip clubs, or a TV that refused to show Fox News. Now recognize we accept this behavior from a product with 40% market share. . . . We have a government, we have parents, we have the ability to vote with our feet, but Apple supercedes all of that in the name of protecting users.").

book, or music that you have purchased and downloaded. Digital property can be as new and strange as a Bitcoin or a magical sword in a massively multi-player online video game, or as old as the bits and bytes of data that represent the numbers in your bank account or stock portfolio. Just like smart property, digital property suffers from a serious conflict with intellectual property. Consider what you own when you purchase a copy of Miike Snow's *Genghis Khan* from the iTunes store. You own the copy – and only that one copy – just as if you purchased a CD. You do not own the copyright, that is, the right to make more copies of it. Courts have found that particular distinction difficult to maintain, and have to a large extent ignored the distinction between digital property rights and intellectual property rights in their decisions. That means Apple can terminate access to your music collection, Amazon can delete books you purchased, and Google Play can make movies you bought vanish.

It should be no surprise that I think the rules for ordinary property ownership should apply to digital and smart property. To make that point, I use the words *traditional* or *old-fashioned* or *everyday* or *basic* to describe property rights as they have been developed over time by the cautious, experimental, iterative process of the common law. As a shortcut, I mean that we ought to own an MP3 the way we own a CD, a smart house the way we own houses now, and a smart car the way we own a regular car. I argue that the traditional rules of personal and real property are entirely practicable and practical for software-embedded smart property and informational objects like digital property.

One final definitional point. I think digital property – which is made up of information – is certainly property. In fact, I think all property is a kind of information: a record of who owns what. But just like all nickels are money, but not all money is nickels, I do not believe that all information, even personal information about us, should be made into property. As I will explore later, property helps us protect our privacy. But this does not mean that I own all information about myself. That is both impossible and unwise. We simply do not permit anyone to own facts. Facts are too necessary for basic survival and functioning. You can't copyright the color of the sky, and you can't patent the law of gravity.

I do believe that control over our smart and digital property will give us a big boost in controlling the data-collecting sensors embedded in them. If we control our devices, we control the stream of information flowing from them. If we control digital houses, we can draw the digital curtains. The distinction is important to keep in mind. Control over our smart and digital property will help us control the flow of information, but we cannot and should not make all information property.

Different Approaches to Property

Property has always meant different things to people of different classes and times. What property means today to a person who is homeless is different from what it meant to a landed aristocrat in sixteenth-century England. Likewise, a modern farmer might think of land when she hears the word *property*, as opposed to the technology-savvy millennial who might think of devices, digital photographs, and MP3s.

There are some identifiable trends, though. Jedediah Purdy, in his masterful book *The Meaning of Property*, identifies three main streams of property thought.[7] His first stream is "libertarianism," or negative liberty: the idea that property means a kind of liberty from government interference.[8] His second stream is efficiency, or what he calls "welfarism": property is an institution that helps to ensure the free flow of goods for minimum transaction costs, such that it allows people to get what they want at the lowest price.[9] Finally, Purdy identifies a stream of human personhood, or identity.[10] The identity view of property requires that we have some stability in our environment so that we can build a home, a family, an identity. Property allows us to surround ourselves with reminders of who we are or wish to be. Here, consider your home, your wedding ring, or your digital avatar. These properties are ways that we express ourselves.[11]

Purdy places these three historical trends of property thought underneath an encompassing principle of freedom, which he defines not in the negative libertarian sense, but as the goal of widening the *range of viable options* for humans. His view is that the three streams of thought represent the goal of letting humans be humans, of expanding the range of capabilities that humans have, and of helping humans see themselves as beings whose decisions matter. In conceptualizing this idea of human freedom, Purdy draws from historical and economic thinkers ranging from Adam Smith to economist and Nobel Laureate Amartya Sen. Sen, in particular, challenged the traditional libertarian view of negative liberty. He focused on what people could actually do, which he termed *capabilities*. Negative liberty is all well and good, but, Sen wondered, what is the point of a right to vote if you cannot drive to the polls? Property is thus to be measured by the yardstick of human capability. Does a proposed property reform expand the range of options for humans? We should adopt it.

---

[7] *See* Jedediah Purdy, The Meaning of Property: Freedom, Community, and the Legal Imagination 19 (Yale University Press 2010).

[8] *Id.* at 19.   [9] *Id.* at 20.   [10] This is also known as the personhood theory of property. *Id.*

[11] *See* Margaret Jane Radin, *Property and Personhood*, 34 Stan. L. Rev. 957, 957 (1982) ("The premise underlying the personhood perspective is that to achieve proper self-development – to be a person – an individual needs some control over resources in the external environment. The necessary assurances of control take the form of property rights.").

Does a property rule reduce the range of options for humans? We ought to reconsider it.

Notably, Purdy's conception of freedom is not purely individual. Property, to Purdy, is an evolving institution within community under conditions of scarcity. You want the thing, and I want the thing, but there's only one thing. How do we decide who gets it, or whether we share, or whether it goes to neither of us? The individual cannot be our sole point of reference for measuring property. Property is a compromise, a necessary point of resolving ongoing tension in reasoning out the creation, movement, and end distribution of resources among people.

This book does not exclusively adopt any one of the three major historical streams of thought – libertarianism, welfarism, or identity. I unapologetically use language from all three, spanning the political divide from right to left. This is because no matter what property means to you or me, the fact is that it is being taken away from all of us. Whether we see property as an expression of untouched liberty from interference, or of flourishing, or of increasing human happiness, matters less than the fact that all of these measures will be reduced if our ability to control our surroundings is diminished by eroding the institutions of property. No matter what property means to you, I want to be on your side.

I do strongly endorse viewing property through the lens of human freedom – not just negative freedom from government interference, which means nothing if one owns nothing – but the actual capability to act. In chorus with Sen and Purdy, I believe that capabilities matter. As applied to property law, I believe that property rules should promote not just the technical right to do something, but the actual ability to do it. Property provides resources and tools. Resources are necessary to turn a technical legal right into a living possibility. Tools enable us to turn legal rights into actions. And, as we will see, I think we will desperately need digital resources and powerful networked electronic tools to fulfill our potential in a networked and technological society. To expand Sen's election day example, in today's wired ecosystem, it's not just a car that is necessary to exercise the right to vote, but access to Google Maps and the ability to find the right polling station using a fast internet search when one ends up at the wrong place (this may have happened to me). When resources are online, we need online resources. And because resources and tools are so critical to expanding our range of options, I want us to use freedom – in the sense of human capability – as our yardstick for measuring the wisdom of property rules.

There is another view of property, though, that is not consistent with human freedom. That view is the locking down of property in centralized, command-and-control feudal or feudal-like systems. In feudal systems, the king owned everything, and everyone else simply managed the king's property based on his permission. Successive users were "subinfeudated," that is, they used the land dependent on and subservient to their lord's grant from the throne. Each successive subinfeudation relied on those above it. And if you were a poor farmer kicked off the land by someone else, your only recourse would be to complain to your lord.[12] Modern property is a reaction against feudal systems of ownership. Modern property severs the control of the grantor of property over the grantee. By contrast, feudal systems relied on that control to enforce strict social hierarchies of power. They "created a form of domination in which subordinates, subject to the arbitrary whim of superiors, adopted tastes, manners, and attitudes to suit their perception of the superiors' wishes."[13]

This book is about the increasing conflict between the "freedom" model of property and the "feudal" mode. If we do not win this war, a few companies will own large tracts of digital assets and everyone else will be a digital peasant. Licensing is the new infeudation, and sublicensing is the new subinfeudation.[14] Software and operating system designers occupy a place startlingly similar to that of a lord, albeit a digital one. Each layer of owner must rely on the owners above them. My phone is an Android Galaxy, and I must ask Samsung's permission to make changes to it. Samsung, in turn, licenses the Android operating system and Google Apps from Google, and must continue to meet license conditions in order for me to use my device. Consider when Amazon deleted Orwell's *1984* and *Animal Farm* e-books from users' Kindles.[15] When a dispute arose between Orwell's estate and Amazon (a third party had placed the e-books on Kindle but did not have the rights to do so), the users' books were erased by Amazon. In short, because the freedom model of property law has not been adequately brought to bear, consumers are dependent on a digital lord, who is dependent on a digital king. Virtual worlds scholar Greg Lastowka observed that users often end up "[l]ike peasants tilling fields around a medieval castle," in an arrangement that ultimately benefits their digital feudal lord.[16] Or, as James Grimmelmann writes:

> Two problems have preoccupied scholars of virtual world law: What is the political relationship between developers and users? And: Should we treat in-world objects as property? We can make progress on both questions by

[12] *See* James Grimmelmann, *Virtual World Feudalism*, 118 YALE L.J. ONLINE 126, 127–28 (2009) ("Crucially, seisin intertwined substance and procedure: the tenant's remedy for disseisin was to appeal to his lord to set matters right.").

[13] PURDY, *supra* note 7, at 13.   [14] *See generally* Grimmelmann, *supra* note 12.

[15] *See generally* Brad Stone, *Amazon Erases Orwell Books From Kindle*, N.Y. TIMES (July 17, 2009), http://www.nytimes.com/2009/07/18/technology/companies/18amazon.html?_r=0.

[16] GREG LASTOWKA, VIRTUAL JUSTICE 153 (Yale University Press 2010).

recognizing that virtual politics and property are inextricably linked, in the same way that feudal politics and property were. It is the tenant/user's relationship with his lord/developer that both creates the property interest and enforces it.[17]

This is an age-old struggle. Adam Smith was driven to resist feudal and other non-free property models (like slavery) because they presented a "path to degradation."[18] Turning back the clock on property law means reversing the advances of freedom, welfare, and flourishing that modern property law has systematically promoted.[19]

If we permit and invest in feudal, non-free property systems, I think we are in danger of setting forth on a path to degradation. It is possible to become detached from the values of property and privacy. We can become inured to the iniquities of power distribution in a digital society. I hear students increasingly parroting the pronouncements of data kings Mark Zuckerberg and Larry Ellison that privacy is dead.[20] These values are increasingly internalized in the culture, and the path to degradation is paved with learned helplessness. As we learn we cannot stop companies from extracting data through our property, we will learn to value privacy less. It's possible that we need some adjustments to our sense of privacy, or that we need new norms for how we use intellectual property. But those should not come from the top down, out of the mouths of digital feudal lords. Our new norms should rise from the bottom up, from how we interact with our devices and with each other.

The Path of Property Law

The common law progresses by careful, cautious, repeated experimentation. What humans deeply feel becomes expressed in deals, then standards, then norms, and finally is recognized in cases and codified in laws. As Robert Cover wrote in his famous *Nomos and Narrative*, rules arise first within communities

---

[17] Grimmelmann, *supra* note 12, at 126.

[18] Jedediah Purdy, *A Freedom-Promoting Approach to Property: A Renewed Tradition for New Debates*, 72 U. CHI. L. REV. 1237, 1254 (2005).

[19] *See id.* at 1253–54 (comparing and contrasting "free labor regimes with slave societies as well as with status-based economies").

[20] *See* L. Gordon Crovitz, *Privacy? We Got Over It*, WALL ST. J. (Aug. 25, 2008), http://www.wsj.com/articles/SB121962391804567765 (noting Oracle CEO Larry Ellison's observation that "privacy . . . is largely an illusion"); Bobbie Johnson, *Privacy No Longer a Social Norm, Says Facebook Founder*, GUARDIAN (Jan. 10, 2010), http://www.theguardian.com/technology/2010/jan/11/facebook-privacy (discussing Facebook founder Mark Zuckerberg's views on privacy norms that have "evolved over time").

without the intervention of attorneys or judges.[21] These rules then percolate up to a point where they come into conflict, and judges must decide which of two rules will continue to bind, and which is destined for the ash heap.[22]

Property's path is particularly tied to technology. As technology progresses, it opens new markets for property. Think of ownership of bandwidth or telecommunications spectrum, ownership of asteroids, or ownership of Bitcoins. In Harold Demsetz's groundbreaking work on the evolution of property rights among Native American tribes, he wrote that the need to propertize beaver-hunting grounds, which were previously open to all, came from the opening of new trading markets.[23] Demsetz wrote:

> We may safely surmise that the advent of the fur trade had two immediate consequences. First, the value of furs to the Indians was increased considerably. Second, and as a result, the scale of hunting activity rose sharply. Both consequences must have increased considerably the importance of the externalities associated with free hunting. The property right system began to change, and it changed specifically in the direction required to take account of the economic effects made important by the fur trade.[24]

Jedediah Purdy writes that one older view of property organized it as a function of animal husbandry: property was first purely personal among hunter-gatherers, then communal among herdsmen, before private real estate was introduced with the private farmer, and the propertization of labor arrived with industrialization.[25] Saul Levmore provides an updated version of this typology, noting the common law of property experiments with new rules to validate human needs for and emotions surrounding property as technology expands into new markets.[26] We had no need to propertize airspace until airplanes, no need to propertize spectrum until radios were invented, no need to propertize space (the US Commercial Space Launch Competitiveness Act was signed the day I wrote this) until commercial exploitation of extraterrestrial water and minerals was a technological possibility. The same is true of the next two immediate steps in property law: property interests in our smart and digital property.

---

[21] *See* Robert M. Cover, *The Supreme Court, 1982 Term – Foreword: Nomos and Narrative*, 97 HARV. L. REV. 4, 11 (1983) (positing "that the creation of legal meaning... takes place always through an essentially cultural medium").

[22] *See id.* at 53–60 (discussing the role of judges in shaping legal norms).

[23] Harold Demsetz, *Toward a Theory of Property Rights*, 57 AM. ECON. REV. 347, 352 (1967).

[24] *See id.*   [25] *See generally* Purdy, *supra* note 18.

[26] *See* Saul Levmore, *Property's Uneasy Path and Expanding Future*, 70 U. CHI. L. REV. 181, 186 (2003) (discussing the "link between interest groups and the apparent expansion of intellectual property rights").

But with the opening of the internet and the electronic frontier, the harmonious development of property norms alongside technological development broke down. The advent of the internet caused us to turn our investments, innovations, and emotions to a largely intangible realm. While the law of intellectual property has advanced by leaps and bounds – many say too far – the law of everyday property has stagnated. Because courts have lacked the analogies, stories, analysis, and imagination to help fulfill human needs and intuitions surrounding digital and smart property, the path of property has stopped or been diverted. Without a significant push, it will not go further. This is because courts too often see everyday property as purely physical, because courts see intellectual property interests as superior to our interests in our smart devices or digital property, and because consumers cannot get access to courts to make the legal arguments necessary to turn norms and standards surrounding digital and smart property into case law. We will never get to where we need to be if we continue to equate property with the physical good itself, and not the piece of information saying who owns the good. This book will, I hope, play a part in pushing us over that hump and getting property law back on track for the future.

DISENTANGLING INTANGIBILITY

What went wrong? Why did property ownership stop developing alongside technology? And why did the development of online rights start turning the clock backward to digital feudalism, rather than continuing the progress of traditional property rights into new electronic markets? In short, courts and policymakers have struggled with how to apply property law to things they can't touch. Unfortunately, in the digital economy, courts, companies, and consumers still see property rights as tied to physical resources, tangible assets, stuff that we can see and touch and move. As the tremendously influential professor of law Grant Gilmore wrote: "Even for a lawyer, the 'what is property?' problem presents no difficulty when you are dealing with goods, chattels, things: if you can see it, count, weigh and measure it, it exists; if you can't, it doesn't. But intangible claims are another matter entirely."[27]

There are two intersecting problems: intangibility is one; the overextension of intellectual property is the other. To put it simply, in the 1980s and '90s, judges and lawyers weren't sure what law seemed appropriate for digital objects

---

[27] Juliet M. Moringiello, *False Categories in Commercial Law: The (Ir)relevance of (In)tangibility*, 35 FLA. ST. U.L. REV. 119, 132 (2007) [hereinafter *False Categories*] (quoting Grant Gilmore, *Article 9: What It Does Not Do for the Future*, 26 LA. L. REV. 300, 301 (1966)).

and physical objects embedded with code. Since one couldn't touch a lot
of these assets, it seemed like intellectual property was the best bet. After
all, for much of history, non-intellectual property – real and personal – was
predominantly tangible. So traditional property law went undeveloped, and
intellectual property law was stretched to cover things it was never meant to
govern. An exchange between Marybeth Peters (the Register of Copyrights
at the time) and attorney John T. Mitchell at a Future of Music Coalition
Summit, as described by Mitchell, illustrates the problem.[28] Peters was asked
whether people who bought music by downloading it were just as entitled
to resell it as were people who bought physical CDs. Peters' immediate,
intuitive response was no, there had to be something tangible in order for
the right to resell to apply. Mitchell replied, somewhat flippantly, "If you
get hit in the head with a hard drive, it will hurt a lot more than a CD."[29]
Peters then changed her response. Yes, she said, legally downloaded music
could be transferred, sold, or given away. The only problem was how to do so if
you had to transfer the physical medium (in this case, the hard drive) in order
to transfer one song. For Peters, one could only resell one's property if it was
physical.[30]

One particularly thorny question is how to sort claims for intangible
resources between normal property and intellectual property. Let's say I paint
a picture. The actual picture and the copyright in the picture are two different
things. A traditional distinction between the thing and the intellectual property rights that attach to it makes a lot of sense. Consider this book: you have
the right to read it, take it with you, sell it to someone else, but not the right
to make as many copies of it as you want and distribute it to anyone you wish.
Ownership of a copy is separate from ownership of the copyright.

But somewhere along the way, the copy/copyright distinction fell apart. In
one particularly well-known set of cases, the same panel of the same federal
court of appeals decided on the same day that while you can resell your
used music CD on eBay,[31] you cannot sell your used software CD on eBay.[32]
Somehow a music CD felt like personal property to the court, whereas the
software CD was just a vehicle for transmitting the software. Even though
identical technologies and media were involved, one felt more physical, by

[28] See John T. Mitchell, Comments of Screen Play Inc. and Rain City Video on Department of
Commerce Green Paper (Jan. 17, 2014), http://www.uspto.gov/ip/global/copyrights/comments/
screenplay_inc_and_rain_city_video_inc_post-meeting_comments.pdf.
[29] *Id.*   [30] *Id.*   [31] UMG Recordings, Inc. v. Augusto, 628 F.3d 1175 (2008).
[32] Vernor v. Autodesk, Inc., 621 F.3d 1102 (2008).

analogy to vinyl, whereas the other felt more intangible, by analogy to software installation.

Courts have struggled with this complexity. Perhaps a good shortcut to understanding this complex area of law is the rule that Marybeth Peters articulated: if there is some part of a property or product that is physical, courts tend to think of regular property law as applying. If there isn't, courts struggle. A fully digital MP3 is not personal property, at least not in the eyes of many courts.[33] A CD is.[34] If you purchase a video game in a box on the shelf at Best Buy, it's your property.[35] If you download it direct to drive, it's not.

This division between tangible and intangible appears all throughout the law. In *Sony Corp. of America v. Universal City Studios, Inc.*,[36] the Supreme Court decided that VCRs were legal, even though some consumers might use them to make illegal copies of TV shows.[37] But when consumers started using software VCRs – programs that permitted them to save streaming video despite the wishes of the streaming parties – the streaming company sued the developer and forced a settlement.[38] The legality of next-generation space- and bandwidth-shifting technologies like TubeMate, which permits users to download YouTube videos while on a cable Wi-Fi connection, thereby avoiding penalties for accessing the same content while on wireless mobile plans, is very much up in the air. The issues are the same: may a company make a product, whether physical (VCRs), partially digital (TiVO), or entirely digital (TubeMate), that permits users to record and manipulate copyrighted content? That legal question doesn't have anything to do with physicality. And yet the less physical a given technology is, the more uncertain courts become about its legality.

---

[33] Capitol Records, LLC v. ReDigi Inc., 934 F. Supp. 2d 640, 660 (2012) (declining to "condone the wholesale application of the first sale defense to the digital sphere").

[34] *See Augusto*, 628 F. 3d at 1180 (concluding that because "UMG transferred title to the *particular copies* of its promotional CDs," it "cannot maintain an infringement action against Augusto for his subsequent sale of those copies" (emphasis added)).

[35] SoftMan Prods. Co. v. Adobe Sys., 171 F. Supp. 2d 1075, 1085 (finding that, where the software was distributed via a boxed collection, "the circumstances surrounding the transaction strongly suggests that the transaction is in fact a sale rather than a license").

[36] 464 U.S. 417 (1984).

[37] *See id.* at 444–45 (finding that the personal use of VCRs to record television shows falls under the "fair use" doctrine).

[38] *See* RealNetworks, Inc. v. Streambox, Inc., No. C99-2070P, 2000 U.S. Dist. LEXIS 1889, at *34–35 (W.D. Wash. Jan. 18, 2000) (enjoining Steambox from "manufacturing, importing, licensing, offering to the public, or offering for sale . . . products that circumvent or attempt to circumvent RealNetworks' technological security measures [and] . . . products that modify RealNetworks' RealPlayer program, including its interface, its source code, or its object code").

INTELLECTUAL PROPERTY TAKEOVER

The hesitation of courts to use the law of traditional property to cover intangible digital assets left a void in the law. Intellectual property rushed in to fill that void, and in doing so, vastly overreached what intellectual property law was designed to do: protect creativity by making sure that those who invent new technology, or compose songs, or write books, can profit from their labors. Ironically, the overreach of intellectual property in the digital age has had varying benefits for creators and innovators. The reign of intellectual property has in some cases had just as many deleterious effects for artists and inventors as it has for owners. Intellectual property has been twisted and stretched to create a system of centralized and feudal command and control, rather than foster experimentation and innovation.

Copies and Copyright

Intellectual property law protects rights to inventions, works, and designs by constraining duplication. You can't replicate a patented invention without the permission of the patent holder. You can't copy a novel without the permission of the copyright holder. Copyright law is one of multiple kinds of intellectual property law. Traditionally, it has been the law of creative expression: music, movies, novels, and poems. It protects the unique expression of ideas, not the ideas themselves. It protects the form of an expression, not its function. A song may make you cry, but it is the pattern of notes, not its effect, that is protected by law.

Copyright is of particular importance to our discussion because, oddly, copyright law came to govern computer code. Computer code, when read by a computer, is a set of 1s and 0s that provides instructions. It is functionally a set of switches, set to off (0) or on (1), and through those combinations, we can tell computers to do pretty much anything.

When a human writes computer code, they generally use a computer language. A computer language is a language that looks enough like a human language (usually English) to give the programmer a leg up on what is happening, but uses enough logical rigor that it can be compiled into a mechanistic set of ones and zeroes for a computer to follow.

So even though a computer reads ones and zeroes, a human programmer writes words that look something like English. A short computer program might appear, at a distance of about six feet, to look like a short poem, but of course the two could not be more different. A program is compiled into a set of instructions that a computer can only execute in one way. A poem embraces ambiguities, nuances, and shades of language to provoke a response in the human reader. A program may be elegant, but its elegance is functional, not literary. This is important, because copyright law protects originality but not functionality (a technical manual is protected, for example, in the phrasing and arrangement of its paragraphs, but not in its functional instructions). In that sense, programs are a lot like lists of ingredients – in other words, a recipe – which aren't protected by copyright law; a program commands its reader (a computer) and a recipe commands its reader (a cook), but neither are particularly expressive beyond their functionality. Yet, despite these differences, programs and poems are protected by the same law: copyright law.

Copyright law is called that because the creator of a new creative work is the only one with the right to make copies of that work. There are other rights, too – like the right to distribute copies of the work – but for now we will stick with the right to make copies. The law of poetry turned out to be a very strange fit for computer programs, because computers do not make copies of programs in order to sell those extra copies or give them to other people. They make copies of programs internally – from storage into active memory – because they need those copies in order to function.

What this means, though, is that the act of turning a computer on is equivalent to the act of pressing "copy" on a Xerox machine. As one might guess, copying something – say, an entire book – without the permission of the copyright holder is copyright infringement. But unlike a Xerox machine, computer software is a necessary part of the device, not a creative work separate from it. Even so, software developers have begun to claim that even if they sell us a device, they have not sold us the right to make the internal software copies necessary to run that device. Rather, they argue, they have merely licensed the right to make necessary copies to us as long as we follow all of their contractual requirements, many of which have nothing to do with legitimate constraints on use of the software.

This highlights the difference between *owning* a piece of software and *licensing* it. In one sense, the distinction between the two is simple: ownership gives the owner the right of exclusive possession, use, and control of an asset – in this case, software. A license, though, is a non-exclusive right. That shouldn't be that big a deal, since it simply means only the licensee can use the one specific copy of the software; other users must buy their own. For our purposes, though, the critical distinction lies in a further detail. If one is a merely a licensee of software, one's ability to make copies of the software is dependent on the one's compliance with all license conditions. A license imposes ongoing obligations on the licensee. And again, that's not that big of a deal for most licenses, for things other than software. Imagine I have bought a book. When I do, I get ownership of the physical copy, but do not have the right to make further copies without the author's permission. Imagine, further, that the author placed all kinds of license conditions on my purchase, such that I would have to follow those conditions if I did want to make another copy of the book. Well, okay. I don't have to make more copies of the book in order to read it, use it, and enjoy it.

But we do have to make copies of software as part of its basic use. Just loading the program requires the making of a copy. Although these are critical distinctions, they have been overlooked, if not disregarded. In fact, turning on or using any device with software embedded in it can be copyright infringement. How have things come to this? The answer begins with a court case from 1993.

MAI and the RAM Copy Doctrine

Like many computer manufacturers in the 1980s, MAI Systems Corporation designed custom software for the machines it made, including operating system software. This meant that – as with all operating systems – the computer automatically loaded MAI's software when anyone pressed the "on" button.

MAI ran into significant financial troubles at the end of the 1980s.[39] To bolster its lagging computer sales, MAI sought to leverage its control over software to permit it to hijack the market for repairing computers it had already sold. Per MAI's license agreement, if you bought a MAI computer, only MAI was allowed to service it. Only MAI could repair it. That way, MAI could make money on servicing fees. To make sure that only MAI would service its computers, the company wrote this requirement into its End User License Agreement. So if you bought an MAI computer, you were contractually bound to only work with MAI to repair your computer.

That contractual protection wasn't strong enough to force MAI's customers to work with MAI for their maintenance needs. If you broke the contract, MAI was out only the profit it would have made on the repair or service. That's how contracts work: if you break a contract, you can only be held liable for the amount of money the other party would have made if you had kept the agreement. For MAI, those damages might not have been worth the cost of a lawsuit. But if the company could find a way to turn the local independent repair guy into a copyright infringer, then it could receive the massive damages set out by the Copyright Act: up to $150,000 per work infringed!

---

[39] *See generally* MAI Sys. Corp. v. Peak Comput., Inc., 991 F.2d 511, 513 (9th Cir. 1993) (discussing the nature of MAI's computer business).

So MAI argued that by turning the computer on, the repair person loaded a copy of MAI's software from storage into active memory – from ROM into RAM. Since the repair person wasn't a licensee, per the End User License Agreement, that copy was unauthorized. Surprisingly, the Ninth Circuit Court of Appeals agreed.[40] A copy loaded into RAM was indeed a copy, and unauthorized use of that copy was indeed copyright infringement.

To reach this result, the Ninth Circuit had to do a lot of surgery to copyright law and ignore a lot of common sense. First, the case just looked bad. MAI was using its power over its operating system not to stop people from making pirate copies, but to prevent an owner from maintaining and repairing her own system, and to freeze out competition for repair jobs. Second, in order for a copy to be the kind of copy that the Copyright Act worries about, it has to be a copy of "more than transitory duration."[41] As copyright scholar Aaron Perzanowski has written, a copy written in sand at the beach or by skywriting probably doesn't count.[42] The copies made when a program is loaded into active memory aren't remotely true copies; they are a representation in active memory that allows the computer to do what it was supposed to do. Moreover, Congress had anticipated this problem. The Copyright Act already contained a 1980 provision stating that owners of a particular copy of software were permitted to make this kind of temporary copy as long as it was an essential step of getting the software to operate.[43] In other words, selling someone an operating system makes absolutely no sense if the buyer doesn't have the ability to load the program.

The Ninth Circuit ignored these problems through questionable reasoning. It hand-waved the requirement that a copy must be of "more than transitory duration," and assumed that loading a program into memory made an actual permanent copy of economic significance that triggered the Copyright Act's prohibitions.[44] Further, the court held that as long as the license (which MAI wrote) *said* that customers didn't own the software but merely licensed it, then the protection that Congress gave to people who owned a specific copy didn't apply. What Congress giveth, the contract taketh away.[45] The decision was the

---

[40] *See id.* at 518 ("Peak's loading of copyrighted software into RAM creates a 'copy' of that software in violation of the Copyright Act.").

[41] 17 U.S.C. § 101 (2012).

[42] *See* Aaron Perzanowski, *Fixing RAM Copies*, 104 Nw. U.L. Rev. 1067, 1095 (2010) ("Text scrawled on a frosted windowpane, skywriting, sand castles, and ice sculptures are all examples of inherently temporary instantiations.").

[43] 17 U.S.C. § 117(a).   [44] *MAI Sys. Corp.*, 991 F.2d at 518.

[45] *See id.* at 517 ("MAI software licenses do not allow for the use or copying of MAI software by third parties such as Peak. Therefore, any 'copying' done by Peak is 'beyond the scope' of the license.").

equivalent of someone trying to sell you your own house on condition that you live in it a certain way. Such a deal only makes sense if that person owns your house to begin with.

Congress put a stop to one tiny part of the *MAI* decision: it amended copyright law to clarify that companies can't stop computer repair people from doing their work.[46] That is why independent computer repair shops are still around. But the deeper holding of *MAI* was still intact. By turning on any device embedded with a computer chip, we run the risk of copyright infringement if we do not use it exactly the way the person who sold it to us says we must. Why? By clicking "I Agree" to get our property to work, we have to agree that we don't actually own large portions of it – we only license it.

There is some hope. *MAI* has been roundly criticized by courts and academics. In a 2008 case, *Cartoon Network v. CSC Holdings*,[47] another appeals court finally refused to follow *MAI*. *Cartoon Network* held that streaming services that use temporary buffers make such short-lived copies that the Copyright Act is not triggered. A copy has to last more than a mere moment, be more than "ephemeral," as the court put it, for it to count as a copy for purposes of the Copyright Act. That is progress. It doesn't undo the damage of the RAM copy doctrine, because RAM copies, while transient and impermanent, can last more than just a few seconds (a RAM copy can last as long as the computer is on). But the decision did finally challenge *MAI*'s faulty reasoning. Maybe more courts will intervene to protect ownership in the era of the Internet of Things, and restore common sense to the law: when you buy something, your ownership rights include the right to turn it on, even if doing so makes a temporary copy in RAM.

DMCA 1201: Locking Owners Out

Companies have also employed a range of technological measures to prevent copying of copyrighted materials. Those measures are called DRM, or digital rights management – it's the code that stops you from ripping your DVD to your computer hard drive, for example. The problem with proprietary company DRM is that it doesn't work. It's a matter of math. What one person can code, another can exploit. For every coder working on DRM, there are millions who have incentives to crack the protection. Under these pressures, even the most carefully engineered DRM controls have fallen to code crackers in a matter of months, weeks, or even days.[48] This principle is why even the

---

[46] 17 U.S.C. § 117.   [47] 536 F.3d 121 (2008).

[48] See Aaron Perzanowski & Jason Schultz, The End of Ownership: Personal Property in the Digital Economy 123–25 (MIT Press 2016).

most over-engineered computer systems in the world can be hacked promptly once the brainpower of millions is brought to bear. No matter how much money Apple spends securing its iPhone, a new hack is out every month.

Predictably, rightsholders began to tire of the DRM arms race. But rather than ask whether the DRM approach in general was working, and rethink the system itself, they went to Congress and asked for legislation to make it illegal for hackers to break DRM. They argued that the battle between hackers and industry was a waste of resources. New DRM schemes spawned new hacks, requiring new DRM schemes. Congress obliged by incorporating section 1201 in its Digital Millennium Copyright Act, the 1998 amendment to U.S. copyright law. The DMCA strengthened intellectual property rights in the emerging digital environment. Section 1201, in particular, prohibits circumvention of technological measures that control access to copyrighted materials. Section 1201 made it illegal to "avoid, bypass, remove, deactivate, or impair"[49] technology that limited access to copyrighted materials – technology such as DRM. The wording of the statute reflects the desire of Congress and rightsholders to stop the hacking of DRM.[50]

But in their haste and zeal to halt DRM hacking, Congress crafted a poorly worded and overreaching statute. The DMCA prohibition is not limited to breaking DRM to make an illegal copy. Simply breaking *any* technological lock on copyrighted material is forbidden, even if that lock is stopping the owner from doing something completely legal. Before the DMCA, for example, the Supreme Court had held that it is fair use – in other words not copyright infringement – to record television shows to watch later. But after the enactment of the DMCA, rightsholders put technological locks on content that prevented this fair use. When people unlocked the locks to make a fair-use copy, rightsholders argued successfully that this was barred under the DMCA.[51] So now, breaking the lock off a broadcast or streamed show to get your Wednesday night *CSI* fix violates copyright law, even though you have the fair-use right to record and watch that show later. It is perhaps unsurprising that after the amendment passed, companies did much more than try to stop

---

[49] Digital Millennium Copyright Act, 17 U.S.C. § 1201(a)(3)(A) (2012).

[50] *See generally* Kim Zetter, *Hacker Lexicon: What Is the Digital Millennium Copyright Act?*, WIRED (June 6, 2016 7:00 AM), https://www.wired.com/2016/06/hacker-lexicon-digital-millennium-copyright-act/.

[51] *See* RealNetworks, Inc. v. Streambox, Inc., No. C99-2070P, 2000 U.S. Dist. LEXIS 1889, at *20–21 (W.D. Wash. Jan. 18, 2000) ("The Streambox VCR meets the first test for liability under the DMCA because at least a part of the Streambox VCR is primarily, if not exclusively, designed to circumvent the access control and copy protection measures that RealNetworks affords to copyright owners.").

actual illicit copying of movies, music, or software – they began to put technological locks on pretty much all of the traditional (and completely legal)
powers of ownership. Since the Act made it illegal to smash those locks off,
owners found themselves locked out of their own property.

Similarly, rightsholders used the DMCA to try to capture secondary markets. One company, Chamberlain, argued that it could use the DMCA to force
its customers to stop buying generic remote controls for its electronic garage
doors – the generic remote circumnavigated controls to Chamberlain's copyrighted software.[52] The printer company Lexmark tried to use the DMCA to
force customers to buy its more expensive ink refill cartridges instead of generic
ones. Lexmark printers require ink cartridges to communicate an authentication code.[53] The company cried copyright infringement when competitors
used Lexmark's software to develop interoperable, cheaper cartridges.[54] The
first attempts to control secondary markets were rebuffed by courts who resisted
use of the DMCA to fundamentally shift the balance of power between company and owner, but of the recent cases, almost all go the company's way.[55]
Owners are locked out.

DMCA section 1201 also reinforced the useless distinction between physical
and digital versions of the same products. Physical VCRs are legal. Purely
software VCRs are often not.[56] Changing the tires on your car is probably still
legal. Running unapproved diagnostic software to see what is wrong with your
tractor is not. Despite Chamberlain's lawsuit, universal remote controls made
by someone other than the manufacturer to interoperate with garage doors are
legal. Pure code that is written to work with other code often is not.[57] Anyone

---

[52] *See* Chamberlain Grp., Inc. v. Skylink Techs., Inc., 381 F.3d 1178, 1204 (Fed. Cir. 2004) (ruling
against a garage door opener manufacturer in its claim against the manufacturer of a universal
transmitter).

[53] *See* Lexmark Int'l, Inc. v. Static Control Components, Inc., 387 F.3d 522, 530 (6th Cir. 2004)
(noting that "Lexmark uses an 'authentication sequence' that performs a 'secret handshake'
between each Lexmark printer and a microchip on each Lexmark toner cartridge").

[54] *See id.* at 529 ("Lexmark claimed that SCC's chip copied the Toner Loading Program in
violation of the federal copyright statute.").

[55] *See, e.g.*, Lexmark Int'l, Inc. v. Impression Prod., Inc., 816 F.3d 721, 774 (Fed. Cir. 2016)
(reversing a judgment of non-infringement and affirming a judgment of infringement, both in
the patent holder's, Lexmark's, favor).

[56] *See* RealNetworks, Inc. v. Streambox, Inc., No. C99-2070P, 2000 U.S. Dist. LEXIS 1889, at
*20–21 (W.D. Wash. Jan. 18, 2000) ("The Streambox VCR meets the first test for liability under
the DMCA because at least a part of the Streambox VCR is primarily, if not exclusively,
designed to circumvent the access control and copy protection measures that RealNetworks
affords to copyright owners.").

[57] *See* Davidson & Assocs. v. Jung, 422 F.3d 630, 642 (8th Cir. 2005) (holding software that
"provide[d] matchmaking services for users of Blizzard games who wanted to play in a multi-
player environment without using [Blizzard's service,] Battle.net," violative of the DMCA).

can sell a used CD.[58] Not so with used MP3s.[59] Owners have the right to modify, change, adapt, and even destroy their physical property, but not their digital or smart property.

The DMCA was not supposed to significantly alter the relationship between intellectual property rightsholders and owners, so it contained a number of exemptions. But those exemptions essentially vanished thanks to some strange court decisions in which courts decided that owners give up their rights under the DMCA when they click the ever-present "I Agree" button, which they must do to use their devices. Courts have held that the "I Agree" screen, which prohibits users from accessing their devices or programs unless they agree to all terms and conditions, acts not only as a legal document specifying terms of use, but also as a technological measure controlling access to the copyrighted program.[60] Therefore, consumers can either hit "I Agree," accessing their devices but giving up all their rights, or they can circumvent technological measures to take control of their device – and be liable for hacking. They are damned either way.

The upshot: modifying or repairing your own property often causes you to infringe copyright and separately be liable for circumvention of access controls. Offline, you would not violate contract or intellectual property law if you took a hammer to your car's GPS. Online, you could face copyright liability for digging the tracker out of your car's code. All in all, DMCA section 1201 is an abject failure. It did not stop illegal copying (there is just as much piracy nowadays; everything can be downloaded via torrent or just by using YouTube, or so I've been told), but it did stop owners from controlling, fixing, repairing, or modifying their own property.

Exhausting Exhaustion

Why would companies want to control what we can do with our own property? Sometimes they want to do this for our own good. A wireless carrier may want to stop users from downloading programs that threaten the stability of the

---

[58] See UMG Recordings, Inc. v. Augusto, 628 F.3d 1175, 1183 (9th Cir. 2011) ("UMG's distribution of the promotional CDs under the circumstances effected a sale (transfer of title) of the CDs to the recipients. Further sale of those copies was therefore permissible without UMG's authorization.").

[59] See id. at 656.

[60] See *Jung*, 422 F.3d at 639 ("Appellants contractually accepted restrictions on their ability to reverse engineer by their agreement to the terms of the TOU and EULA."); Bowers v. Baystate Techs., 320 F.3d 1317, 1327 (Fed. Cir. 2003) ("The shrink-wrap license agreement prohibited, *inter alia*, all reverse engineering of Mr. Bowers' software, protection encompassing but more extensive than copyright protection, which prohibits only certain copying.").

device. But sometimes they want to do this for *their* own good. Some of those downloaded programs may actually make a device more safe – but interfere with the company's ability to deliver targeted advertising. This control may be exercised for more nefarious purposes. Volkswagen, for example, argued that it needed to be able to control the software on people's vehicles because that would help them protect the environment by monitoring pollution emissions. The company turned out to be less than trustworthy on this point – VW actually used its control over vehicle emissions testing software to fool tests and lie to regulators.[61]

When a company tries to control what it has sold, it runs up against a basic principle of law called "exhaustion." Normally, when a company sells you something, it has "exhausted" certain of its intellectual property rights, and can't control what you do with the thing you just purchased. For example, smart devices are created using a lot of patents. But when those patents are made into an object, the object encapsulates all those rights.[62] When you buy a device, you get the right to use all the patents that are bound up in it as part of using your new gadget.[63] Exhaustion is under attack and fading fast. Scholars Aaron Perzanowski and Jason Schultz have written an extensive text, *The End of Ownership*,[64] that provides a fascinating analysis of the current jurisprudence of exhaustion, and details how companies extend their power over assets they have already sold by terms in license agreements and contracts. Perzanowski and Schultz demonstrate that companies' attack on exhaustion has permitted ever-more-intrusive control over digital and smart assets. Unless some radical change is coming, they argue, we are looking at the end of ownership as we have known it.

Consider a book: you get the right to read the book, and sell it to someone else if you wish, even though the owner of the copyright is normally the only person who can distribute copies of the book.[65] Or consider trademark, another major kind of intellectual property. Although I can't paint Nike's

---

[61] *See* Andreas Cremer & Valerie Volcovici, *Volkswagen Shares Plunge on Emissions Scandal; U.S. Widens Probe*, REUTERS (Sept. 21, 2015), http://www.reuters.com/article/usa-volkswagen-idINL5N1R0TU20150921 (noting that "the German carmaker admitted it had rigged emissions tests of diesel-powered vehicles in the United States").

[62] *See generally* 1-1 Chisum on Patents § 1.02 (2015) (discussing patented products).

[63] *See, e.g.*, Quanta Comput., Inc. v. LG Elecs., Inc., 553 U.S. 617, 625 (2008) ("The longstanding doctrine of patent exhaustion provides that the initial authorized sale of a patented item terminates all patent rights to that item.").

[64] PERZANOWSKI & SCHULTZ, *supra* note 48.

[65] *See, e.g.*, Kirtsaeng v. John Wiley & Sons, Inc., 133 S. Ct. 1351, 1355 (2013) (noting that "once a copy of [a copyrighted novel] has been lawfully sold (or its ownership otherwise lawfully transferred), the buyer of that copy and subsequent owners are free to dispose of it as they wish").

famous "swoosh" logo on my own products, I can certainly display the logo which it put on the shoes I just bought (and I can also resell those shoes).[66] One way to think about it is that your personal property right in something is like a box. We can put patent rights in that box representing all the inventions that were necessary to build your device. We can put copyrights in that box, representing all the coding necessary to make the software to get the device to run. We can dress up the device with trademarks, such as Apple's logo. Then we close the box, tie it up with a bow, and say: "Here. If you would like to buy this, you get this box. No strings attached."

That's how things are supposed to work. It's how things work for books you buy at the bookstore or (for now) cars you buy at the dealer. You, as the owner, don't need to worry about all the intellectual property that went into making your property, it's just your property. The way lawyers talk about that is to say that various rights of the intellectual property rightsholders have been exhausted. Done.

Principles of exhaustion appear throughout intellectual property law.[67] One specialized but well-known version of the exhaustion principle is called the "first sale" doctrine.[68] Copyright holders get the right to distribute copies of their works. In the era of printing presses and factories and trucks carrying books to bookstores, control over distribution channels was important, and was separate from the right to make copies of the work. Congress decided that the right to control distribution ended when the book was finally sold.[69] At that point, the distribution right was exhausted. So, we can sell our used books to whomever we wish, and the rightsholder can't stop us. That's why your corner bookstore sells used books.

Online, though, that right doesn't exist.[70] If you order a physical copy of a book from Amazon, you exhaust the rights of the copyright holder. Not so if you buy an electronic copy. If you buy a physical book, the publisher has no control over you. If you buy an e-book, you're under their control. If you buy a

---

[66] *See, e.g.,* NEC Elecs. v. CAL Circuit ABCO, 810 F.2d 1506, 1509 (9th Cir. 1987) ("Once a trademark owner sells his product, the buyer ordinarily may resell the product under the original mark without incurring any trademark liability." (citing Prestonettes, Inc. v. Coty, 264 U.S. 359 (1924))).

[67] *See, e.g.,* Allison v. Vintage Sports Plaques, 136 F.3d 1443, 1448 (11th Cir. 1998) (describing the application of exhaustion to "the three principal forms of intellectual property rights").

[68] *Id.*

[69] *See* 17 U.S.C. § 109(a) (2012) (providing "the owner of a particular copy" of a copyrighted work the right "to sell or otherwise dispose of the possession of that copy").

[70] *See, e.g.,* Michael S. Richardson, Comment, *The Monopoly on Digital Distribution,* 27 Pac. McGeorge Global Bus. & Dev. L.J. 153, 167 (2014) (observing that "tangible personal property receives first sale protection, whereas intangible digital property receives no protection under the federal court system").

CD from Amazon, the publisher can't stop you from selling the CD on eBay or anywhere else.[71] But if you buy the same song – the same album – the very same bits and bytes of music, but have it delivered to you electronically instead of by CD, then you're a digital peasant. That's what the users of the used MP3 website ReDigi found out when they tried to sell their legally purchased, used MP3s.[72] The rightsholders, arguing that there is no first sale doctrine for digital products (because they are intangible and must be copied to move them from buyer to seller), sued ReDigi out of business.

To be fair to the rightsholders, they may feel the need to eliminate consumers' first sale rights to compensate rightsholders for the increased risk of piracy for digital products. They may feel that since they are losing sales to illegal copying, they are justified in taking over secondary markets for used property. If that is the argument, though, reducing owners' rights is the wrong way to go about it. The trade is too crude. Why should a customer who buys a legal copy have reduced rights because others break the law? Do we reduce property rights in houses because they can be broken into, or cars because they can be stolen? A better way to prevent piracy is not to reduce owners' rights, but to invest in systems that both support strong property rights for buyers and protect sellers' intellectual property interest in preventing illicit copies – more on how to do that later.

In an age of iPods, it is absurd to require people to keep their music on CD or vinyl if they wish to retain it as property. The change in medium should not affect our property rights. Nothing much changed when we moved from 8-track tapes to cassette tapes to CDs. Yet the shift in storage medium from CDs to hard drives has been turned into an opportunity to cut short rights in what we have always owned. Rightsholders don't want you to be able to sell your used goods. They want each person who wants to buy a device, movie, music, book, and eventually car or house or mini-Segway footboard to have to come and buy a brand-new one from them. That is, they want to destroy our property interests in order to make more money in aftermarkets.

Antitrust and Aftermarket Control

The control that rightsholders have over personal property is a real problem when manufacturers try to use code to block competitors out of related

[71] *See* Capitol Records, LLC v. ReDigi Inc., 934 F. Supp. 2d 640, 656 (S.D.N.Y. 2013) (noting that the Copyright Act permits the "the resale of CDs and cassettes").

[72] *See id.* at 660–61 (granting the copyright holder's motion for summary judgment against ReDigi on "direct, contributory, and vicarious infringement of its distribution and reproduction rights").

markets. My Epson printer, for example, limits my ability to use printer cartridges made by anyone else. Since I bought one Epson product, Epson wants to use it to force me to buy more. Epson printers are coded with chips that recognize corresponding chips in Epson printer cartridges. If the printer doesn't recognize the chip, it complains and tries to get me to buy "authentic" cartridges, by which it means cartridges manufactured by Epson itself.

We have long limited monopolistic lock-in through antitrust law. Antitrust attempts to regulate the unfair profits a company can make if it has a monopoly on a good or service. By extension, it also steps in if a company has a monopoly in one area and then tries to extend it to another. Many decades ago, when Kodak tried to use its monopoly over the camera market to take control of the film market, antitrust law stepped in.[73] And when a pharmaceutical company required users of its schizophrenia-treating medicine to also purchase its blood-monitoring services, despite the existence of many alternatives, antitrust law again stopped that abuse of power.[74] We tend to think that a monopoly in one market is enough. We don't need monopolies spreading to other markets.

Online, though, antitrust law has lost much of its force. In the 1990s, the Department of Justice prepared an antitrust enforcement case against Microsoft on the basis of Microsoft's brutal power play for the browser market.[75] Then-leading browser Netscape had been excluded from original equipment manufacturer deals, clearing room for Microsoft Explorer to take over.[76] The case ultimately resulted in a settlement between Microsoft and the Department of Justice, though many have argued that Microsoft suffered little more than a slap on the wrist for its actions.[77]

[73] *See* United States v. Eastman Kodak Co., 853 F. Supp. 1454, 1459 (W.D.N.Y. 1994) (discussing a 1954 consent decree entered after the United States "charging Kodak with violating the Sherman Act by its practices relating to the sale of color film" in the U.S., "which forbade, among other things, tying or otherwise connecting in any manner the sale of [Kodak's] color film to the processing thereof" (internal quotation marks omitted)).

[74] *See* Milt Freudenheim, *Company News; Antitrust Settlement By Sandoz*, N.Y. Times (June 21, 1991), http://www.nytimes.com/1991/06/21/business/company-news-antitrust-settlement-by-sandoz.html (detailing a settlement between the company and the FTC, after the FTC "said the tie-in arrangement had raised the price of clozapine," a "drug that could help people with schizophrenia").

[75] *See* Stan J. Liebowitz & Stephen E. Margolis, Winners, Losers & Microsoft: Competition and Antitrust in High Technology 248–55 (Independent Institute 1999) (discussing allegations that "Microsoft's integration of its browser into [its] operating system [was] largely predatory").

[76] *Id.* at 247–48.

[77] *See* Amy Harmon, *U.S. vs. Microsoft: The Overview; Judge Backs Terms of U.S. Settlement in Microsoft Case*, N.Y. Times (Nov. 2, 2002), http://www.nytimes.com/2002/11/02/business/us-vs-microsoft-overview-judge-backs-terms-us-settlement-microsoft-case.html?pagewanted=all ("[T]he judge imposed few new restrictions that would slow Microsoft's

Why let Microsoft off so easily? Antitrust in rapidly evolving fields can be a tricky thing to handle. The idea of market dominance has evolved significantly since the turn of the millennium. Now, antitrust regulators are as likely to wait for the next paradigm shift to naturally upset a technological monopoly as they are to enforce. So, the reasoning goes, it may not matter much that Microsoft dominates the market for PC operating systems.[78] PCs are a dated technology, and Microsoft is decidedly behind the curve in developing mobile operating systems, where both Apple and Google have staked a strong claim. If technological shift is fast enough, antitrust enforcement in its traditional form is less useful.

There are problems with this narrative, of course. Microsoft may have fallen behind competitors in the mid-2010s, but that was a decade and a half too late for Netscape or any of the other tech companies – would-be giant-slayers – whose corporate skeletons line Silicon Valley. Frank Pasquale writes in his book *The Black Box Society* that although the 1990s and early turn of the millennium were no doubt a time of fast technological foment, there is no reason to think that the new giants of the social media and search landscape – Facebook and Google – can be displaced any time soon.[79] Search and identity are locked down, and there is no serious competition.

Beyond that, there is a specific difficulty that affects our discussion here, a problem not of market monopoly but of consumer lock-in. Harking back to my Epson printer, consider a printer company that wants to lock in its customers. The company has no monopoly in the printer market. There are many different computer printers out there. No one company controls a dominating market share. However, once a customer buys a printer from our hypothetical company, the company has an opportunity. If it can assert control over the property it has manufactured and sold, by means of embedded software, it can control whom its customers do business with in the future. This is precisely what Lexmark did – I mentioned this earlier – in the well-known case *Lexmark v. Static Control*.[80] As discussed, Lexmark wrote software that required specific authentication from the printer cartridge to the printer.[81] This

---

aggressive push into new markets. . . . Still, she granted almost none of the core proposals the states raised during an eight-week trial [in 2002].").

[78] *See* LIEBOWITZ & MARGOLIS, *supra* note 75, at 14–15 (discussing Microsoft's monopoly on the PC market in the 1990s).

[79] *See* FRANK PASQUALE, THE BLACK BOX SOCIETY: THE SECRET ALGORITHMS THAT CONTROL MONEY AND INFORMATION 92–98 (Harvard University Press 2015) (discussing the dominance of Google and Facebook in their respective markets).

[80] Lexmark Int'l, Inc. v. Static Control Components, Inc., 387 F.3d 522 (6th Cir. 2004).

[81] *See id.* at 529–30 (discussing Lexmark's "Toner Loading Program" and "Printer Engine Program").

went a step further than Epson did with my printer: a Lexmark printer refused to run with non-Lexmark cartridges.[82] This way, Lexmark could stop competitors like Static Control from refilling and refurbishing printer cartridges and selling them back to the consumer at lower cost. Lexmark's theory of the case was that by including a copy of Lexmark's authentication program (which was, as mentioned, the only way to get the cartridge to talk to the printer), Static Control committed copyright infringement.[83]

Lexmark lost the copyright case, because the Sixth Circuit Court of Appeals wasn't ready to tar Lexmark's off-brand competitors with the brush of copyright infringer. But Lexmark promptly turned to patent law, arguing that its patent licensing agreements with distributors permitted it to block sellers of refurbished (and refilled) ink cartridges that were first sold overseas. This time, before the Court of Appeals for the Federal Circuit, it won on a very technical ground: Lexmark argued that it didn't exhaust its patent rights when it sold overseas, even though it arguably would have exhausted its rights when it sold in the United States.[84] The point is, Lexmark doesn't care how it takes over the secondary market: copyright law, patent law, traffic law, whatever. Lexmark's goal was to capture the market for cartridges once someone bought a Lexmark printer. That is lock-in.

Companies don't want to just sell us something once. They want to control our property so that they can force us to keep buying more and more from them. Recall the lock-in pressure Chamberlain exerted on customers who bought its garage doors – it tried to prevent them from buying generic remote controls. Recall MAI's efforts to control computer repairs; John Deere has recently employed a similar logic in requiring farmers to only repair their tractors at a John Deere-approved mechanic. If you own an iPhone, you are familiar with Apple's infamous "walled garden" ecosystem: Apple products only work with Apple products; even the charger is unique to Apple. The urge to use the power of copyrighted software to hijack secondary markets is a major driving economic force behind the war on your property. Companies can simply pretend to sell you a car, or a house, or an MP3, or a movie, then

---

[82] *See id.* at 530 ("If the code calculated by the microchip matches the code calculated by the printer, the printer functions normally. If the two values do not match, the printer returns an error message and will not operate, blocking consumers from using toner cartridges that Lexmark has not authorized.").

[83] *See id.* at 529 ("Lexmark claimed that SCC's chip copied the Toner Loading Program in violation of the federal copyright statute.").

[84] *See* Lexmark Int'l, Inc. v. Impression Prod., Inc., 816 F.3d 721, 727 (Fed. Cir. 2016) ("[A] U.S. patentee, merely by selling or authorizing the sale of a U.S.-patented article *abroad*, does not authorize the buyer to import the article and sell and use it in the United States, which are infringing acts in the absence of patentee-conferred authority." (emphasis added))

make more money by essentially forcing you to do more and more business with them.

There's a funny coda to the history of DRM – the access control technologies that brought us section 1201 of the DCMA. DRM continues to proliferate. After all, the DCMA and its prohibitions against circumnavigating access controls have been a boon to rightsholders. But the music industry – one of the original proponents of DRM – has shifted its perspective. Apple is famously credited for freeing the music market from DRM.[85] But as Aaron Perzanowski and Jason Schultz write, that is not quite the entire story.[86] At first, Apple dominated the market, and the major music rightsholders were content to work with them. After all, Apple was much better than Napster. But after a while, the rightsholders began to think about what they'd done.[87] Apple users could only play their music on Apple devices. DRM technology locked users' legally purchased music inside the Apple ecosystem. (I don't know if you ever looked at your Apple music files during those years. If you tried to open the file outside of iTunes, it was just gibberish.) Eventually, the major recording labels realized they had made a mistake. Users were locked into iTunes and Apple. Consumers lacked the basic right to move their music from one service to another. This raised switching costs, and as Apple came to dominate the market for retail music sales, the rightsholders were faced with the prospect of losing bargaining power against Apple. Rightsholders realized why Apple had such a strong focus on the "walled garden," the ecosystem of Apple products that work seamlessly with each other, but really terribly with anything else. Once a company's music was inside Apple's walled garden, consumers would be locked in. It would be expensive and hard for them to switch.[88]

So the music industry changed course. The rightsholders negotiated with Amazon to do something new: sell music with no DRM so that it could be migrated to any service.[89] This was some serious competition to Apple's

---

[85] *See, e.g.,* John Markoff, *Jobs Calls for End to Music Copy Protection,* N.Y. TIMES (Feb. 7, 2007), http://www.nytimes.com/2007/02/07/technology/07music.html?_r=0 (noting that Apple "jolted the record industry . . . by calling on its largest companies to allow online music sales unfettered by antipiracy software").

[86] *See* PERZANOWSKI & SCHULTZ, *supra* note 48, at 133–34 (discussing the history of Apple and DRM technology).

[87] *See id.* at 133 ("To hear Steve Jobs tell it, the labels insisted on DRM, and Apple played along. . . . [But] the labels came to regret their insistence once they discovered that DRM benefitted Apple much more than it did copyright holders").

[88] *See id.* at 133–34 ("Apple's FairPlay-protected tracks, which consumers collectively spent tens of millions of dollars buying, couldn't be played on competing hardware.").

[89] *See id.* at 134 (discussing how the record labels "free[d] themselves from the chains of DRM" with help from Amazon).

closed-off universe. Recognizing this, Steve Jobs made his famous pronounce-ments against DRM, Apple started selling DRM-free music (for a modest markup), and consumers everywhere benefited.[90] The basic property right to transfer property solved a tangled market and restored power to consumers, who were no longer locked in.

Outside the music industry, lock-in remains a compelling and ubiquitous force. In 2006, Blizzard Entertainment, maker of the famous massively multi-player game *World of Warcraft*, distributed an investors' report discussing the financial reliability of its games.[91] Blizzard boasted that once users began to build their avatars (digital selves within the game), make friendships, and earn valuable digital property, they would be locked in to Blizzard's products. Bliz-zard wrote: "Advantages that accrue to highly successful MMORPGs [include] high consumer switching costs – the player has to leave their characters and friends!"[92] In short, players were locked in.[93]

Companies don't just want to control your property to force you to buy extras, add-ons, or supplies from them. They also want to control your property to keep you from selling it to anyone else. The markets are, to the company, pretty similar. Imagine a car manufacturer like GM, which tried – unsuccessfully – to use its control over software embedded in the car to control which mechanics can work on the car.[94] Such a manufacturer could also decide to take over the used-car market. It could do so by making the software inside its cars only licensed to the first buyer, and requiring that any secondary buyer pay the company for her own license. This is the same theory that dominates the online music business right now: courts have decided that consumers are not allowed to resell digital music that they have legitimately bought and paid for. Why would record companies do this? Because they want to sell two copies of the music – one to you, and one to a friend – instead of letting you buy a copy and then sell or trade or give it to a friend when you are done with it. Imagine if a car company did the same, and either took a cut

---

[90] *See* James Niccolai & Martyn Williams, *EMI Drops DRM for Music Sold Through iTunes*, PCWORLD (Apr. 2, 2007), http://www.pcworld.com/article/130308/article.html (indicating that consumers benefit from DRM-free music "because any player would be able to play music from any online retailer").

[91] Vivendi Games, Introduction to Vivendi Games (EX-99.1) (June 2006), *available at* http://www.sec.gov/Archives/edgar/data/1127055/000095012306007628/y22210exv99w1.htm.

[92] *Id.* at 15.

[93] Joshua A.T. Fairfield, *Anti-Social Contracts: The Contractual Governance of Virtual Worlds*, 53 McGILL L.J. 427, 470 (2008).

[94] *See* Thomas Fox-Brewster, *DMCA Ruling Ensures You Can't Be Sued for Hacking Your Car, Your Games or Your iPhone*, FORBES: SECURITY (Oct. 27, 2015, 3:38 PM), http://www.forbes.com/sites/thomasbrewster/2015/10/27/right-to-tinker-victory/#375ca92238ae.

of every purchase or rendered the car undriveable by revoking the software licenses.

Traditional antitrust law doesn't seem to be a great fit for this problem. For one thing, tech companies rarely hold monopolies in their primary markets. For another, even if they did, we might reasonably expect to see some (not all) of these companies lose their dominant positions in the usual high-technology market roil. And finally, antitrust law is a slow process, and one that doesn't particularly help consumers in the short term.

What is needed is a robust sense that this attempt to command downstream markets by trying to control what the company has already sold contravenes long-standing notions of what it means to sell something. What is needed is a strong sense that once a consumer buys something, she may sell it to someone else without asking permission of the manufacturer. What is needed is a strong set of principles laying out not only what companies may *not* do once they've made a sale, but what the new owner *may* do. While we figure out antitrust theory, ordinary people need ordinary property rights. In short, we need traditional, good-old-fashioned property law.

The threat to consumer wealth is not just market domination, but consumer lock-in. As things stand, once a company has sold you one thing, it can use the power of contracts, intellectual property licenses, and anti-hacking laws to force you to either abandon the thing you first bought, or else continue making purchases exclusively from that firm. This is exactly what happened with Apple's DRM-scrambled music. If you wanted your music all in one place and playable on one device, you had to buy more music from the iTunes store. The way to solve consumer lock-in and restore competition, as the music battle between Apple and Amazon shows, is by restoring to consumers' basic property rights over digital and smart property.

CONTRACT WITHOUT CONSENT

As we have seen, part of the problem is that intellectual property was stretched to cover cases it was never designed to govern. Another problem is that doctrines that have traditionally constrained the powers of intellectual property rightsholders, like exhaustion, are getting weaker. But none of the above would have come to pass without a similar overextension of online contract law. The holding of *MAI* rested on the contract between the parties, which the court interpreted as a mere license, not a sale. DMCA 1201 is problematic only if the contract is deemed a piracy countermeasure – if so, accessing the program while avoiding the contract violates the law. Exhaustion is whittled away in license agreements that grant rightsholders powers long after the transaction has been concluded. And all by themselves, through their raw number and power, online contracts have changed the balance of power in law between rightsholders and consumers. To exaggerate only slightly: the most important social contract of the twenty-first century is not the U.S. Constitution, it is the Facebook Terms of Service.

Catch 22.0

Perhaps, like me, you read Joseph Heller's *Catch-22* in high school. In this book about impossible choices during World War II, a pilot could be excused from flying combat missions if he were mentally unfit, but any pilot who did not want to fly was by definition mentally fit.[95] It's a double bind; colloquially, "damned if you do, damned if you don't." That's where owners of smart and digital property are now. Copyright law and anti-hacking law – the RAM copy doctrine and section 1201 of the Digital Millennium Copyright Act among them – play a large part in this double bind, but the ties that bind them are contract law. To use our property, we have to sign contracts that give up key rights and ownership interests.

Here's how it works: you have to sign a stack of contracts just to activate a device. When you bring your new device home from the store and power it up for the first time, you are presented with a bunch of screens that ask you to agree to various terms and conditions. We don't read those terms and conditions. Nobody does and nobody could. But you have to agree to them. If you don't, you are a copyright infringer. Remember, per the RAM copy doctrine, you made a copy of copyrighted material when you turned your device on – you loaded copyrighted material from storage into active memory. And if you make that copy without a license – if you don't click "I Agree" to the terms and conditions of the rightsholder – then you've infringed copyright. More practically, if you don't agree, your device will turn into an expensive paperweight.

So you hit "I Agree" to avoid being a copyright infringer and to actually use your device. What did you agree to? The contracts are different, but they have quite a few things in common. First, they state that you do not own the software that came with your device and that makes it run. You just license it. The Copyright Act gives owners certain rights, including the right to make a copy of a computer program in order to use the machine. But when you click "I Agree," you give up those ownership rights. As soon as you agree that you do not own what you just bought, you open the door to all kinds of other

---

[95] JOSEPH HELLER, CATCH-22 56 (Simon & Schuster 1961).

controls by the manufacturer. As a non-owner, you cannot make copies, even as a necessary part of using the product, without doing exactly as the licensor demands.

What's more, you give up all kinds of rights to sell your property, to modify your software, to control who can access your data, and to make changes to your own device. It's kind of like agreeing not to repaint your new car without the dealer's permission. In fact, you may even give up your rights to act in certain ways while using your device. In one famous case, a video game manufacturer claimed its users were infringing copyright by breaking the rules of the game.[96] That case involved cheating, but computer games have a host of rules – sometimes even ones that say that you have to be nice.[97] So, to follow this logic, if you are not nice while playing the game, you could be accused of infringing copyright. You loaded a copy of the game from storage into active memory while not following every single term of the long and unreadable license.

Moreover, many of these contracts (in fact, pretty much all of them if the contract is with a major operating system provider or telecommunications carrier) take away your right to go to court to argue about it.[98] Let's say you disagree about whether you have broken one of the rules of the license. For example, you think you should have the right to back up your software for security purposes, or encrypt your communications with a third-party program, or take your tractor to a local dealer instead of a licensed one, but the licensor disagrees. So the licensor revokes your license: now you can't use your own property. It's a pain if the device is your smartphone; but what if the device is your farm's harvester?[99] You can't even go to court to argue that the licensor's interpretation is wrong, or that it misunderstands Congress's protections, or that you should be able to do what you want with your own property.[100]

---

[96] MDY Industries, LLC v. Blizzard Entertainment, Inc., 629 F.3d 928 (2010). This case is discussed in detail in Chapter 8.

[97] For instance, the license agreement for the popular MMORPG World of Warcraft provides in part that the game owner may "take such disciplinary measures as it sees fit up to and including termination and deletion of the Account" if players transmit language that "is deemed to be offensive, including without limitation content or language that is unlawful, harmful, threatening, abusive, harassing, defamatory, vulgar, obscene, hateful, sexually explicit, or racially, ethnically or otherwise objectionable." *World of Warcraft Terms of Use*, BLIZZARD ENT., http://us.blizzard.com/en-us/company/legal/wow_tou.html (last updated Aug. 22, 2012).

[98] *See, e.g., id.* (providing that "either you or Blizzard may elect to have [a] Dispute . . . finally and exclusively resolved by binding arbitration").

[99] *See* Kyle Wiens, *We Can't Let John Deere Destroy the Very Idea of Ownership*, WIRED (Apr. 21, 2015 9:00 AM), http://www.wired.com/2015/04/dmca-ownership-john-deere.

[100] *See* Jessica Greenberg & Robert Gebeloff, *Arbitration Everywhere, Stacking the Deck of Justice*, N.Y. TIMES (Oct. 31, 2015), http://www.nytimes.com/2015/11/01/business/dealbook/

You have to go to arbitration instead, because that's what you agreed to when you signed the contract. What's more, many arbitration agreements not only force consumers out of court, but require them to complain one at a time, instead of sharing the costs of lawyers as a class.[101] Unsurprisingly, very few consumers actually manage to arbitrate. Over a five-year period, only sixty-five of Verizon's 125 million customers, seven of Time Warner's seven million customers, and six of Sprint's fifty-seven million customers – roughly one per ten million, or 0.00001% – managed to arbitrate their disputes. And two-thirds of those few customers who do arbitrate, lose.[102] Is it reasonable to think that only one out of fifty-seven million Sprint customers has a viable grievance with a telecommunications carrier every two-and-a-half years? This is not a credible system of dispute resolution.

Finally, let's say you've decided that clicking "I Agree" and giving up your rights is a bad idea. And you're good enough with computers that you can get your device to work without doing so. That's when you encounter another wrinkle in the catch-22: thanks to DMCA section 1201, you've broken copyright law. You just hacked a technological lock.

Contracts Everywhere!

Companies' ability to bind consumers by contract has grown more powerful with the advent of information technologies. As if clicking "I Agree" to fifty-page documents that no one can read were not enough, companies now claim the right to bind consumers who do nothing at all. I'm sure you have seen websites that say, "By continuing to use this website, you agree to tracking by cookies." That is not an argument that usually works. Let's try it: Dear reader, by reading this book, you have already agreed to give me all your money. Nope. Didn't work. But it does online. Many online contracts are considered enforceable simply because you used the webpage. In the case of smart property, you are sometimes held to have consented to the extraction of your data merely because you used the device – a device that you already purchased and paid for.

When we walk about our daily lives, we don't have to sign contracts just to do basic things. You can buy a pair of shoes at a store, drive down the street, enter your home, all without signing a single contract. But if you do

---

arbitration-everywhere-stacking-the-deck-of-justice.html (discussing the impact of arbitration clauses on ordinary consumers).

[101] *See id.* (noting "two Supreme Court rulings, in 2011 and 2013, that enshrined the use of class-action bans in contracts" and virtually eliminated class arbitrations).

[102] *Id.*

those things using electronic devices, suddenly you are presented with Terms of Use, End User License Agreements, or the simple contractual "I Agree" button at every step. Buy a pair of shoes from an online store, and a court will say you have agreed to multiple contracts by the time you are done, even if you never saw a word of them. Drive down the street in your software-enabled car, and you are bound to a huge number of contracts. Even more if you use your Android or iPhone to get you there with Google Maps. And to run the smart appliances in your own home? More contracts!

This creates a particular problem. The law says that we can do practically anything with contracts. For example, there is a background rule that says we can't go around hitting each other. That's the basic rule of tort law: no hitting. But I can agree to let you hit me in a contract. That's called a boxing match. So the general rule of tort law can be undone by a specific contractual agreement. We can do the same thing with property. The basic rule of property law is: no stealing. If you want my goods, you have to negotiate with me and get me to agree. This is what Guido Calabresi and A. Douglas Melamed call a "property rule," in their landmark article *Property Rules, Liability Rules, and Inalienability: One View of the Cathedral.*[103] But you and I can agree to let you have my property in a contract. That's what's called the closing of a real estate transaction. Again, the general "no stealing" rule can be modified by the specific agreement to let you take my property in a specific case. The same goes for criminal law (I can't actually agree to let you murder me, but that's a specific case), or constitutional law (without a warrant, the police can't search your house unless you agree to let them, in which case they can). In each case, contractual rules are specific exceptions to the general rule.

But what if enough companies could put enough contracts in our path, controlling enough of the world around us that we would have no choice but to agree to their terms? The contract rule would become the general rule. It would not only replace the outcome of a specific deal. Contracts would replace property – and every other form of law. With contracts embedded in more and more objects we encounter, and greeting us at every step, surrounding all of our actions taken online and, increasingly, many actions we take offline, this is precisely what is happening. Our property has been taken from us by contracts that we must sign in order to use our own property. Our right to a day in court

---

[103] *See* Calabresi & Melamed, *supra* note 1, at 1092 ("An entitlement is protected by a property rule to the extent that someone who wishes to remove the entitlement from its holder must buy it from him in a voluntary transaction in which the value of the entitlement is agreed upon by the seller.").

has been taken from us in the same contracts.[104] We cannot protest how our data – extracted from the devices around us – are used. We have signed away our data, our property, and our privacy just to be able to function in day-to-day life.

All of this is to say: this book focuses on property law online. But for personal property to survive and thrive in the twenty-first century, the law must significantly alter its understanding of what it means to write a contractual exception to a rule. When both parties want to write such an exception, it works well. But when contracts are forced, they are corrupted. Forced contracts are no contracts at all. It is not enough to say that if we don't like the contract, we need not click "I Agree." For one thing, the "I Agree" stands in the way of our using our own property. That is a holdup, not a contract. For another, if we permit contractual provisions embedded throughout ordinary life to govern, law will lose its significance. My distress over this is not simply as a professor of law who wants to preserve his profession. Rather, it comes from a sense that default rules should benefit all of us. Contract provisions, on the other hand, benefit the person who wrote them. If we are not cautious, the default rules of property, common decency, and constitutional ordering that have been tested by millions of people over generations will be discarded in favor of a contract written by a corporate attorney in the last few years to benefit her client and no one else. That is not going to be a pleasant society to live in.

And if the above strikes you as too strong, check the "I Agree" contracts in your phone, tablet, or computer. You'll be surprised at what you find.

PROPERTY IS DEAD – LONG LIVE PROPERTY!

The free model of property is being replaced by a new digital feudalism. Court confusion over the respective roles of intellectual and traditional property has intensified the problem. Judges' unwillingness to rein in online contracts has left consumers out in the cold – these same contracts prevent consumers from even to going to court to challenge these agreements. The decentralized freedom of an individual property owner is being increasingly replaced by a centralized system of intellectual property licensing. This turns back the clock to a time when a few held the reins of power, and the many only had claims on resources through their relationships with the few. That's how it is now: we only have claims on our digital and smart property through our license relationships with intellectual property rightsholders.

---

[104] *See supra* notes 98–102 and accompanying text (discussing the prevalence of arbitration clauses in consumer contracts).

   Although all of this is cloaked with a thin layer of freedom of contract – you
are free to not click "I Agree," and not use your device, after all – in truth, it is a
perversion of the idea of freedom. Jedediah Purdy applies the term "Hobson's
Choice," a choice where only one option is presented, to describe unfree
decisions in sheep's clothing.[105] "I Agree" is a textbook Hobson's choice. In
line with the thinking of Amartya Sen, a choice between "terrible," "worse,"
and "god-awful" is not freedom in any human sense of the word. We need to
expand consumers' range of real choices. To do that, we will need to bring
digital and smart property back to life. And the need is all the more urgent
because, as the next chapter describes, the laws that have until now only
governed music, movies, and software are coming to govern everyday life as
sensors and software are seeded throughout our environment.

[105] Jedediah Purdy, A Freedom-Promoting Approach to Property: A Renewed Tradition for New
   Debates, 72 U. CHI. L. REV. 1238, 1260 (2005).

3

Surrounded

"It's impossible to move, to live, to operate at any level without leaving traces, bits, seemingly meaningless fragments of personal information."

– William Gibson[1]

"Everyone who had ever lived was literally surrounded by the iron walls of the prison; they were all inside it and none of them knew it."

– Philip K. Dick[2]

In testimony delivered to the Nevada legislature, T. Candice Smith recalled driving down crowded Interstate 15 in Las Vegas when her car was turned off abruptly by her auto lender. As Smith later told the New York Times, "The worst thing ever to happen to someone is to be driving on a freeway, the car is going, like, super fast, and your car just instantly powers down."[3] Smith's lender was one of a number of subprime auto lenders who use "starter interrupt devices" to remotely disable cars if their customers, many of whom struggle financially, miss a payment.[4] One woman observed that she had to schedule her life and driving around her payments. "It's like they control my life," she noted. She held up the small device that connected her car to the internet. "This thing rules my life."[5]

Subprime auto loans have been a cash cow ever since their cousins, subprime mortgages, became more heavily regulated.[6] Lenders figure that

---

[1] William Gibson, *Johnny Mnemonic, in* THE SCIENCE FICTION CENTURY 939, 948 (David G. Hartwell ed., 1997).

[2] PHILIP K. DICK, VALIS 48 (Houghton Mifflin Harcourt 2011) (1981).

[3] Sean Patrick Farrell, *The Remote Repo Man*, N.Y. TIMES (Sept. 25, 2014, 5:19 AM), http://www .nytimes.com/video/business/100000003095109/the-remote-repo-man.html.

[4] *Id.*   [5] *Id.*

[6] *See* Helaine Olen, *Subprime Loans Are Back*, SLATE (May 2, 2016, 3:47 PM), http://www .slate.com/articles/business/the_united_states_of_debt/2016/05/why_subprime_auto_loans_are_

because borrowers need cars to keep their jobs, they will do almost anything to make their car payment.[7] And that's doubly so if a remote GPS-enabled device disables the car if a payment is missed. This eagerness to turn a car off has caused some lenders to skirt state law. Where state law often gives a consumer thirty days to make a car payment without defaulting, starter interrupt devices often shut the car down two days after a missed payment.[8] This "tough-love approach"[9] results in control over the borrower's life. Whether she can take a sick child to the hospital or get to work to afford the next car payment is entirely dependent on the tender mercies of the subprime lender.[10] And the devices create a huge security flaw: everything can be hacked, as two researchers demonstrated when they were able to remotely turn off a reporter's car on the freeway.[11] "I was driving 70 mph on the edge of downtown St. Louis when the exploit began to take hold," wrote *Wired* reporter Andy Greenberg.[12] The hackers turned on the air conditioning full blast, cut the transmission, and replaced the console display with their own picture, just to put the finishing touches on the experience.[13] Mind you, they did this by exploiting the Jeep Cherokee's sophisticated on-board internet-accessible computer. But a starter interrupt device is a one-stop-shop for converting your "dumb" car into a rolling hackable coffin. After her experience on I-15, Smith paid for her next car with cash. "I would never get another car that has a GPS or PassTime device on it again, under any circumstances, unless they were to agree to take the GPS system off," she said.[14]

Here's another account from the front line of the Internet of Things: in 2015, the FTC brought a complaint against Nomi Technologies.[15] Nomi tracked users' cell phones as they moved around stores.[16] Nomi claimed that users could opt out of the tracking via a website and in the store, but in fact offered no in-store opt-out. Companies like to know where you go. Perhaps you and other shoppers linger too long in front of the chocolate section before finally

booming.html (noting that "fewer than 15 percent of new cars sold in the last quarter of 2015 were paid for outright").

[7] *See id.* ("Financial experts believe because our autos are such a lifeline to our financial lives, people will pay their monthly loan bills over almost any other bill.").

[8] *See* Farrell, *supra* note 3 (discussing the discrepancy between state regulations and the threats contained in letters accompanying starter interrupt devices).

[9] *Id.*

[10] *See id.* (observing the concerns of drivers with starter interrupt devices).

[11] *See* Andy Greenberg, *Hackers Remotely Kill a Jeep on the Highway – With Me in It*, WIRED (July 21, 2015, 6:00 AM), https://www.wired.com/2015/07/hackers-remotely-kill-jeep-highway/.

[12] *Id.*   [13] *Id.*   [14] Farrell, *supra* note 3.

[15] Complaint, *In re* Nomi Techs., Inc., No. C-4538 (F.T.C. Aug. 28, 2015).

[16] *See id.* at 1 (finding that "Nomi use[d] mobile device tracking technology to provide analytics services to brick and mortar retailers through its 'Listen' service").

stepping away through a supreme act of willpower. The store needs to know this so that it can step up advertisements for delicious chocolatey temptations.[17] Nomi tracked shoppers' phones by gathering the media access control (MAC) address, a unique identifier to each phone, as well as the strength of the Wi-Fi signal and other identifying information from the device.[18] Nomi did disguise the MAC address by using a mathematical hash function, but it kept the same number for each shopper.[19] It is as though John Smith were tagged as "Shopper 1," and kept that same number every time he came back into the store. The FTC argued that Nomi violated its privacy promises to consumers by tracking them without informing them, and by failing to provide consumers the promised in-store opt-out.[20]

A third dispatch: Oral Roberts University, a private, evangelical university in Tulsa, Oklahoma, mandated that its incoming freshmen class purchase and wear Fitbit fitness trackers as part of its freshman fitness requirement.[21] In the entry-level class Health Fitness I, students are expected to log ten thousand steps per day. The steps tracked in the app counted for 20 percent of the student's grade. In prior years, ORU had required students to log their daily exercise in journals. Now, freshmen must grant an ORU-linked account access to data from the Fitbit, including heart rate and steps tracking data. Although ORU does not require students to enable GPS tracking, a large number of the Fitbits sold to students do track and report location. And a University of Toronto study shows that fitness trackers like Fitbit leak location information to third parties through the broadcast of a unique Bluetooth identifier – even when the tracking application is shut down and a phone's Bluetooth is shut off.[22]

These three stories highlight the emerging risks of the Internet of Things, or IoT. In Smith's story of being shut down on the superhighway, we see the dangers of handing over control of our property to remote entities that do not

---

[17] *See id.* at 2 ("Nomi uses the information it collects to provide analytics reports to its clients about aggregate customer traffic patterns....").

[18] *See id.* (detailing Nomi's technological methods).

[19] *See id.* ("Hashing obfuscates the MAC address, but the result is still a persistent unique identifier for that mobile device.").

[20] *See id.* at 3 (charging Nomi with violations of "Section 5(a) of the Federal Trade Commission Act").

[21] Sam Machkovech, *Evangelical University Requires Fitbit Ownership, Data Syncing for Freshmen*, Ars Technica (Feb. 1, 2016, 4:05 PM), http://arstechnica.com/gadgets/2016/02/evangelical-university-requires-fitbit-ownership-data-syncing-for-freshmen.

[22] *See* Alex Gillis, *Fitness Tracker Flaws Exposed by U of T's Citizen Lab and Open Effect*, U. Toronto (Feb. 2, 2016), http://www.utoronto.ca/news/fitness-tracker-flaws-exposed-u-ts-citizen-lab-and-open-effect (reporting that "seven fitness trackers studied leak personal data that enable anyone near a device to track a user's location over time").

have our best interests at heart. In the story of Nomi, we see how technology we carry with us – our smartphones – can interact with technology that is built into the infrastructure we encounter. In the story of ORU, we observe real tension between the enormous value of IoT devices to consumers and users at the edge of communications networks, and the inevitable pull of that data to the center for use by companies, organizations, or governments. And for an added kick, one can observe that mandated adoption and central administration of IoT devices reduces personal security and privacy by providing a target-rich environment for hackers of all stripes.

We are surrounded. Computers are embedded in the spaces around us. We carry them with us in the form of smartphones and fitness trackers. We encounter them when we enter computerized spaces like the workplace, the home, supermarkets, shopping malls, and traffic intersections. If we do not come to the sensors, they come to us – towers reach out to our phones and, increasingly, drones and autonomous vehicles will come to where we are. Finally, if we seek to escape this world of escalating surveillance by escaping into virtual worlds and online environments, we find that we have escaped the frying pan by leaping into the fire. Computerized virtual environments are the perfect panopticon: worlds in which the entire world itself is a camera.

The buzzword "Internet of Things" is made up of a mix of tech trends. Sensors proliferate. Devices have gotten smaller and more mobile. Standards like bluetooth and RFID (radio-frequency identification) permit gadgets to connect with one another. Devices have gotten better at interacting with the environment through cameras, GPS, and motion sensors. Virtualization technology has improved so that humans can experience three-dimensional virtual spaces with just a smartphone, two lenses, and a cardboard box, not to mention the sophisticated virtual reality headsets now coming into vogue.[23] Converging communications technology then means that each of these objects can speak with many others and with large pools of processing power maintained elsewhere online – the so-called cloud.

Lurking behind these stories should be the question, what does it mean when we have no ability to control the devices and spaces, packed with computers and sensors, that surround us? Property rights allow humans to make demands on resources and to control their surroundings. Our houses are the best example: we build and modify them in order to create a small bubble of warmth and light in an inhospitable world. When cold rain drums on the roof,

---

[23] *See, e.g.*, Brian X. Chen, *Oculus Rift Review: A Clunky Portal to a Promising Virtual Reality*, N.Y. TIMES (Mar. 28, 2016), http://www.nytimes.com/2016/03/31/technology/personaltech/oculus-rift-virtual-reality-review.html (discussing the "much-hyped Oculus Rift system").

we are thankful that we can patch leaks to keep dry and build fires to keep warm.

Property law cannot be permitted to be swallowed up by information systems. If it is, we will lose the ability to make decisions about the world around us. We need the digital equivalent of the ability to patch leaks and build fires. We are in danger of digital exposure. We are at risk of digital homelessness. The Internet of Things will bring vast benefits, but if we cannot make demands on digital resources, then we are merely tenants, to be evicted from use of these digital resources at the whim of our digital feudal lords.

Of course, the Internet of Things also comes with large benefits. It will be wonderful to organize physical space with the same ferocious efficiency and completeness that we have used on the internet. I often lose my car keys. These days I can find them again with an application that tracks a dongle that I have hung on my keyring.[24] This saves me so much anger and stress. I did the same to my wallet and my laptop. I should do the same for my car.

But to reap the benefits of these information-enriched devices, we will have to trust IoT systems enormously. IoT data exposes our most vulnerable moments. It is not about us sitting at a desk. It is about us at the therapist, in bed, at the doctor, at church, and in a bar. It is not about how we act in one context, but in every context. Given that, IoT appliances do not do enough to earn our trust. I would like to have a health-tracking watch, but the risk of handing personal health information off to an advertising consortium is simply too high. I don't want my healthcare data networked that much. I'd be happy to have it stay local, near me. I want to see the charts and data, not have them handed off to my employer, for example, or my insurance company, or pill advertisers.[25]

THE ELEMENTS OF THE INTERNET OF THINGS

The Internet of Things creates an information-linked and information-responsive reality. The current waves of sensor proliferation, device connectivity, miniaturization, mobile computing, embedded computing in infrastructure, and virtual reality augmentation all flow toward one purpose: to bring the efficiency, organizational structure, and raw computing power of the internet ecosystem to bear on realspace.

---

[24] *See* Jefferson Graham, *What's Cool in Tech? Tile, Nuzzel, Service*, USA TODAY (Apr. 24, 2016, 11:16 PM), http://www.usatoday.com/story/tech/2016/04/24/whats-cool-tech-tile-nuzzel-service/83463360 (discussing Tile, a "little white square" that "syncs to a specific device").

[25] *See* Scott R. Peppet, *Regulating the Internet of Things: First Steps Towards Managing Discrimination, Privacy, Security, & Consent*, 93 TEX. L. REV. 85, 123–25 (2014).

Think of it as hyperlinking and hashtagging reality. You will be able to Google your shoes when you lose them. Just as the internet organized and linked information to other information, the Internet of Things links the real world to information and organizes the results. In many senses, the real world itself is information. "Where were you when you took that picture?" is information. "Where should I turn left to get to the store?" is information. "Who within one hundred feet of me meets my romantic profile's criteria?" is information. Where objects are is information, what people do is information, and what devices perceive is information. All that real-world information is not (yet) connected to computing power. So the Internet of Things embeds processing power within the real world and provides processing power for humans to carry with them as they move through the world. Increasingly, the sensors are placed on robotic platforms so that sensors and processors can move, and so that digital information can interact with analog reality. Humans will interact with information attached to real-world landmarks, places, and spaces through augmented interfaces. Your smartphone already tells you when to turn left. In a few years your glasses may tell you who in a crowded bar shares your taste in music.

The project of the Internet of Things is not to connect the world's devices; it is to harness internet technologies and informational architectures to have direct effect in the real world. A better name might be the "Internet of Everything," or the Eschaton (with apologies to Charles Stross)[26] – but frankly the Internet of Things is already one buzzword too many. I doubt it will be used in a decade. We will simply come to accept that information technologies have a deeper reach into realspace than they did before.

This emerging information-enriched reality relies on a few technological trends, detailed below. The proliferation of sensors is the first step. Connectivity is another easy candidate. Linked sensors and devices drive the explosion of the Internet of Things. Mobility and miniaturization matter because people will primarily interact with the IoT through their mobile and wearable processors. Smartphones are the point of interaction for many technologies, like Nomi's. I add robotics for the simple reason that the Internet of Things will act upon objects and spaces in realspace through robots. Roombas and self-driving cars are core IoT devices. Finally, I discuss augmented reality interfaces because they represent our ability to link information to realspace, and to perceive

---

[26] *See id.* at 89 n. 14 (detailing the "Internet of Everything"). In Charles Stross's novels, the "Eschaton" is a god-like artificial intelligence. *See generally* CHARLES STROSS, SINGULARITY SKY (Ace Books 2003).

information overlaid on top of realspace. For purposes of this book, I gather all these topics under the Internet of Things.

Sensors

Internet of Things scholar Scott Peppet notes that "[s]ome estimate by 2025 over one *trillion* sensor-based devices will be connected to the Internet or each other."[27] We wear sensors. Smartwatches, smart glasses, virtual reality headsets, and a vast array of fitness and health trackers record our environment and intimate details.[28] We carry them: smartphones have compasses, cameras, accelerometers, and microphones. We drive them. Cars are increasingly rolling sensor platforms, with the vast majority now containing Event Data Recorders (devices that record driving data in the event of a crash) or more sophisticated and longer-term GPS recorders.[29] And wherever we go, sensors are already there waiting for us, in street corner cameras, pressure-sensitive streets, and smart power grids that can tell with 96 percent accuracy what movies we watch.[30]

These sensors are extremely sensitive. One developer utilized the increasingly sensitive accelerometers within smartphones to create an app that can "record ground shaking from an earthquake, with the goal of creating a worldwide seismic detection network that could eventually warn users of impending jolts from nearby quakes."[31] Smartphone cameras are now capable of taking pictures so massively detailed that police have been able to catch child pornography perpetrators by identifying the ridges of their fingerprints on the edge of pornographic photographs they took.[32]

Increased sensitivity creates challenges for users who try to control what their device does. Researchers at Stanford University found that the gyroscope sensors in iPhones and Androids (the sensors that automatically reorient your screen when you move the phone from vertical to horizontal) are sensitive enough to capture acoustic signals – speech – in the area of the phone,

---

[27] Peppet, *supra* note 25, at 98 (citations omitted). [28] *Id.* at 98–103.

[29] *See id.* at 104–06. [30] *Id.* at 110.

[31] Robert Sanders, *New App Turns Smartphones Into Worldwide Seismic Network*, BERKELEY NEWS (Feb. 12, 2016), http://news.berkeley.edu/2016/02/12/new-app-turns-smartphones-into-worldwide-seismic-network.

[32] FED. BUREAU OF INVESTIGATION, PSP FINGERPRINT EXPERT IDENTIFIES CHILD PORNOGRAPHY PRODUCER BY ANALYZING RIDGES IN PHOTO (Aug. 12, 2015), https://www.fbi.gov/contact-us/field-offices/pittsburgh/news/press-releases/psp-fingerprint-expert-identifies-child-pornography-producer-by-analyzing-ridges-in-photo.

without using the microphone.[33] Phone manufacturers do not require user consent to access the gyroscope, which means that the sensor is a wide-open channel.

Sensor Fusion and Algorithmic Inferences

By implication, the increased number, sensitivity, and reach and range of sensors drastically increase the conclusions data researchers can draw. Two sensors can help algorithms make three conclusions. Devices can record different parts of our life and algorithms meld the results together to get even more information than each data set would have alone.[34] This relies on two components: first, the increase of data caused by sensor proliferation, and second, the depth of inference made possible by big data data-mining and algorithmic inferences.

"Sensor fusion" is a well-known phenomenon whereby two sensors generate more information together than they would separately, added together.[35] Scott Peppet's core example is the two sensors of our eyes. Whereas each alone does not perceive depth, together our eyes perceive in three dimensions.[36] Sensor fusion lies at the heart of the cross-device tracking industry. Consider the innovative combination of sensors and identifiers used by SilverPush, the market leader in cross-device tracking via audio beacons.[37] In a report sent to the FTC, the Center for Democracy and Technology noted that when users encounter a SilverPush advertiser on their computer, the advertiser plants a cookie in the browser – and plays an ultrasonic inaudible sound. Users can't hear the sound, but any devices they own using apps with SilverPush software *can* hear it. These audio beacons, which are also embedded in TV commercials, pair with the browser cookie to identify which devices belong to a single person. This is valuable information for companies, who can learn "which ads the user saw, how long the user watched the ad before changing the channel, which kind of smart devices the individual uses, along with other information that adds to the profile of each user that is linked across devices."[38]

---

[33] *Gyrophone: Recognizing Speech from Gyroscope*, Stan. Sec. Res. (last visited July 8, 2016) https://crypto.stanford.edu/gyrophone/.
[34] *See* Staff, *Sensors and Sensitivity*, Economist (June 4, 2009), http://www.economist.com/node/13725679.
[35] *See* Peppet, *supra* note 25, at 93, 120–21.   [36] *Id.*
[37] Calabrese et al., *Comments for November 2015 Workshop on Cross-Device Tracking*, Ctr. for Democracy & Tech. 4 (Oct. 16, 2015), https://cdt.org/files/2015/10/10.16.15-CDT-Cross-Device-Comments.pdf.
[38] *Id.*

SilverPush's technology raises several distinct issues. Its technology actually physically invades the space of the user, transmitting audio beacons from one device to another, from the television to the smartphone to the computer or whatever other processors and sensors are available to pick it up. It uses multiple devices at a time. The linkage of devices serves as a unique identifier. So perhaps I am the only person in the airport with a Samsung Galaxy S6 running Android 6.0.1, an LG Urbane smartwatch, and Tile tabs on my keys and watch. You get the point. The more devices we carry, the more it is likely that we are the only person in an area carrying that particular configuration, and the more data points about us the devices can independently corroborate.[39] That identifies us perfectly even with no other unique identifier. So we are identified by our wearables, and tracked over time and space by the multiple sensors. This in turn permits sensors to gather more information about us.

Big data algorithms can combine information from sensors to draw deep inferences.[40] Peppet writes:

> [R]esearchers are beginning to show that existing smartphone sensors can be used to infer a user's mood; stress levels; personality type; bipolar disorder; demographics (e.g., gender, marital status, job status, age); smoking habits; overall well-being; progression of Parkinson's disease; sleep patterns; happiness; levels of exercise; and types of physical activity or movement.[41]

A sensor I encounter in one town can link its data to a sensor I encounter an hour later in another town. Big data algorithms then can combine information from both worn and encountered sensors to make broader deductions about me.[42] If these combined sensors note that I travel from my place of work to a physical therapist's office at 10:30 a.m. every Thursday, alongside the purchase of a pair of tennis elbow braces from Amazon.com, an algorithm might reasonably conclude that I have health problems and that my health insurance premiums ought to rise.

Connectivity

Data moves through the Internet of Things in two distinct ways. One flow is between small processors at the edges, where data are rich and processing power is still relatively weak. The other flow is between the edge and the core, where data can be moved to the center of the processing network in order to

---

[39] *Id.* at 94.
[40] *See generally* Frank Pasquale, The Black Box Society: The Secret Algorithms That Control Money and Information (Harvard University Press 2015).
[41] *See* Peppet, *supra* note 25, at 115–16 (citations omitted).   [42] *Id.* at 117–18.

perform much more powerful operations. For example, when you purchase something using Apple Pay, information moves from your phone to the payment console. It is a small amount of information: a cryptographic token that Apple has created to identify the specific transaction. That token is communicated from your phone to the reader through near field communications, and the merchant then communicates the token back to Apple to settle the transaction. In some cases, data move between points at the edge, and can stay there. A friend can send you a document directly, one device to another. But much more often, data are routed through the core. Users do so for the convenience and power of the more powerful processing capabilities available in the cloud. Providers do so because of the wealth to be skimmed from that data when they are used for advertising.

The battle for personal property in the Internet of Things is partly a battle over these two flows. Do our data stay near us, and are they used purely for the purposes we wish, or are they communicated to many other actors, only some of whom are processing the data as we wish it to be processed? Do our devices help us, or do they spy on us? Do they do what we tell them to do, or do they accept instructions and over-the-air software updates at the demand of remote entities who do not necessarily want what is best for us?

Edge systems and core systems use different connectivity standards. Edge networks rely on advances in near field communication (NFC) protocols.[43] Bluetooth permits close-range low-bandwidth information transfer, sending, and receiving.[44] Radio-frequency identification permits identification of passive devices that don't need to receive information.[45] It's a low-energy way for devices to identify themselves to larger nodes in the network. Another broad standard is Wi-Fi itself. Now universal, Wi-Fi was originally just another possible way to link up computers. Its universality follows Metcalfe's famous law – the more devices and access points that use it, the more valuable the standard is. Similarly, wireless standards have converged. Long Term Evolution (LTE) standards promise to help bridge the gap between the two major types of basic phone technology, CDMA and GSM, making devices that simply reach out to the internet on their own (and don't need a Wi-Fi hotspot or the like) ever more attractive.[46]

Broad adoption of good standards means that innovators can easily add devices to the edge of the network. Manufacturers who can license Bluetooth can link up with other Bluetooth-enabled devices. The emergence of these

---

[43] *See* DANIEL MINOLI, BUILDING THE INTERNET OF THINGS WITH IPv6 AND MIPv6: THE EVOLVING WORLD OF M2M COMMUNICATIONS 147–56, tbls. 6.2 & 6.3 (Wiley 2015).
[44] *Id.*   [45] *Id.*   [46] *Id.*

standards means that developers can bring their devices to market with some sense that they will be able to interact with other IoT objects. These standards are the foundation, the essential building blocks of the Internet of Things. On the other hand, standards can become tools of expropriation. Companies that own a specific standard can use the standard like a scalpel, to cut consumers off from other devices. Ever wonder why your Apple or Samsung device speaks smoothly and easily to other devices by the same manufacturer, but has tremendous problems with other systems? That's why.

Mobility and Miniaturization

If connectivity forms the strands of the IoT information web, mobile devices are the nodes where the strands most often connect. In the past decade, we have completely changed how we use the internet. We used to use it more or less like a typewriter. Now we wear it. We do not type to communicate with it, we speak, we gesture, we move the device itself around to activate its motion sensors. We do not sign in to services: the device itself serves as proof that we are who we say we are. It authenticates itself through unique identifiers. Changes in miniaturization, mobility, identity attribution, and sensor technology mean that the shift to mobility has done much more than provide us with powerful, small computers. It has fundamentally changed the way we get information from networked systems, and how those systems get information about us.

The same advances in miniaturization that let us put the 2005 equivalent of a high-end computer in your smartphone now lets us shoehorn the equivalent of a quite capable 1990s computer into pretty much anything. This matters for packing a powerful punch into a small mobile computing device, as the next section will discuss. But it matters even more when we can put tiny microprocessors in printer ink cartridges, light bulbs, jewelry, soda cans, and more. Most consumer goods can be linked. Low-cost, small processors will enable owners to seed microprocessors throughout their property. An emerging example is Nomi's "Listen" technology, mentioned earlier, which relies on computers embedded throughout participating stores. As the technology gets better, the sensors will get smaller. Imagine Nomi-style technology deployed throughout a mall, or around a downtown, to map everywhere everyone goes, how long they linger in front of each storefront, with whom they speak, and so forth.

A few figures on miniaturization are worth noting. Moore's Law is a rough approximation, but it has held for long enough. The law states that the number of transistors in a dense, integrated circuit doubles approximately every two years.[47] This constant doubling yields surprising results not only in terms of speed but also in terms of size. Today's iPhone 6 has many millions of times the processing power of NASA in 1969.[48] The latest Samsung Galaxy phone comes with 32 gigabytes of storage space, while the 1983 IBM PC-XT Model 286, costing nearly $4,000 at the time, came with a 20-megabyte hard disk – that's a 160,000 percent increase.[49] And, lest you think these results only occur when we look at decades-old technology, the first iPad, released in 2010, featured 256 megabytes of RAM, which pales in comparison to the newest model's 2 gigabytes (2048 megabytes) of RAM.[50]

Mobile computing means mobile signaling of identity. Mobile devices identify us through a wide range of unique tags: media access control (MAC) addresses, universally unique IDs (UUIDs), even static IP addresses.[51] Verizon assigned a unique identifier to all outgoing data requests made by a user, so that anyone who knew the identifier could track the user's web browsing wherever she went online, without the user's knowledge or even ability to do anything to stop it other than use a virtual private network, or VPN.[52] Although Verizon claimed that it gave "customers choices about how [it] use[d] their data,"[53] the FCC found that the company failed to disclose the practice for

[47] Gordon E. Moore, *Cramming More Components onto Integrated Circuits*, ELECTRONICS, Apr. 19, 1965, at 114, 115.

[48] *See* MICHIO KAKU, PHYSICS OF THE FUTURE 23 (Doubleday 2011) ("Today, your cell phone has more computer power than all of NASA back in 1969, when it placed two astronauts on the moon.").

[49] *Compare Your Guide to the Galaxy: Samsung's Newest Phones at Verizon*, VERIZON (2016), http://www.verizonwireless.com/archive/mobile-living/tech-smarts/new-samsung-galaxy-phones/, *with* Winn L. Rosch, *The AT Clone from IBM*, PC MAG. (Jan. 13, 1987), at 155–56.

[50] *Compare Apple iPad Wi-Fi*, GSM ARENA, http://www.gsmarena.com/apple_ipad_wi_fi-3828 .php (last visited May 5, 2016), *with Apple iPad Pro 9.7*, GSM ARENA, http://www.gsmarena .com/apple_ipad_pro_9_7-7984.php (last visited July 8, 2016).

[51] *See* MICHAEL R. ARKFELD, ELECTRONIC DISCOVERY & EVIDENCE § 3.24 (Law Partner Publishing 2016) (observing that "[i]nternet and computer geolocation can be performed by associating a geographic location with the" IP address, MAC address, and embedded software numbers such as UUID, among other technologies); Christopher Soghoian, *An End to Privacy Theater: Exposing and Discouraging Corporate Disclosure of User Data to the Government*, 12 MINN. J.L. SCI. & TECH. 191, 210 (2011) (noting that "Sprint Nextel assigns each Internet-connected wireless handset a static IP address").

[52] *See* Andrea Peterson, *FCC Cracks Down on Verizon Wireless for Using 'Supercookies'*, WASH. POST (Mar. 7, 2016), http://www.washingtonpost.com/news/the-switch/wp/2016/03/07/fcc-cracks-down-on-verizons-supercookies/?hpid=hp_hp-cards_hp-card-technology %3Ahomepage%x2Fcard ("The Federal Communications Commission is cracking down on Verizon Wireless for using a powerful type of code to track its customers around the Internet.... [that] is almost impossible to disable and could allow almost anyone to follow users around the Web.").

[53] *Id.*

nearly two whole years after it was first implemented.[54] Verizon's move was like putting a virtual radio tag on all its users' movements, making sure they could be tracked in the internet wilderness. Another tracking method is called app fingerprinting. App makers can often identify a person uniquely by the combination of applications she has already installed. Think about it – how many people have the exact app combination that you have downloaded on their phones? Likely just you. Similarly, through a process called browser fingerprinting, a person's online browser can be tracked.[55] Here's an example of the headers that my browser is currently broadcasting:

user-agent: Mozilla/5.0 (Windows NT 10.0; WOW64; rv:45.0) Gecko/
    20100101 Firefox/45.0
accept: text/html,application/xhtml+xml,application/xml;q = 0.9,*/*;q = 0.8
accept-language: en-US,en;q = 0.5
accept-encoding: gzip, deflate, br
dnt: 1
connection: keep-alive

One real irony is that since I have set my "do not track" flag in my browser – you can see that in the line "dnt: 1" – I am now *more* identifiable, since I'm now "that guy who always sets his do-not-track flag" in addition to all the other browser characteristics I transmit to each website. It's the same mathematical principle that drives sensor fusion: the more pieces of data one can gather from my devices about me, the more certain one can be that it's uniquely me, even though each piece of data might be shared with a range of other people. Of course, there are tracking cookies and web bugs and flash cookies, and all kinds of other shenanigans, but even with those cleared or not enabled, the series of customizations individuals make in setting up their browser or device very often results in the ability to identify them nearly perfectly.

Online and offline identifiers combine. Imagine walking into a grocery store. You pause in front of the protein powder in the healthcare section, since you have been thinking of exercising more. You have already checked brands of powder online, and you check the price of the powder you want to buy, to make sure you're getting the best deal. You are being a responsible consumer.

54 Press Release, FCC, FCC Settles Verizon "Supercookie" Probe, Requires Consumer Opt-In for Third Parties (March 7, 2016), *available at* http://apps.fcc.gov/edocs_public/attachmatch/DOC-338091A1.pdf.
55 *See* Calabrese, *supra* note 37, at 4 ("[A]dvertisers can use a form of probabilistic tracking called browser fingerprinting to identify a user . . . . Modern web browsers are highly customizable . . . . creating in essence a unique signal that websites can use to uniquely identify the user.").

But you've also revealed your exercise plans to website operators, who know who you are through cookies, ISP trackers, and browser fingerprinting; to the maker of your healthcare app, which is able to identify you through your account and app fingerprint; and to the store owners, who are able to use tools like Nomi's Listen technology to track your phone's MAC address, signal strength, and so on.

Mobile computing follows us across contexts. We are by now familiar with the idea that gathering multiple types of information can yield far greater insight than gathering a lot of the same kind of information. That is why, as Helen Nissenbaum puts it, we try to control information flows by channeling them into the appropriate contexts.[56] We want to keep our work persona at work, our home persona at home, and what happens in Vegas, in Vegas. Perhaps you've had the experience of working with someone for a long time. You feel like you know them. Will you learn more about them by working with them for another day or by visiting them at home? One can learn much more by gathering information from multiple contexts. Pervasive web tracking surveillance only showed what we were like when we were seated at a computer. At home, perhaps, and at work, perhaps, but still, the online environment was a context of its own. Mobile devices follow us across all our contexts, to our club meetings, to rehab, to the doctor, to our parent–teacher conferences, to our homes, on our vacations, to our business meetings, and to the spa. Data drawn from this range of contexts are not just quantitatively greater, but qualitatively more exhaustive and intrusive than data from one context alone.

Infrastructure

In the coming years, sensors will mushroom across and throughout infrastructure: smart homes, smart workplaces, and smart cities. Mobile and infrastructural components work together. Consider the sensors in Nomi's Listen technology. Those sensors were installed in supermarkets and stores, embedded into the environment. They were waiting for consumers to walk in the door with their phones. Smart roads interact with smart cars. Cell towers interact with smartphones. In the not-so-distant future, a smart refrigerator might order groceries to be delivered by drone. This interaction between mobile and static sensors and processors gives the IoT its unique character, as bridge for data

---

[56] *See* Helen Nissenbaum, *Technology, Values, and the Justice System: Privacy as Contextual Integrity*, 79 WASH. L. REV. 119, 154–55 (2004) (discussing the "right of privacy as a right to control information about oneself" and noting that "it is crucial to know the context . . . . [w]hen we evaluate sharing information with third party users of data").

about the real world which can then be indexed and linked in information systems.

Smart Homes

In 2013, a couple in Houston, Texas, woke up to the sound of a strange man cursing at their two-year-old daughter. Someone had hacked the internet-enabled camera and baby monitor in the child's room. The hacker began cursing the parents when they entered the room as well.[57] It was clear he could see them.

Smart devices are spreading in the home: Roombas, baby monitors, scales that tweet your weight, robotic lawnmowers, Samsung's Smart TVs, Amazon's Echo, and many hundreds more. But as the baby monitor hack shows, there is a troublesome gap between the intimacy of the home and the open connectivity (and lax security) of IoT devices. My friend Joel Reidenberg, a well-known privacy scholar at Fordham University Law School, recounted how his water utility company came to his house wishing to install a new smart meter. Professor Reidenberg refused entry to the technicians until they informed him of the specifications of the meter. As it turned out, the meter was not secured. Anyone from the street could have been able to read detailed information from it. He preferred to keep his old, ostensibly "dumb" meter. And he is not wrong: unencrypted IoT devices leak data to anyone who cares to read it. Researchers in Germany have demonstrated that it is possible to find out what media a homeowner is watching, to chart power usage so as to tell when the homeowner is away or asleep, and even to remotely turn on meter sensors like smart TV cameras to spy into the home.[58]

Or, consider the FTC's first internet-connected device case.[59] TRENDnet made internet-connected cameras for home security and baby monitoring. The FTC alleged that TRENDnet's cameras lacked a range of basic security precautions:

---

[57] *See* Alana Abramson, *Baby Monitor Hacking Alarms Houston Parents*, ABC News (Aug. 13, 2013), http://abcnews.go.com/blogs/headlines/2013/08/baby-monitor-hacking-alarms-houston-parents/.

[58] *See* Dario Carluccio & Stephan Brinkhaus, Smart Hacking for Privacy, 28th Chaos Communication Conference (Dec. 30, 2011), *available at* http://youtu.be/YYe4SwQn2GE (discussing the use of smart meters as surveillance devices); Erica Fink & Laurie Segall, *Your TV Might Be Watching You*, CNN (Aug. 1, 2013, 11:32 AM), http://money.cnn.com/2013/08/01/technology/security/tv-hack ("The flaws in Samsung Smart TVs . . . enabled hackers to remotely turn on the TVs' built-in cameras without leaving any trace of it on the screen.").

[59] *See* Complaint at 1, *In re* TRENDnet, Inc., No. C-4426 (Feb. 7, 2014), *available at* http://www.ftc.gov/system/files/documents./cases/140207trendnetcmpt.pdf (charging a company that among other things sold "Internet Protocol ("IP") cameras" with violating the Federal Trade Commision Act).

[TRENDnet] transmitted user login credentials in clear text over the Internet, stored login credentials in clear text on users' mobile devices, and failed to test consumers' privacy settings to ensure that video feeds marked as "private" would be in fact private. As a result of these alleged failures, hackers were able to access live feeds from consumers' security cameras and conduct "unauthorized surveillance of infants sleeping in their cribs, young children playing, and adults engaging in typical daily activities."[60]

"Typical daily activities" indeed. Utilities, appliances, sensors, towers, and wireless networks combine to create a framework within which IoT appliances can move and operate. At the same time, they implicate property law in its oldest sense. These sensors are often built into, embedded within, or bolted onto real property. The shopping mall can install tracking sensors because it owns the mall. The homeowner can install smart thermostats and automated airflow fans because it is her house.

Smart Workplaces

As with much technology, it was industry that made first use of the IoT.[61] The Port of Hamburg in Germany is a wonderful example. The second-largest port in Europe, it is nevertheless 110 kilometers up the Elbe River from the North Sea. Space is at a premium. The *Speicherstadt* ("storage city") is a UNESCO World Heritage Site, a city-within-a-city of brick warehouses surrounded by canals. Because some of the largest transports cannot navigate the Elbe, and because river traffic is so constrained, Hamburg has invested heavily in computing technology and embedded sensors to streamline the movement of goods through the port. Tracking sensors and big data analytics parse truck arrival times, offloading, and tasking of cranes and equipment. Hamburg's smartPort platform, intended as a platform for future ports, includes sensors embedded in "ships, containers, trucks, cranes, access roads and streetlights."[62] By 2020, the smartPort platform will accommodate a million connected devices.

Future workplaces will be saturated with sensors. "[W]orkplace sensors create new streams of data about where employees are during the workday, what they are doing, how long their tasks take, and whether they comply with

---

[60] FTC, INTERNET OF THINGS: PRIVACY & SECURITY IN A CONNECTED WORLD 32 (Jan. 2015), https://www.ftc.gov/system/files/documents/reports/federal-trade-commission-staff-report-november-2013-workshop-entitled-internet-things-privacy/150127iotrpt.pdf (quoting Complaint, *In re* TRENDnet, Inc., *supra* note 59, at 5).

[61] *See* Ryan Calo, *Robots and Privacy*, in ROBOT ETHICS: THE ETHICAL AND SOCIAL IMPLICATIONS OF ROBOTICS 187, 187 (Patrick Lin et al., eds., MIT 2011) [hereinafter *Robots and Privacy*].

[62] Tom McNichol, *The Industrial Internet Comes to the Loading Docks*, REWRITE (June 10, 2015), http://rewrite.ca.com/us/articles/application-economy/the-industrial-internet-comes-to-the-loading-docks.html.

employment rules."[63] Already, hospitals connect an employee's identification badge to sinks and hospital beds, and buzz the badge if an employee has not washed her hands before approaching the bed.[64] Banks use sensor badges to determine the movement and attitudes (expressed in tone of voice) of call-center employees.[65] Delivery companies monitor their fleets through GPS trackers. Companies can even tell who is a respected member of a team by monitoring who turns toward or away from that employee, using infrared-enabled badges.[66] Similar data enable employers to find out who is likely to leave a company or get a promotion.[67] Peppet quotes MIT Professor Alex Pentland: "We've been able to foretell, for example, which teams will win a business plan contest, solely on the basis of data collected from team members wearing badges at a cocktail reception."[68]

Employers are also pressing ever further into the devices of their employees. The "bring your own device" movement, which reduces corporate costs and increases efficiency by encouraging employees to bring and use their own familiar devices, causes employers to (perhaps entirely reasonably) want to enable security features and tracking capabilities on employee phones. If an employee receives work email on her personal smartphone, she must accept a range of constraints set by her employer. If she is lucky, the office administrator merely requires that she set a password to lock her phone. Many employers, like mine, require more, including the ability to wipe the phone remotely at the employer's discretion.

From these brief examples one can draw two conclusions. First, removing a company's ability to control its own smart-factory, port, fleet, or other workplace would be a business-ending loss. If a software company were able to remotely shut down a smart port or smart factory in the event of a dispute with its customer, it could wreak economic havoc and gain a crushing bargaining advantage. Second, employees in the smart workplace and increasingly at home are constantly surrounded and evaluated by their employer's sensors.

Smart Cities

Cameras on every street corner give the city eyes.[69] Pressure sensors under roads give a city a sense of touch.[70] Sound and vibration sensors detect leaks

[63] *See* Scott Peppet, *supra* note 25, at 111.   [64] *Id.*   [65] *Id.*   [66] *Id.*   [67] *Id.*
[68] *Id.* (citations omitted).
[69] *See* Alexey Medvedev et al., *Citywatcher: Annotating and Searching Video Data Streams for Smart Cities Applications, in* INTERNET OF THINGS, SMART SPACES, AND NEXT GENERATION NETWORKS AND SYSTEMS 144, 144 (Sergey Balandin, Sergey Andreev & Yevgeni Koucheryavy eds., Springer 2014) ("Modern cities have large networks for surveillance cameras including CCTV, street crossings and the like.").
[70] *See A Summary of Vehicle Detection and Surveillance Technologies use in Intelligent Transportation Systems,* FED. HIGHWAY ADMIN., http://www.fhwa.dot.gov/policyinformation/pubs/

in water pipes.[71] Weight sensors alert city employees when garbage bins are full.[72] Flow sensors adjust street lamps according to pedestrian traffic.[73] The city of Hamburg has signed a memorandum agreement with Cisco to extend the smartPort sensor and parsing network throughout the city.[74] The rollout will include smart streetlights, traffic optimizing sensors, environment and infrastructure sensing, and citizen services delivered via virtual kiosk.[75]

One significant component of smart cities is the smart grid. According to the U.S. Department of Energy, "[m]uch in the way that a 'smart' phone these days means a phone with a computer in it, smart grid means 'computerizing' the electric utility grid."[76] Smart grids are two-way technology. They offer the utility remote control over the endpoints of the grid, and let the endpoints report back to the utility. So "it includes adding two-way digital communication technology to devices associated with the grid.[77] Each device on the network can be given sensors to gather data (power meters, voltage sensors, fault detectors, and so on), plus two-way digital communication between the device in the field and the utility's network operations center."[78] This offers real improvements in efficiency. It also offers real dangers. A single point of failure (the utility's control center) means that utilities become more enticing hacking targets. Researchers can tell, via power fluctuations, what movies a homeowner is watching, when she is at home, or what room in the house she might be in. After all, the lights and heat are on.

Smart-city technology is particularly well (or poorly, depending on your point of view) suited for government use. Governments can use smart-city technology to improve traffic flows, increase fuel efficiency, reduce crime, and monitor buildings for signs of danger. On the other hand, turning an

vdstits2007/04.cfm (last visited May 11, 2016) ("Pneumatic road tube sensors send a burst of air pressure along a rubber tube when a vehicle's tires pass over the tube. The pressure pulse closes an air switch, producing an electrical signal that is transmitted to a counter or analysis software.").

[71] *See* Gerhard P. Hancke et al., *The Role of Advanced Sensing in Smart Cities*, 13 SENSORS 393, 403–05 (2013) (discussing smart water distribution systems).

[72] *See id.* at 417 (noting a Barcelona initiative to remotely monitor "the content of bins, which enable the development of an improved garbage collection system, therefore optimizing garbage collection services").

[73] *See id.* at 416 (discussing the use smart systems in Songdo, South Korea, an "ubiquitous city" planned from 2001).

[74] *City of Hamburg and Cisco Launch Plans for Smart City of the Future and Lay Foundation for a Partner Ecosystem*, CISCO (Apr. 30, 2014), https://newsroom.cisco.com/press-release-content?type=webcontent&articleId=1414144.

[75] *Id.*

[76] *Smart Grid*, DEP'T OF ENERGY, http://energy.gov/oe/services/technology-development/smart-grid (last visited July 5, 2016).

[77] *Id.*   [78] *Id.*

entire city into a system of sensors can pose serious problems for citizens' privacy and independence. Consider New York City's "domain awareness" system, developed in conjunction with Microsoft.[79] The system combines sensors from street cameras with sensors on police officers' belts, permitting comprehensive surveillance of people and packages moving about the city. One can hardly blame New York for being cautious. But domain awareness systems are spreading across the country. People are worried about what police might do with this data.[80] Oakland's efforts to install a domain awareness center met with strong protests.[81] The protestors have a point. Massive public infrastructural surveillance is disturbing and the reach and scale of the technology is new. Legal rules are not in place, and the potential for abuse is significant. In the Ukraine, cell tower systems have already been subverted to report the identity of phones carried by political protesters, who then received messages from police threatening reprisals.[82]

Cameras, pressure sensors, microphones, and other increasingly sensitive detectors are now part of the everyday cityscape – and beyond. The question is whether our cars, phones, Fitbits, and other personal sensors will help us to combat the constant surveillance we meet as we travel, or whether they will be co-opted as an active and important part of that network.

Robotics

If we do not come to the sensor network, it will come to us, by way of robots. Robotics covers a range of automation behavior. For purposes of the Internet of Things, I prefer Professor Ryan Calo's view: robots are capable of sensing the world around them, processing that information, and taking action in the world.[83] This often yields concrete, physical results: a robotic arm in a factory or a Roomba vacuuming the house.

---

[79] *See* Press Release, NYC Office of the Mayor, Mayor Bloomberg, Police Commissioner Kelly and Microsoft Unveil New, State-of-the-Art Law Enforcement Technology That Aggregates and Analyzes Existing Public Safety Data in Real Time to Provide a Comprehensive View of Potential Threats and Criminal Activity (Aug. 8, 2012), *available at* http://www.nyc.gov/portal/site/nycgov/menuitem.c0935b9a57bb4ef3daf2f1c701c789a0/index.jsp?pageID=mayor_press_release&catID=1194&doc_name=http%3A%2F%2Fwww.nyc.gov%2Fhtml%2Fom%2Fhtml%2F2012b%2Fpr291-12.html&cc=unused1978&rc=1194&ndi=1.

[80] *See* Martin Kaste, *In 'Domain Awareness,' Detractors See Another NSA*, NPR (Feb. 21, 2014), http://www.npr.org/sections/alltechconsidered/2014/02/21/280749781/in-domain-awareness-detractors-see-another-nsa.

[81] *Id.*

[82] *See* Andrew E. Kramer, *Ukraine's Opposition Says Government Stirs Violence*, N.Y. Times (Jan. 21, 2014), http://www.nytimes.com/2014/01/22/world/europe/ukraine-protests.html.

[83] *See* Ryan Calo, *Robotics and the Lessons of Cyberlaw*, 103 Calif. L. Rev. 513, 529 (2015) [hereinafter *Lessons of Cyberlaw*] ("There is some measure of consensus, however, around the

Automation, sensing, decisional autonomy, and physicality are the hall-marks of robotics.[84] A Google autonomous car is a robot. It senses the road and the obstacles around it, combines information from databases and online sources – Google Maps among other things – and processes that informa-tion to make decisions. At other times, the car is directed by a human. At that point it's not robotic. Drones, like cars, can be robots sometimes, and just remote-controlled machines at other times. It's ironic that machines are cyborgs before people are. Most of them are a hybrid of human and machine decision making at any particular time.

Robots are mobile sensor platforms.[85] They must be, in order to make decisions about and act upon their physical surroundings. The rich data from mobile sensors does not merely serve to let the robot act, however. It also makes the robot a node in a surveillance network. As Calo writes, our first use of robotics was industrial automation. But our second was surveillance.[86] Robots can follow us into the spaces between other sensors. Perhaps we are on camera at the mall, and our cellphones can be tracked by cell site location information as we drive home, but we can still leave the mall or leave the phone behind. Robots permit long-term, persistent, mobile surveillance.

Robots can fill the gaps of other sensor networks, rounding out details and permitting observation over time. As Calo writes, the "mobility, size, and sheer, inhuman patience" of robots makes them ideal not only for performing their rote automated tasks, but also for closing sensor loopholes in the Internet of Things.[87]

Virtuality

I hesitate to include virtuality in a discussion of the Internet of Things, but believe it to be necessary. At first, virtualization technology seems to be the opposite of the IoT. While the IoT embeds computing power in physical space, virtualization technologies use computing power to create virtual places and

---

idea that robots are mechanical objects that take the world in, process what they sense, and in turn act upon the world.").

[84] *See id.* at 532 (noting that the functions of robots "generally require[] a physical presence" and that "the processing capabilities of robots translate into the tantalizing prospect of original action").

[85] *See id.* at 530 (noting that "robots can leverage data from any sensor").

[86] *See Robots and Privacy, supra* note 62, at 187 ("Robots are, first and foremost, a human instrument. And after industrial manufacturing, the principle use to which we've put that instrument has been surveillance.").

[87] *Id.* at 191.

spaces. Google Cardboard, for example, combines a smartphone with a simple cardboard headset to create a surprisingly good three-dimensional 360-degree virtual reality.[88] The user places her phone sideways in the headset. The phone projects two different images that create the three-dimensional effect when received by each eye. The phone's sensitive motion sensors permit the image to change when the user moves her head, thus creating a full virtual environment around the user.[89] In 2015, politically minded Samsung Gear VR headset owners could catch a 360-degree view of a CNN live-stream of the October Democratic primary debate.[90]

Both virtualization technology and embedded computers link the real world to information. Consider two ways of advertising your store. You could put a beacon in your store that communicates with passing smartphones to display an advertisement. That is a classic embedded computer approach – exactly what Nomi did. The other alternative would be to have an app on the user's phone that displayed an advertisement when the user reached the GPS coordinates of your store. In both cases, the consumer approaches the store and sees an advertisement on her smartphone. She may not know which method was used.

Data tagging, especially geotagging, is an important part of the Internet of Things.[91] Consider a photograph tagged with the location it was taken, or a Yelp review keyed to the geolocation of a restaurant. Data tagging can tie virtual assets – a review, a slogan, an advertisement, a sign, even a virtual reality experience – to a physical location. In 2010, the Museum of Modern Art in New York City created an augmented reality exhibition. As they walked through the museum, users could view a virtual overlay to the physical exhibits

---

[88] *See* Leena Rao, *Google Cardboard Virtual Reality Viewers Go International*, FORTUNE (May 11, 2016, 12:25 PM), http://fortune.com/2016/05/11/google-virtual-reality-viewers ("Google has used Cardboard, made literally from cardboard, as an inexpensive and easy way to popularize its virtual reality technology on Android phones.").

[89] *See* JT Ripton, *Google Cardboard: Everything You Need to Know*, TECHRADAR (Dec. 18, 2014), http://www.techradar.com/us/news/phone-and-communications/mobile-phones/google-cardboard-everything-you-need-to-know-1277738 ("You can even move your head around, and the images will respond as if you're in the same place as what's displayed on your screen.").

[90] Brian Stelter, *How to See CNN's Democratic Debate in Virtual Reality*, CNN (Oct. 13, 2015, 11:42 PM), http://money.cnn.com/2015/10/13/media/cnn-virtual-reality-democratic-debate-stream.

[91] *See generally* Kirill Krinkin & Kirill Yudenok, *Geo-coding in Smart Environment: Integration Principles of Smart-M3 and Geo2Tag*, *in* INTERNET OF THINGS, SMART SPACES, AND NEXT GENERATION NETWORKING 107 (Sergey Balandin, Sergey Andeev & Yevgeni Koucheryavy eds., Springer 2013) (discussing "geo-tagging and smart spaces" in the "modern mobile market").

through their smartphones.[92] In 2016, Pokémon GO took the world by storm: suddenly, businesses, museums, and even residences found themselves to be hotspots for virtual creatures and their flesh-and-blood hunters. Data tagging and embedded computing work together to create the Internet of Things. Often it does not matter whether a mobile sensor is responding to an embedded processor (the Nomi model) or a geolocation (the MOMA and Pokémon models). This method of laying an experience on top of the physical world is called augmented reality (think here of the computer-generated first-down line created in every football game broadcast). It uses virtual reality to augment real life. A fun example is an application created to project a solution onto any Rubik's cube, for those who missed out on the '80s craze.[93]

Augmented and virtual reality technologies provide us with an interface to create and innovate. Consider Google's Tilt Brush, which permits artists to draw and paint fantastical designs in three dimensions.[94] These works of art can then be experienced by others who use the tools of augmented reality. A virtual installation like the MOMA's might be placed in the center of your favorite restaurant. A street might be filled with gorgeous virtual graffiti, only available to those who are at that place and able to access the geolocated information.

I include virtualization technology in this discussion of the Internet of Things because geotagging makes the IoT possible, and because augmented reality directly affects our interface with the IoT. Consider the core IoT application: Google Maps. It overlays a simple two-dimensional virtual experience – the map – on top of physical reality, to help us know where we are. For a more immersive experience, consider the New York Times' virtual reality project. Times reporters and videographers go to places we can't go, then transport us there using Google Cardboard. These stories offer a vivid sense of space and a powerful physicality. In one, the reporter discusses the killing of a young Mexican man by a border patrol agent who fired through a border fence.[95] The agent claimed the young man was throwing rocks, a common tactic used by drug gangs to distract law enforcement. It is powerful to stand where the

[92] See Oct 9th 2010 AUGMENTED REALITY Art Invasion, SNDRV, http://www.sndrv.nl/ moma/?page=details (last visited May 12, 2016) ("The [exhibition] will not be visible to regular visitors of the MoMA, but those who are using a mobile phone application called 'Layar Augmented Reality browser' on their iPhone or Android smartphones, will see numerous additional works on each of the floors.").

[93] See Kelsey D. Atherton, Solve a Rubik's Cube With Augmented Reality, POPULAR SCI. (May 31, 2016), http://www.popsci.com/solve-rubiks-cube-with-augmented-reality.

[94] See Tilt Brush by Google, https://www.tiltbrush.com/ (last visited Sept. 30, 2016).

[95] Mark Binelli, 10 Shots Across the Border, N.Y. TIMES (Mar. 3, 2016), http://www.nytimes.com/ 2016/03/06/magazine/10-shots-across-the-border.html.

young man stood, and be able to get a sense of the physical space. No one knows the truth, but when a viewer stands in that space, albeit virtually, it is hard to imagine that anyone would try to throw a rock over a fence of that height. Don't take my word for it, though. Look for yourself. You can: that's the power of the technology.

IoT devices can be "geofenced" as a way to tie the device to physical geography. Geofenced devices or apps function only within certain GPS parameters. Consider the viral (and virulent) collegiate gossip app Yik Yak.[96] It permits a user to post anonymously (or, more accurately, pseudonymously, since Yik Yak records the user's telephone number) to anyone within a 1.5-mile radius of their location. If a student is at college, she sees only the pseudonymous posts of people in her area. As with many anonymous forums, Yik Yak rapidly accumulated a reputation as a sewer, with users posting threatening, bullying, or simply extremely negative comments to those within their immediate area. In response, Yik Yak offered to geofence the app off from any institution that requested it. If a user enters the geofenced area, Yik Yak no longer works.

Geofencing can also be used malevolently. By definition, when a smartphone enters a geofenced area, an advertiser learns the current physical location of the user. For example, when women entered abortion clinics, they were bombarded with advertisements from anti-abortion advocacy groups, which used geofencing technology to target advertisements at clinic locations.[97] Eight hundred thousand women received the specifically tailored advertisements while sitting in abortion clinics.[98] Whatever one thinks of the underlying political debate, advertisers intervening directly into an intimate medical environment based on the direct connection of electronic device to physical geography and cross-linkage to vast data on online browsing, offline travel, and purchasing history should be outside any bounds of ethical responsibility.

---

[96] *See* Caitlin Dewey, *How Do You Solve a Problem Like Yik Yak?*, Wash. Post (Oct. 7, 2014), https://www.washingtonpost.com/news/the-intersect/wp/2014/10/07/how-do-you-solve-a-problem-like-yik-yak/.

[97] *See* Sharona Coutts, *Anti-Choice Groups Use Smartphone Surveillance to Target 'Abortion-Minded Women' During Clinic Visits*, Rewire (May 25, 2016, 6:52 PM), https://rewire.news/article/2016/05/25/anti-choice-groups-deploy-smartphone-surveillance-target-abortion-minded-women-clinic-visits/.

[98] *See* Christina Cauterucci, *Anti-Abortion Groups Are Now Sending Targeted Smartphone Ads to Women in Abortion Clinics*, Slate: XXfactor (May 26, 2016, 4:31 PM), http://www.slate.com/blogs/xx_factor/2016/05/26/anti_abortion_groups_are_sending_targeted_smartphone_ads_to_women_in_abortion.html.

PROPERTY IN THE INTERNET OF THINGS

What does dusty property law have to do with the new and shiny Internet of Things? The earlier discussion establishes that it will be important for owners to (1) control the sensors embedded in infrastructure, especially the home; (2) control the sensors in devices; (3) control the flow of information between the moving and static parts of the IoT; and (4) control the user interfaces that mediate our perceptions. If we can strengthen property rights, we can strengthen these specific forms of owner control.

First, property rights allow us to control the sensors embedded in infrastructure. As things stand, the owner of a house can still make some basic decisions about the sensors embedded in her house. She may give away many of those rights when she clicks "I Agree" or signs a contract when she buys a smart thermostat, or a smart fan, or internet-enabled babysitting cameras, but she still has final say over what comes into her house and what stays out. Professor Reidenberg's confrontation with his utility company is a good example. His power to exclude the utility repairman until the company gave him adequate information about the smart meter demonstrates the power of local property over locally installed infrastructural sensors.

Second, stronger property rights would enable owners to control the sensors in devices. These rights are shrinking, but they are still there. No one will tell you that you cannot put a sticky note over the camera of your laptop to protect your privacy. You could probably unscrew the backplate of your smartphone or smart television and swap the components out. At the limit, no matter what license you have signed, you can probably throw a device out the window, put your work-required pedometer in the dryer to confuse it, or disconnect the GPS tracker that comes in your car. You can put your Roomba in a closet if you are worried about the fact that it maps your home and shares that information with others.[99]

Companies do try to stop users from repairing or modifying their devices. Gamers who sought to modify their Playstations were hunted by Sony, which sent subpoenas to service providers and YouTube, trying to discover the identity of everyone who watched videos on how to perform the modifications.[100] But consumers still feel strongly justified in modifying, repairing, and in general asserting control over their devices. When individual owners exercise their property rights, they push back against the control of intellectual property

---

[99] *See* Valentina Palladino, *iRobot's Roomba 980 Maps Your Home While Making Your Floors Sparkle*, ARS TECHNICA (Sept. 17, 2015, 9:10 AM), http://arstechnica.com/gadgets/2015/09/irobots-Roomba-980-maps-your-home-while-making-your-floors-sparkle/.

[100] *See* David Kravets, *Judge Lets Sony Unmask Visitors to PS3-Jailbreaking Site*, WIRED (Mar. 4, 2011), https://www.wired.com/2011/03/geohot-site-unmasking/.

rightsholders in their smart and digital property. Property rights resist intellectual property overreach, and strengthening them will increase that resistance.

Third, stronger property rights would enable owners to control the flow of information between their wearable and mobile devices and the infrastructure-embedded sensors they encounter. Consider the FTC's action against Nomi, where shoppers' cell phones were tracked upon entering a shop or supermarket. An owner with weak ownership rights might not be able to modify her phone to stop broadcasting to Nomi's trackers, because she cannot give the relevant permissions to applications that block such access. An owner with stronger ownership rights could do so by downloading and giving root access to software that manages wireless access points and blocks contacts with tracking hotspots. As for those owners that have no idea that such things are going on inside their devices, the property rule of trespass would create a simple rule of exclusion: unless the owner is aware of and okay with what you are doing, keep out.

Fourth, stronger property rights in smart property will enable us to protect our own perception. Our devices filter how we see the world. In the case of the Oculus Rift, Google Cardboard virtual reality headsets, or augmented reality games like Pokémon GO, this is literally the case. We see the world through the screen of the device. Other devices affect our perceptions more indirectly. We must be able to trust that our GPS application takes us where we wish to go, and does not choose the route based on the desires of advertisers to route us to the local shopping district.

Viewed from sixty thousand feet and more abstractly, property enables local-area decision making. You and your neighbor don't have to ask someone else whether you can build a shed on the neighbor's field – you buy the field from your neighbor and build the shed. Traditional property is decentralized and local. Intellectual property is centralized and global. In the Internet of Things we see the two networks discussed above. One is centralized and global, the other is decentralized and local. I was at a conference in Germany and emailed my presentation slides to the conference moderator – who was sitting right next to me. It struck me as strange that for a document to move three feet, it must travel across the transatlantic cable to my university's home servers in the United States, back across the cable to Germany, and finally come to rest three feet away. That is how favored the core-centralized model of computing is, currently. But networks can be, and in some cases are, local. We can move documents from one node at the edge to another node at the edge. We can move a file from a smartphone to a tablet without having to go through the core network. It's possible, but unnecessarily inconvenient. With the Internet of Things, we could build a much more robust edge network. Many of the connectivity protocols of the IoT are local, device to device. (The new industry buzzword for this is "fog computing," as opposed to the cloud.) We can expect such technology to get better as local devices find more and more value in talking with each other.

Intellectual property fits well with cloud computing, license servers, broadband connections, and centralized control. Consider Apple Music. The music resides in the cloud and streams to the user, who is licensed to hear it. Thanks to relatively inexpensive broadband access, burning bandwidth to listen to her music is of little consequence to the consumer. The music never leaves Apple's hands, and the consumer doesn't get a copy, so Apple can prevent the consumer from reselling her music, and can revoke or remove access to the music if the consumer stops paying for the service.[101]

Traditional property law fits well with devices, edge networks, bluetooth, RFID, local sensors, and decentralized control. Consider your smartwatch, your fitness tracker, and your smartphone. They link with each other, forming a small network that serves your purposes. Of course, they also report the information to a bunch of other companies and advertisers, but that is part of the problem we are trying to solve. They don't need to do that to function. They are perfectly capable of forming a small, local, useful network of devices to keep track of your health data for your benefit. The same goes for a linkage between your smart thermostat and the fans in your home that circulate air to balance temperature in rooms that are being used, or to control window blinds to maximize or minimize solar heating, and so on. Those functions are local. The companies that make these devices want your data for testing purposes, to improve their products, or to sell to advertisers. But access to the core network is not necessary for the devices to serve you.

At the same time, the owners of the intellectual property inside these embedded processors and sensors claim the ability to control them. The utility company wished to switch Joel Reidenberg's water meter without informing him that it was installing an insecure smart meter. Sometimes the conflict of interest between owner and software provider becomes even more stark. One high-profile Bitcoin startup intended to sell Internet of Things appliances that would use the chips within those appliances to mine Bitcoin (more on how that works in Chapter 7) and send the proceeds to the developer.[102]

[101] See *iTunes Store Terms and Conditions*, APPLE INC. (last updated Oct. 21, 2015) ("When your Apple Music Subscription term ends, you will lose access to any feature of the Apple Music Service ... accessible through the Apple Music Service or stored on your device, and any songs stored in your iCloud Music Library.").
[102] See Izabella Kaminska, *Meet the Company That Wants to Put a Bitcoin Miner in Your Toaster*, FIN. TIMES: ALPHAVILLE (Apr. 30, 2015, 4:28 PM), http://ftalphaville.ft.com/2015/04/30/2127543/meet-the-company-that-wants-to-put-a-bitcoin-miner-in-your-toaster/.

This brings the law of intellectual property directly in conflict with the law of real property. If license terms and conditions are to be believed, the user cannot ever truly own the software-enabled device she purchases. Within property law, the law of fixtures says that once you install something permanently, so that it cannot be easily removed from real property, it is part of the real property. Let us imagine a factory installed with a smart heating system. Sensors detect where heat is in the building, and turn fans on and off to circulate air for maximum heating and cooling effect, depending on which rooms are occupied. If the fans were merely "dumb" fans, there would be no question that the heating system would be part of the real estate, and could be sold with it. But these fans are smart, and subject to the usual licenses. Can the owner sell the factory with its heating system intact?

Now imagine that in our factory very nearly everything is chip-enhanced: the water system (to increase efficiency of water use in the restrooms), the manufacturing machines, the lighting system (to increase electrical efficiency), the automated forklifts and smart sensors in the floor that guide them, and the tracking chips that help to automatically register the movement of inventory. It is easy to imagine a modern factory that is made up of hundreds, if not thousands of overlapping license conditions. Trying to sell that firm, if one of the intellectual property owners objects on the grounds that its licenses are non-transferrable, is not an easy prospect.

Michael Heller, a well-known property scholar, proposed the idea of the property anticommons.[103] The idea is simple. The tragedy of the commons occurs when everyone can use a resource. So everyone takes as much as they can, and the resource is soon depleted. But the tragedy of the anticommons is where too many people have the right to block each other from using a resource. There, the resource is not overused, it is underused.[104] Imagine if, instead of owning a car, one person owned the steering wheel, another owned the wheels, a third owned the engine, and a fourth owned the brakes. It would be very nearly impossible to purchase the car because at least one of the four would hold out for a too-high price, as predicted by legal scholars Melamed and Calabresi.[105] This creates a property tragedy of the

---

[103] Michael A. Heller, *The Tragedy of the Anticommons: Property in the Transition from Marx to Markets*, 111 HARV. L. REV. 621 (1998).

[104] *See id.* at 624 ("When there are too many owners holding rights of exclusion, the resource is prone to underuse – a tragedy of the anticommons.").

[105] *See* Guido Calabresi & A. Douglas Melamed, *Property Rules, Liability Rules, and Inalienability: One View of the Cathedral*, 85 HARV. L. REV. 1089, 1106 (1972) ("Often the cost of establishing the value of an initial entitlement by negotiation is so great that even though a transfer of the entitlement would benefit all concerned, such a transfer will not occur.").

anticommons, where no one uses the resource instead of too many people using the resource.[106]

Intellectual property embedded in real property creates an anticommons problem. Whereas before, if a property owner purchased something and affixed it to her property, she would be the owner of both the real property and the affixed personal property, she must now worry about all sorts of licenses that control the software embedded within the property. That can make the property very difficult to value and sell. In the worst-case scenario, it can undermine its value as property altogether: one must negotiate with each property holder and each license holder in order to buy a factory, or a machine, or a building.

OUT OF (OUR) CONTROL

The Internet of Things represents the seeding of computing power and sensors throughout our environment and within and around our bodies. It is the process of enriching reality with information, and acting on information within reality. It includes health-tracking bands, pacemaker implants, babysitting cameras, fake Wi-Fi stations that track supermarket shoppers, and accelerometer-enabled augmented reality.

Property law has always been about allocating and commanding resources. We need to be able to command resources in the physical world. We need to be able to get food and shelter. Beyond basic needs, humans desire to alter and shape their environment to their preference. Give a teenager a room, and she will paint it. Give a gamer a computer and she will mod it. Give an adult a four-wheel-drive truck and she will want to drive it offroad.

The centralization of the license-server, intellectual property, cloud-based model of the Internet of Things compromises our ability to command data-enriched resources and control the devices we wear, carry, and encounter. This costs us financially, emotionally, and as a society. We are degraded financially when we lose money, beaten at the economic game of poker by those who use our devices to see our cards. We are degraded emotionally as relationships of equality give way to centralized control. And we are degraded in terms of our ability to see ourselves as active agents, as people whose choices matter, when we are forced into specific uses (or abuses) of our own property by those who subvert it for their own profit. In short, we lose in every way.

---

[106] See Heller, *supra* note 104.

4

So What?

In May 2016, a man named James Pinkstone reported that he had lost over twenty years of carefully collected music and rare recordings from his computer.[1] He had signed up for Apple Music's streaming service, and claimed that Apple replaced his meticulously curated recordings with different streamed versions. When Pinkstone contacted Apple support, he was informed there was nothing that could be done, and that indeed the system was designed to work like that. To be clear, it is likely that the problem was caused by Apple misidentifying filenames of music that it had in a streaming library, that Apple Music does not delete files without giving the user some choice, and that Pinkstone probably could have avoided the problem if he had set the complicated controls correctly. But that is the point: Apple weans its customers from owning music and teaches them to stream it, while exerting control over what is easier or harder to store or stream. By the exercise of slight pressures and careful use of complexity, "Apple Music represents a clumsy and inscrutable attempt to blur the line between 'owning' a song and merely streaming it."[2]

In an article about the Pinkstone incident, one reporter wrote that the complexities of transferring music left him with only the music Apple had sold him. The rest was lost in the difficulties of converting from device to device, library to library, software version to software version. He wrote:

> At some point between then and now, iTunes became a total black hole to me. I stopped understanding what it did when I downloaded a song and dragged it into my library. I didn't get how it related to Apple Music, or what

[1] Leon Neyfakh, *Apple Destroyed My Will to Collect Music*, SLATE (May 9, 2016, 5:55 AM), http://www.slate.com/articles/technology/technology/2016/05/will_apple_music_complete_itunes_destruction_of_my_will_to_collect_music.html.
[2] *Id.*

role iCloud played in managing my data. Above all I couldn't get my head around syncing – the mysterious and maddening process I had to go through whenever I wanted to put specific songs on my iPhone. None of it made sense to me, and when I thought for too long about the impact iTunes was having on the texture and structure of my music consumption, I was overcome with a bitter sense of loss.

I used to love collecting music.[3]

Why should we care that our property rights are fading online? One might reasonably ask whether it is better to stream than to own, as long as it's cheaper. So what if we don't own our books, but merely rent them through Amazon Kindle? So what if we don't own our movies, but merely rent them through Netflix? Perhaps it is no big deal if we don't own our smartphones, tablets, laptops, self-driving cars, or network-controlled houses, and instead essentially rent them from the telecommunications carriers or operating system designers. What's so bad about this future without ownership?

Our independence is at stake. If we become digital tenants living at the mercy of digital landlords, we lose our ability to act on our own. If a person owns her own house, she has a reserve of value upon which she can call. She can turn down a job she doesn't like and wait for one that she prefers, because she is not immediately pressed for living space. If a person owns her own computer, she need not bow to her carrier or the advertising networks. She can research, think, write, and connect with others as she wills. A homeowner can turn her property into a cat sanctuary. A renter is subject to her landlord's aversion to cats. An owner of music can listen to it where and when she wishes. A mere licensee of music may find that her music has been quietly deleted from her cloud storage without her knowledge or consent. An owner of banned books can still read them if they become politically or economically unpopular. A licensee of e-books that are suddenly banned may find that they are not available any more.[4]

To the founders of the United States, the independent farmer who answered to no one was the core political foundation of the polity.[5] In the founders' view, the independent yeoman farmer could be trusted to vote for what was best in the abstract, not what was best in his own self-interest, precisely because he depended on no one. That view of the world is not without its problems. We have moved beyond requiring people to own property to vote (or to be of a

---

[3] *Id.*   [4] See Chapter 2 for a more detailed discussion of this incident.

[5] *See* WALLACE HETTLE, THE PECULIAR DEMOCRACY: SOUTHERN DEMOCRATS IN PEACE AND CIVIL WAR 15 (University of Georgia Press 2001) (discussing how Thomas Jefferson envisioned the "ideal yeoman" being "the cornerstone of a virtuous society").

certain race or sex, for that matter). Yet there is no question that people who can fall back on property benefit from independence of action and thought. People who depend on others for their life and livelihood tend to alter their political views to conform to the views of the people who hold control over their lives. That is dangerous for our democracy.

Consider another angle: the Uber ride-sharing service knows when you will accept insanely high surge pricing.[6] Uber's head of economic research shared that riders will accept surge pricing up to 9.9 times higher than the usual fare if their mobile phone battery is about to die. Riders accept this deal because they cannot risk being stranded, and so cannot wait to see if the surge pricing will ebb. Uber knows that the user's battery is dying because the Uber app receives battery information intended to help maximize battery life by moving to low-power mode. (For what it's worth, Uber's spokesman promised that Uber would not abuse this knowledge.[7])

Our economic well-being depends on our ability to control who does what on our devices. If a corporation can mine data about us by turning our own smartphones and smart homes against us, it can gain an insurmountable advantage in bargaining with us. In economic language, the corporation can capture the entire transactional surplus. The price for a cab ride will spike when our battery is low. The price of gasoline (or a fast recharge) will spike when our smart car is low on fuel. The price of a plane ticket already spikes when we comparison shop online (or if we shop for it using an Apple product).

In Chapter 2, I discussed the three major streams of property thought: property provides freedom from interference (libertarianism); property provides "freedom from want,"[8] ensuring the most good for the most people (welfarism); and property provides freedom of self-expression (identity). Although they come at it in different ways, these three historical understandings of property reflect an approach that is oriented toward human freedom: property is able to, and should, widen the range of viable human options for people. In this chapter, I examine the implications of property as a means of increasing and honoring human freedom in the digital age. Property is important because it makes us free; it is important because we use it to define our identities; and it is important because it is a measure of wealth and a hedge against exploitation.

---

[6] *See* Madison Malone Kircher, *Uber Knows When You'll Pay Surge Pricing, But Promises Not to Use It Against You*, N.Y. MAG.: SELECT ALL (May 19, 2016, 5:14 PM), http://nymag.com/selectall/2016/05/uber-knows-exactly-when-youll-pay-surge-pricing-promises-not-to-use-info-against-us.html?wpsrc=nymag.

[7] *Id.*

[8] President Franklin D. Roosevelt, Annual Message to Congress (Jan. 6, 1941), *in* 87 Cong. Rec. 44, 46 (1941).

But if we don't get digital and smart property ownership right, these values are at risk.

INDEPENDENCE

Property secures our ability to act by enabling access to resources. It provides us with a way to exercise individual decision making that is independent from, and in some cases directly opposed to, the determinations of society. As prominent Yale law professor and property scholar Charles Reich has written:

> One of [the functions of property] is to draw a boundary between public and private power.... It is as if property shifted the burden of proof; outside, the individual has the burden; inside, the burden is on government to demonstrate that something the owner wishes to do should not be done. Thus, property performs the function of maintaining independence, dignity and pluralism in society by creating zones within which the majority has to yield to the owner.[9]

Independence of Action

Property is a demand on resources that society respects. If I need a car, how can society decide whether I just get to hop into one of them out in the parking lot and take off? To the uninformed observer, it is not possible to tell whether, when I drive away, I am the car's owner or a thief. What we can do depends on the degree to which society respects our demands on resources: our property. It doesn't matter much if GM tells me that I technically own my car if I cannot fix it without asking GM's permission. It doesn't matter much that Samsung tells me that I technically own my smart television if the TV won't stop listening to conversations in my house when I tell it to.

Some intrusions into our ability to use our property may benefit us. I may prefer that my car not beep at me when I forget to put my seatbelt on immediately, nor automatically lock the doors when I start to drive. Those are small ways in which our property does not respond to our wishes, and those minor invasions of our right to use our property as we wish aren't a big deal, and make us safer.

But as we take more and more rights away from owners, we hollow out the meaning of property. We make it an empty promise. Society no longer promises to allow us the digital equivalent of hopping in the car and driving away. It constrains what we can do. It holds back a lot of rights to take action,

---

9 Charles A. Reich, *The New Property*, 73 YALE L.J. 733, 771 (1964).

and this stops us from doing what we want to do, when and how we want to do it. When society permits holdouts, caveats, reserves, hidden clauses, and other legal chicanery to deplete property rights, we don't just have problems of consumer confusion (people don't know what they are buying) or potential consumer deception (people thought they were buying more than they were). We reduce the range of human independence to act.

That can be a real problem. Consider bionic prosthetics, many of which are controlled by software.[10] One group of researchers has even developed a "cyber expert system" that automatically "tunes" prosthetics to account for bodily changes.[11] If we take to heart the arguments advanced by John Deere and others, individuals dependent on these prosthetics may not even own their own limbs. Or consider other medical devices: you may think you own the pacemaker that regulates your heartbeat, yet there are limits to what you can do. The device reports to its manufacturer, and through it, to government. In one case, reported by the Washington Post, a man was charged with arson because of data pulled by law enforcement from his pacemaker.[12] Investigators argued that he could not have escaped his house with his belongings without stressing his heart, and used the evidence of his implant to bring charges.[13] But while government can track every beat of your heart, you may not be able to get certain data feeds from your device to keep track of how you are doing. Jason Schultz and Aaron Perzanowski tell the story of Dana Lewis, who needed to hack her insulin pump in order to incorporate a potentially life-saving innovation.[14] Because she was unable to hear her device's alarm, she "built a new program that displayed blood sugar levels with new louder alarms and a snooze button."[15] She and her partner even used the data sent by the device to

---

[10] *See, e.g.*, Geoff Brumfiel, *The Insane and Exciting Future of the Bionic Body*, SMITHSO-NIAN MAG. (Sept. 2013), http://www.smithsonianmag.com/innovation/the-insane-and-exciting-future-of-the-bionic-body-918868/?no-ist ("Improved software, longer-lasting batteries and smaller, more power-efficient microprocessors – the technologies driving the revolution in personal electronics – have ushered in a new era in bionics.").

[11] *See* Stephen Feller, Software Tunes Powered Prosthetic Legs Automatically, UPI (Sept. 29, 2015, 10:53 AM), http://www.upi.com/Health_News/2015/09/29/Software-tunes-powered-prosthetic-legs-automatically/4241443533421.

[12] *See* Cleve R. Wooston, Jr., *A Man Detailed His Escape From a Burning House. His Pacemaker Told a Different Story.*, WASH. POST: TO YOUR HEALTH (Feb. 8, 2017), https://www.washingtonpost.com/news/to-your-health/wp/2017/02/08/a-man-detailed-his-escape-from-a-burning-house-his-pacemaker-told-police-a-different-story/.

[13] *Id.*

[14] *See* AARON PERZANOWSKI & JASON SCHULTZ, THE END OF OWNERSHIP: PERSONAL PROPERTY IN THE DIGITAL ECONOMY 152-53 (MIT Press 2016) (discussing a diabetic's efforts to modify her glucose monitor).

[15] *Id.* at 152.

create a unique algorithm to predict her insulin needs, a potential violation of the manufacturer's intellectual property rights.[16] As Schultz and Perzanowski rightly note: "No IP law, and certainly not one designed to stop consumers from sharing movies online, should stand in the way of patients adapting equipment they own to keep them alive."[17] What if the upgrade to "Heart 2.0" is too expensive? Or, conversely, what if your pacemaker force-updates, eliminating your customizations and settings, the way that many Windows users were "upgraded" to Windows 10 against their will? Our independence of action makes these questions too important to leave to license terms and intellectual property law.

Independence of Thought

Where ownership of real estate might establish independence of means, ownership of digital and smart property establishes independence of thought. Scholars come at this from a few different directions. Cass Sunstein points out that if we only interact with others who believe the same as we do, we become more polarized in our views.[18] Similarly, Eli Pariser notes in his book, *The Filter Bubble*, that a world in which information is tailored just for us is a world in which we learn little, and a world in which whoever controls the information flow pulls our strings.[19] If I tell you something you already know, you haven't learned anything. No information has passed from me to you. So when Google filters our smartphone search results to return familiar and comforting news, we are quite literally learning less. (Google can do this, of course, because of its deep access to our devices and search profiles.) Worse, by exclusively consuming information that fits with our worldview, we reinforce our errors and deepen our intellectual isolation.

Other theorists approach this independence of thought issue from the perspective of privacy. Julie Cohen notes that we need to give citizens "breathing room," a place to experiment with being different from other people, and find out what makes us truly human.[20] Paul Schwartz talks about a "constitutive"

---

[16] See *id.* at 153 (noting that the unique algorithm would "automate and adapt based on the data her device was sending out" and "could even predict her insulin needs 30, 60, and even 90 minutes in the future").

[17] *Id.*

[18] See Cass Sunstein, Going to Extremes: How Like Minds Unite and Divide (Oxford University Press 2009).

[19] See Eli Pariser, The Filter Bubble: How the New Personalized Web is Changing What We Read and How We Think 16 (Penguin Books 2011) ("When you enter a filter bubble, you're letting the companies that construct it choose which options you're aware of.").

[20] Julie Cohen, *What Privacy Is For*, 126 Harv. L. Rev. 1904, 1906 (2013).

element of personal privacy – that it protects the democratic decision making and processes that underlie our society.[21]

Independence of thought requires both information and space. We need public information spaces to learn new things. We need private information spaces to experiment and become ourselves. And to think clearly, we need the raw materials. We need the books, the music, and the artworks that exemplify and spur innovation. In the digital age, that includes the digital and smart devices we rely on to help us and let us think. We need to have access to these things even when someone else does not want us to have them. We need to own them.

Think about your book collection. When I first presented these ideas at academic conferences, academics (of all people!) were skeptical about the value of owning books. They were much more focused on the academic values of freedom of expression, and the technological values of access to knowledge. After all, if you can access information, and express yourself as you will, then what is the value of owning a particular (usually out-of-date) copy of that information yourself?

Books matter because they help to define us – think about the aspirational books that line your shelves, the ones you want to read, but haven't yet – they challenge us, they provide constant reminders of what we have learned (oh, yeah, I remember, it's in that book!), and, according to some studies, they even help our children succeed academically merely by being in the house.[22]

Physical books serve as a buffer against censorship. Take, for example, Henry Miller's *Tropic of Cancer*, famously banned in the 1930s from publication anywhere in the United States. The book was published thirty years later by a publisher willing to face the ensuing obscenity lawsuits, culminating in a victory before the U.S. Supreme Court. But during the thirty-year interim, people smuggled in copies. Frances Steloff, proprietor of the Gotham Book Mart, challenged censorship by importing both *Tropic of Cancer* and D. H. Lawrence's *Lady Chatterley's Lover*.[23] When someone bans a book, nothing happens to the actual copies. The book continues to exist. Copies of the book, scattered on bookshelves across the country, act as a physical buffer against forgetting knowledge. Bookshelves don't back up much in terms of exabytes

---

[21] Paul M. Schwartz, *Privacy and Democracy in Cyberspace*, 52 VAND. L. REV. 1609, 1613 (1999).

[22] *See* M. D. R. Evans et al., *Scholarly Culture and Academic Performance in 42 Nations*, 92 SOC. FORCES 1573, 1592 (2014) (finding that "books in the home have a positive 'payoff' in improved test scores throughout the world").

[23] *See* Herbert Mitgang, *Frances Steloff Is Dead at 101; Founded the Gotham Book Mart*, N.Y. TIMES (Apr. 16, 1989), http://www.nytimes.com/1989/04/16/obituaries/frances-steloff-is-dead-at-101-founded-the-gotham-book-mart.html?pagewanted=all.

of information, but they do back up what we find most important, including much that would not otherwise be preserved. But when someone bans a copy of an e-book, license agreements allow the publisher to take it away at the drop of a hat. When power over books concentrates in the hands of a few e-book publishers, it becomes easier for governments to effect bans for political ends.

We should care about property interests in the online context not just as a measure of physical wealth, but also as a measure of intellectual access. Even if we do not crack open the books we own, they provide a meaningful backstop to efforts to deny access to information. Even if we do not watch the movies we own on DVD, or listen very often to some of our CDs, they provide a valuable price check to firms that must compete against the secondary market for used DVDs and CDs on eBay. This ensures that they remain available at a reasonable price for those who do need them for thought or research. Even if we do not read our Kindle collection, Amazon should not be free to delete it. These intellectual, cultural, and artistic resources preserve our independence of thought, creativity, innovation, and access to common (or uncommon) culture.

It is important not to take this too far. Tailored information access can often recommend things to us that people like us have enjoyed, and that we end up enjoying too. That's why Amazon's "People who bought ... also bought ..." recommendation engine is so effective. And new technology and the constant access provided by mobile devices and the Internet of Things make sharing and common culture more accessible than ever before. Yet at the same time that we have unprecedented present access to information, we have less information than ever about who shapes that information as it comes to us, how and why they shape it, and to what end. Moreover, we have no guarantees that present access will be future access. When your Netflix subscription runs out, the show's over.

IDENTITY

Property does not merely define what we can do. We use it to define and remember who we are, to make a record in object form of our identity, our history, and our growth. Property law icon Margaret Jane Radin writes:

> Most people possess certain objects they feel are almost part of themselves. These objects are closely bound up with personhood because they are part of the way we constitute ourselves as continuing personal entities in the world. They may be as different as people are different, but some common examples might be a wedding ring, a portrait, an heirloom, or a house.[24]

---

[24] Margaret Jane Radin, *Property as Personhood*, 34 STAN. L. REV. 957 (1982).

I have always looked at the bookcase in my parents' house as a reminder of the lives they have led. That bookcase contains books in German from their study abroad in college, books in French from their time as educators in Africa, books in Nepali from their time in mission work. There are books they have gathered at each stage in life, books they received from their parents, some of them *written* by their parents. There are still books on the lower shelves – where my children take them down and read them – that were given to me as a child. My youngest often brings me books with my name scrawled in them in a seven-year-old's penmanship.

My grandfather, Grant Stoltzfus, was a professor and scholar. His life was marked by a lifelong love of learning. To hear my mother tell it, Grant "had a study with two huge bookcases and several small ones, full of books. He had read most of them, he pulled them out to quote from them when we were having a discussion or he had a point to make. His learnedness defined him in a big way, we children were surrounded by these books and got our love of learning from their presence and [Grant's] interaction with them."

I never knew my grandfather, who suffered a heart attack when I was a year old. After he passed away, my mother and her siblings kept his books. "[T]hey sustain me by being visible on the shelves," my mother wrote to me. Grant knew he would continue the intellectual conversation with his children and grandchildren through his notes in his books. So although I never spoke with my grandfather, my own intellectual life has been guided by the titles, by the selection, by the range and languages, by the underlining and marks written in the margins of books that I pulled off the shelf.

The bookcase is more than a compendium of information – it is a reminder of places we have been, thoughts we have encountered, and the people we were and were with when we encountered them. Often *who* a book is from is more important than *what* it says. I have religious texts inscribed with my grandmother's name, novels from my grandfather, computer science textbooks from my father, and language-learning texts from my mother. Often the first thing I do when left alone in someone else's house is look at their bookcase. I want to know what is important enough to them that they have chosen to announce it to the world in object form. It saves a lot of small talk, and provides something worthwhile and enriching to talk about.

Objects of many kinds serve this purpose. It is no mistake that we call some things "mementos" or "souvenirs" – they are not merely physical representations of our memories, they are memories themselves. Sometimes the memories are gone, or nearly gone, until an object recalls them to us. Each of us has had the experience of a watch handed down from our father, or a musical instrument handed down by a grandmother. A wedding ring is a reminder. It is nearly impossible to walk through a home or a place experienced as a

child and not have some reaction to the environment. That reaction may be
negative, it may be positive, but it is without doubt a part of us. This sense of
property as an intrinsic part of our identity doesn't square well with a view of
the world that puts a price on everything.

For this identity function of property, William Blackstone's "sole and
despotic dominion" makes more sense.[25] Certainty and long-lastingness take
the place of purely economic incentives. No one values as I do the dog-eared
copy of *Good Luck Arizona Man* that my father read to me as a child. Using
market pricing to allocate that particular resource would be disastrous. What
the market is willing to pay has nothing to do with the anguish of a person cut
off from the objects and places that make up who they are. A person exercising
sole and despotic dominion over her wedding ring, to wear, use, lose, destroy,
or pass on to her children as she sees fit, is a better solution than considering
the ring to be merely the placeholder for a price.

Smart and digital property also carries this emotional freight of identity.
Many of the initial legal disputes over virtual property centered on who owned
the social media accounts of deceased soldiers.[26] The bereaved families wanted
access to those memories as property of the deceased soldier's estate. The
companies argued that the social media accounts were just contractual services
that would not pass on to the family. Nora McInerney Purmort wrote movingly
for Slate magazine that her phone was "a time machine to a place where my
husband is still alive."[27]

A lot of the branding that surrounds our digital devices plays to our sense
of self. iProducts sell one vision of the self. BlackBerries (at least before the
company's steep decline) sold a different one. More, it is entirely possible
to build relationships and meaningful attachments to fully digital spaces and
experiences. When Blizzard Entertainment updated the look of World of
Warcraft avatars, players complained. They had become attached to the old
models, and missed the digital forms in which they had invested so much
energy. The music to *Super Mario Bros.* takes a generation back to bedrooms,
basements, and living rooms. Oddly enough, one of the major features players

---

[25] See 2 WILLIAM BLACKSTONE, COMMENTARIES *2.
[26] See, e.g., Ariana Eunjung Cha, *After Death, a Struggle for Digital Memories*, WASH. POST,
Feb. 3, 2005, at A1 (noting that, when it comes to data stored on the internet, "[t]here are no
clear laws of inheritance, meaning Internet providers must often decide for themselves what
is right."); *see also* Joshua A.T. Fairfield, *Virtual Property*, 85 B.U. L. REV. 1047, 1056 (2005)
(discussing the disputes between ISPs and the families of deceased soldiers).
[27] Nora McInerney Purmort, *Please Don't Ask Me to Put Down My Phone*, SLATE (May 24, 2016,
11:54 AM), http://www.slate.com/articles/life/family/2016/05/my_phone_is_a_time_machine_to_
where_my_husband_is_still_alive.html.

of video games and virtual worlds look for is "housing" – the ability to own and decorate their own spaces. And speaking of video games, I have many memories of worlds that do not exist, fond memories of Skona Ravine, and Tatooine, and Blackwing Lair.

We should be wary of a future in which our ability to express ourselves through control over and preservation of our environment is severely compromised due to the questionable economic claims of intellectual property rightsholders. We should be concerned when companies claim that the digital equivalent of our family members' letters and journals will not pass to us. We should be worried that we cannot pass on our books or music collections to our children. These things are much more than a mere license to look at intellectual property. They are a part of us.

WEALTH

So what if our property is being used to economically profile us? After all, it just means we see and have to ignore some annoyingly personal ads – or perhaps it might even direct us to things we never knew we wanted. But the real difficulty comes in forcing us to negotiate with people who have already used our devices to learn everything about us, from what we want to how much we can afford to pay. Shopping online using a device controlled by other parties is like playing poker with someone who can see your cards: you're just not going to win.

The process is called "price discrimination." Some economists and politicians claim that the more a company knows about us, the better deals we get.[28] A 2015 White House report asserted that, although price discrimination can be misused,[29] the more companies know about their buyers, the better the deals will become. The report claimed that above all, poor people benefit from price discrimination.[30] Here is why they say this: imagine you could charge each person a different price for a widget that cost you $20 to make. Since the widget costs you $20, you wouldn't charge any less than that. Above that point, though, you might be willing to sell the widget for anywhere from $21 on up.

---

[28] *See generally* Irina D. Manta & David S. Olson, *Hello Barbie: First They Will Monitor You, Then They Will Discriminate Against You. Perfectly.*, 67 ALA. L. REV. 135 (2015).

[29] *See* EXECUTIVE OFFICE OF THE PRESIDENT, BIG DATA AND DIFFERENTIAL PRICING (2015), *available at* https://www.whitehouse.gov/sites/default/files/whitehouse_files/docs/Big_Data_Report_Nonembargo_v2.pdf ("Economics suggests that many forms of differential pricing, such as senior citizen discounts at the box office or tiered pricing for air travel, can be good for both businesses and consumers. However, the combination of differential pricing and big data raises concerns that some consumers can be made worse off, and have very little knowledge why.").

[30] *See id.; see also* Manta & Olson, *supra* note 26, at 179.

However, if you sell it to Fred for $21, you would lose out on the money you would have earned if Wilma were willing to buy it for $2,100. You could solve this problem if you could tell the difference between Fred and Wilma, and charge each of them a personalized price: sell to Wilma at $2,100 and then to Fred at $21.

So, the usual logic goes, unless you can soak Wilma for $2,100, you will be unwilling to sell to Fred at $21. Or, put another way, if you must only choose one price, you might only be willing to sell to the Wilmas of the world, and you would sacrifice the sale to the Freds of the world. After all, you would prefer to take the profit from a sale to someone like Wilma. So the White House report follows the standard line: assuming (and this is a big assumption, as we'll see later) that the reason Fred is only willing to pay $21 is because he is poor, then the way to make sure Fred gets a chance to buy the widget is to enable the seller to charge different people different prices.

To see the standard model in action (and in a positive light), consider the economic model of nonprofit universities. Assume the list price for a year at a private college is $50,000. Few students pay this price, however. During the financial aid process, students fill out extensive forms revealing their family's finances. Using these disclosures, the colleges apply a formula to determine the family's expected contribution – that is, the real price that the student and her family must pay. The list price minus the amount the family actually pays is called the "discount."

Why would any family reveal information that causes them to be charged a higher price, other than the fact that they are required to do so during the applications process? One reason is the belief that discounting permits nonprofit universities to serve students who would not be able to pay full price, or even most of the discounted price. Roughly put, a university can afford to take on a student for free if it takes on a student who pays full price. They balance out, and we generally see this as a positive thing. The ability to charge an artificially inflated price to those who can afford it permits selling the same product for next-to-nothing to those who can't.

This works as long as a university remains dedicated to transferring the surplus it generates on a full-price sale back to students who cannot afford to go to college. But when the profit model changes, so do the incentives. A for-profit school – or a for-profit entity of any kind – has little incentive to redistribute the consumer surplus it takes at the top end to consumers who need it at the bottom end. So if the cost of educating a student is $30,000 per year, a profit-driven university would not be incentivized to redistribute the top-end payments from students who might pay $50,000 a year to those who can only pay $15,000. A school not motivated primarily by profit might.

Efficiency

At stake is the economic concept of efficiency. Economists worry that if Fred can't buy the widget, valuable trade wealth is lost. Trade makes everyone better off. If I have a $5 bill and you have a huge cup of coffee, and I would like the coffee more than the money, and you would like the money more than the coffee, then trading is a great way to make everyone happier at a pretty low cost – the cost of handing each other what we have. Economists say that it is inefficient if we don't trade. In the case of Fred and Wilma and your widgets, if you only sell to Wilma but would be willing to sell to Fred at $21 if you could, then the inability to charge different people different prices causes the inefficient loss of the potential sale.

The failure to make the sale is a cost – what economists call a "deadweight loss." This is because nobody gets the value of the trade, not the seller, not the buyer. Society loses out on the chance for everyone to become a little better off. It is this loss to society that traditional economics seeks to avoid. But that is not the only loss possible. Let us say that I am willing to pay *up to* $5 for that cup of coffee. But coffee is not all that expensive. Let us say that you are willing to sell the coffee for *as low as* sixty-nine cents. So I might get a great deal if I buy the coffee for sixty-nine cents. You might get a great deal if I buy the coffee for $5. Neoclassical economists do not care who gets this value as long as the trade happens. They don't even care if sellers exploit information they have gathered about buyers to make sure that they, the sellers, get the best deal.[31] So if you can figure out how much I'd pay for that coffee, standard economics would say "Go ahead," caring little about any exploitation required to do so. But nobody likes to be exploited. As experiments in behavioral economics confirm, we naturally resist exploitation. And that results in efficiency losses of other sorts.

Exploitation

While price discrimination can, under good circumstances, yield more deals for more people who need them,[32] in practice this idea falls short. In theory, price discrimination can help expand the size of the pie.[33] In practice, it often just helps the seller get a bigger slice.

Knowing more about the buyer doesn't necessarily encourage a seller to charge a buyer less – it helps the seller charge the maximum that each customer is willing to pay. Trades are beneficial precisely because the buyer values the

---

[31] Richard A. Posner, Economic Analysis of Law (Seventh Edition) 9–11 (Wolters Kluwer 2007).
[32] *See, e.g.*, Manta & Olson, *supra* note 26, at 179–87.   [33] *Id.*

property that she purchases more than the seller values it. If I buy a pair of used dress shoes on eBay, I may value the shoes at $25, because the alternative is paying $300 for new Allen Edmonds Park Avenues. The seller may value the $25 more than the shoes, because she bought them at an estate sale for $2, and they have several scratches on the right toe. So we trade, and each of us is happier. The amount by which we are both happier is called the surplus. The buyer and seller split the surplus. Let's say I would have been willing to buy the shoes for up to $50. If I buy them at $25 (never mind the darned shipping costs), and the seller would have been willing to sell them for $2.01, then I get $25 of the surplus from the trade, and the seller gets $22.99 of the surplus. A pretty good deal for both of us! (And true, I'm wearing the shoes as I write.)

But what if the seller knew I was willing to spend up to $50 for the used shoes? The shoes are only worth that much to me, no more. The seller would charge $50 for the shoes. The trade would happen, and that's efficient to an economist, but I would no longer be getting a good deal – I would be paying the very maximum that I'm willing to pay. The seller captures the entire surplus.

Fair enough, but what if the seller didn't know exactly that $50 was my cutoff? What if the seller knew instead that, one, the school year was starting soon and I didn't have any dress shoes to teach my classes, two, that there were no shoe stores offering good deals on shoes within a fifty-mile radius of where I live, and three, that the maximum I had paid in any prior shoe auction was $50. In the game of economic poker, it seems like the seller has read my hand.

This is how machine learning algorithms operate, although at a far more advanced level of complexity. Imagine that an algorithm could compute that, due to some twenty-seven different facts about your life, you were willing to pay up to a certain amount for a good or service at a given time in a given place, and given certain circumstances. Algorithms can, and they do. All the free apps that we use on our smartphones and tablets and laptops are not truly free. There is a reason the Android flashlight app wants to know your geolocation.[34] It is worth money, because a seller that knows where you drive each day can vary rates, times, and offers to yield higher returns than a seller that does not have such information. The same goes for every other fact gathered about us through our smartphones, tablets, laptops, or other smart devices. A seller that knows that most of our friends have bought Common Projects low-top sneakers

[34] *See* J. D. Biersdorfer, *Shining a Light on Nosy Apps*, N.Y. TIMES (Oct. 24, 2014), http://www.nytimes.com/2014/10/24/technology/personaltech/shining-a-light-on-nosy-apps.html (noting that "there has been at least one case in which the Federal Trade Commission found the maker of an Android flashlight app guilty of collecting personal information from users without proper notification").

(thanks to information exchange between e-commerce and social networking sites) can charge us a higher price on well-made white leather sneakers than can a seller that does not know that fact about us. And the information can be used for more than just ads: consider the practice of targeting specific voters based on the magazines they read, the cars they drive, or the websites they visit.[35]

Anna Bernasek and D. T. Mongan write in their 2015 book, *All You Can Pay*, that this question of who takes the consumer surplus is one of the most important inquires in the modern economy.[36] Their first chapter, "The Prize," demonstrates that extracting consumer surplus is the goal of much of the innovation in the smart property and big data markets. They describe how perfect price discrimination – the ability to tune a price to "all we can pay" while simultaneously providing an individualized product at a different price to each consumer by perfect product discrimination – has raised prices and made American consumers significantly poorer. Bernasek and Mongan used the story of Perrier, which successfully shipped water from France to the United States, and sold bottled sparkling water to an entire nation with enormous free water resources.[37] By clever market segmentation and market differentiation, Perrier was able to sell people a product they could get for free at the nearest tap. (While writing this chapter, I jokingly suggested to my brother that the next thing would be selling people bottled air. He pointed out that "oxygen bars" already exist. And now at least one start-up really *has* begun selling bottles filled with fresh air from the Rockies.[38])

The view that price discrimination serves the poor is not borne out in reality. For example, a *Washington Post* exposé detailed how the poor pay more for everything, from milk and bread to financial services and basic utilities.[39] The poor pay more because of the risk of nonpayment, because of the cost of operating grocery stores in impoverished areas, and pretty often, purely because

---

[35] *See generally* John Sides, *The Real Story About How Data-Driven Campaigns Target Voters*, WASH. POST (July 9, 2015), http://www.washingtonpost.com/blogs/monkey-cage/wp/2015/07/01/the-real-story-about-how-data-driven-campaigns-target-voters.

[36] *See* ANNA BERNASEK & D.T. MONGAN, ALL YOU CAN PAY 15 (Nation Books 2015) (describing "the consumer surplus" as "the ultimate prize for firms").

[37] *See id.* at 6–11.

[38] *See* Katie Hunt, *Canadian Start-Up Sells Bottled Air to China, Says Sales Booming*, CNN (Dec. 16, 2015, 8:09 PM), http://www.cnn.com/2015/12/15/asia/china-canadian-company-selling-clean-air ("A Canadian company selling air bottled in a ski resort says it's now seeing huge demand from Chinese customers.").

[39] *See* DeNeen L. Brown, *The High Cost of Poverty: Why the Poor Pay More*, WASH. POST (May 18, 2009), http://www.washingtonpost.com/wp-dyn/content/article/2009/05/17/AR2009051702053.html ("The poorer you are, the more things cost. More in money, time, hassle, exhaustion, menace.").

they have few options and constrained time frames. Cable One, for example, was exposed for using predictive analytics to determine which customers were poor (or, euphemistically, "hollow") and then providing worse or no customer service to those customers.[40]

The standard economic model assumes two things that cannot both be true at the same time. First, it assumes that a person has so little money that their purchase limit is real, that is, that Fred only offers $21 because he has no ability to offer more. Second, it assumes that this poverty does not imply any pressure to buy, or any desperation in economic circumstances that could be exploited to raise prices. So while the standard economic model indicates that knowing more about someone would be a great way to charge them less for it, in reality, knowing more about them enables sellers to charge more. This ability is only magnified by the large data sets gathered through the many channels discussed earlier – the apps and sensors and trackers that remember your shopping history, your schedule, your messages, and your daily habits.

Price discrimination can be used to exploit people at their weakest points. Equifax, one of the three big consumer credit reporting agencies, sold lists of customers who were behind on their mortgages to predatory lenders, who not only used the customer lists to market expensive financial products to financially distressed consumers, but also sold the lists onward to other companies, some of which had been under law enforcement investigation for their lending practices.[41] When you are late on your mortgage is precisely when you are the most vulnerable to a pitch for a new loan, no matter how bad its terms might be.

But we despise exploitation. Amazon learned this the hard way when it attempted to introduce differential pricing.[42] Consumers quickly learned that they could get different prices by going to different links. The backlash not only caused Amazon to stop the practice, but caused CEO Jeff Bezos to publicly apologize and promise that Amazon would not introduce differential pricing

[40] See Harold Feld, *Broadband Privacy Can Prevent Discrimination: The Case of Cable One and FICO Scores*, PUB. KNOWLEDGE (June 1, 2016), https://www.publicknowledge.org/news-blog/blogs/broadband-privacy-can-prevent-discrimination-the-case-of-cable-one-and-fico.

[41] See *FTC Settlements Require Equifax to Forfeit Money Made by Allegedly Improperly Selling Information about Millions of Consumers Who Were Late on Their Mortgages*, FTC (Oct. 10, 2012), https://www.ftc.gov/news-events/press-releases/2012/10/ftc-settlements-require-equifax-forfeit-money-made-allegedly (noting that Equifax "improperly sold lists of consumers who were late on their mortgage payments").

[42] See Anita Ramasastry, *Web Sites Change Prices Based on Customers' Habits*, CNN (June 24, 2005), http://edition.cnn.com/2005/LAW/06/24/ramasastry.website.prices/ (detailing how an Amazon customer "watched the price of a DVD offered to him for sale drop from $26.24 to $22.74" when he deleted the cookies on his browser that marked him as a regular customer).

again.[43] Coke planned in 1999 to introduce a vending machine that would raise prices in hot weather.[44] Again, the backlash was significant, and Coke abandoned the idea. Even the "happiest place on earth" is not immune to the practice–Disneyland Paris allegedly charged different prices to patrons depending on their nationality.[45]

Companies engage in price discrimination using a variety of data. For instance, researchers found that the Princeton Review charged students different prices for the same online tutoring services, depending on their zip code.[46] Those in the Northeast paid $3,240; those in eastern Pennsylvania, northern Virginia, Maryland, Delaware, and much of California, Illinois, and Wisconsin paid $3,000; and those in the rest of the United States paid $2,760.[47] In another case, Dell charged different prices for a "512 MB memory module" based on whether the customer self-identified as a large business ($289.99), individual ($275.49), government agency ($266.21), or small business ($246.49).[48]

Behavioral science validates the notion that people strongly dislike being treated unfairly, and really hate getting a worse deal than someone else. Numerous studies show that people reject unfairness and exploitation, even if they would be better off if they just accepted it.[49] In the well-known ultimatum game, one subject divides a pot of money and the other decides if they will receive the payout as divided or if both will get nothing at all. Under standard

43 *See Bezos Calls Amazon Experiment 'a Mistake,'* BizJournals (Sept. 28, 2000), http://www.bizjournals.com/seattle/stories/2000/09/25/daily21.html ("'We've never tested and we never will test prices based on customer demographics,' said Bezos.").

44 *See* Constance L. Hays, *Variable Price Coke Machine Being Tested*, N.Y. Times (Oct. 28, 1999), http://www.nytimes.com/1999/10/28/business/variable-price-coke-machine-being-tested.html.

45 *See* Michael Addady, *Disneyland Paris Probed for Charging Brits and Germans More Than the French*, Fortune (July 29, 2015), http://fortune.com/2015/07/29/disneyland-price-discrimination ("The park has been accused of charging customers more based on their country of origin. The Financial Times reports that French customers paid €1,346 ($1,486), British customers paid €1,870 ($2,065), and German customers paid €2,447 ($2,702), all for the same package.").

46 Keyon Vafa et al., *Price Discrimination in The Princeton Review's Online SAT Tutoring Service*, Tech. Sci. (Sept. 1, 2015), http://techscience.org/a/2015090102.

47 *See id.* (reporting the prices quoted by The Princeton Review using 32,989 zip codes). The curious reader may visit the website to enter their zip code to see how much they would have been charged under this price regime. *Id.*

48 *See* R. Preston McAfee, *Price Discrimination*, in 1 Issues in Competition Law and Policy 465, 465 (ABA Section of Antitrust Law 2008).

49 *See* Barbara J. King, *Feeling Down? Watching This Will Help*, NPR (Feb. 27, 2014, 12:54 PM), http://www.npr.org/sections/13.7/2014/02/27/283348422/that-s-unfair-you-say-this-monkey-can-relate (discussing the experiment).

economic models, if player A divides the pot as $0.99 for himself, and $0.01 for player B, then player B will accept the deal.[50] After all, a penny is better than nothing. But in reality, and in the lab, players reject this deal as unfair. They would rather earn nothing than be treated unfairly.

Humans are what the experimental literature calls "inequity averse." They despise coming in last, or even significantly second best. In fact, experiments show that people would rather be treated equally – and poorly – than be better off but come in second best. Recent experiments show that this tendency to demand fair treatment extends beyond humans. Startling experiments with Capuchin monkeys show that the monkeys are willing to perform a simple task – handing a rock to a researcher – if they both receive cucumbers as a reward.[51] But if one monkey receives grapes (yum!) for the same task while the other receives only cucumber slices, the underpaid monkey goes ape. Not only does the monkey demonstrate anger at the unfair treatment, she further – and this is the important part – refuses to perform the task that she had previously been willing to perform for cucumber as long as she was fairly treated.

Unfairness is not just unethical, it's inefficient. Recall that neoclassical economists don't sit up and take notice until A and B do not trade. At that point, society has lost the value of the trade. When people refuse a deal because they have been exploited, or are being offered a worse deal than their neighbor, the same thing happens. The trade does not go through. That is a deadweight loss for society. The Amazon buyers who were up in arms over being offered a worse deal than someone else show the same natural reaction as the angry Capuchin monkey. No grapes? No deal.

The bottom line is, if we negotiate with entities that can use our own devices to spy on us, we will lose. Furthermore, once we know this, we may react to the inequity by refusing to trade with the person, or the company, who is exploiting us. Our trust has been betrayed. Worse yet, if we don't stop trading, we initiate a vicious circle. Thanks to the data gathered in the first negotiation, the second negotiation may go even worse. The more that our smart property is used to subvert our economic interests, the worse the deals will become. Eventually, we might agree to buy items without any ownership rights at all.

Property as Repository of Wealth

A major role of property in its most traditional sense is that it acts as a hedge against uncertainty and as a repository of value. We buy stocks and bonds to

---

[50] *See* David Easley & Jon Kleinberg, Networks, Crowds, and Markets: Reasoning About a Highly Connected World 313 (Cambridge University Press 2010) ("Since B will accept any positive offer, A should pick the division that gives B something and otherwise maximizes A's own earnings.").

[51] *See* King, *supra* note 48.

prepare for retirement. We buy our house so that when we retire we have some place to live rent-free. We buy cars, rather than rent them, because when we own a car, we do not have to care about the rental agency's requirements, or read and honor the fine print of a lease agreement. Businesses purchase capital goods to produce more goods, to expand the business, to build the firm.

Access to information, whether that information is in the form of software, music, art, CDs, reports, books, or databases, is a kind of wealth. It is a hedge against ignorance. This wealth is not in the least metaphorical. Thomas Piketty, the French economist, notes in his award-winning book *Capital in the Twenty-First Century*, that the single greatest force for reducing wealth inequality is the distribution of knowledge and skills.[52] Books, especially textbooks, do that. One very concrete way to protect access to knowledge is to protect robust markets for the kinds of property that spread knowledge despite the restrictions of intellectual property rightsholders. Take, for example, the Supreme Court's decision in *Kirtsaeng v. John Wiley & Sons*.[53] There, a publisher of textbooks attempted to stop the resale of copies legally made and purchased abroad. (Why? Price discrimination. The books were sold abroad at a lower cost than they were sold to students in the United States.) The Supreme Court held that consumers' ownership rights trumped the publisher's intellectual property interests, which were exhausted after the first sale.[54] In cases like *Kirtsaeng*, we see the value of robust consumer ownership rights in securing low prices for knowledge and guarantees for the persistence of that knowledge. Books spread knowledge, and ownership of books helps that knowledge spread. If Piketty is right that diffusion of knowledge reduces inequality, then there is a direct argument for protecting knowledge distribution via vigorous protection of consumer ownership of books. If *Kirtsaeng* were extended to digital property, then all sorts of knowledge, in the form of e-books, textbooks and reference texts, technical manuals, and training guides, would be even cheaper and more widely distributed, strongly promoting diffusion of skill and information.

Property also protects wealth because it restrains price increases. How much can Netflix increase the price you pay to watch a movie that you already own on DVD? It represents a kind of reserve wealth for citizens. The existence of a robust secondary market for digital and smart property lowers up-front prices. Take the market for video games. Companies have been trying to limit resale of games for years. Microsoft planned to ban entirely the resale of games on the

---

[52] Thomas Piketty, Capital in the Twenty-First Century 22 (Arthur Goldhammer trans., Belknap Press 2014).

[53] 133 S. Ct. 1351 (2013).

[54] *See id.* at 1361 (finding that "one who *owns* a copy *will* receive 'first sale' protection, *provided*, of course, that the copy was '*lawfully made*' and not pirated" (citing 17 U.S.C. § 109)).

Xbox One to try to eliminate the aftermarket.[55] Gamers did not respond well, and Microsoft backed down.[56] Likewise, textbook vendors sell books with one-time use codes to limit the usefulness of the book when resold.[57] Companies don't want to compete against their own used products when trying to sell new ones. But the aftermarket is beneficial for consumers. That's why eBay works: each dollar a consumer does not have to pay is a dollar in her bank account.

Distributional effects can be ignored for a while. As long as someone captures the value of the trade, society as a whole is better off. But over time, the distributional unfairness builds, and dangerous inequity snowballs. Recall that economics argues that an efficient trade is one in which everyone who trades is made better off (even if the surplus that they divide is distributed overwhelmingly to one party) and no one is made worse off. Certain strains of modern economic thought hold such "best of all worlds" efficiency to be the only way we as a society can be certain that a trade should go through.[58]

In fact, in this line of economic thought, one perfectly efficient state of affairs would be if one person or company owned everything. Since there could be no more trades that would make everyone better off, we'd have traded ourselves into an optimal world. This would be perfectly efficient; it would also be a miserable way to live. As Piketty has noted, accumulated wealth leads to the accumulation of more wealth.[59] Permitting companies to take wealth and property from consumers merely means that consumers have less to trade in further rounds. Eventually, this creates precisely the kind of online serfdom we are being sold today as licenses, subscriptions, or limited-time offers. A limited view of economic efficiency creates many good ideas for maximizing short-term wealth, but it is not good for society in the long term. Permitting one party to capture the entire consumer surplus is not a positive feature of the free market but a corrosive force that will cause the very market freedom

---

55   *See* Nigram Arora, *Microsoft Gives in to Gamers on Xbox One Used Games, Connection Requirement*, FORBES (June 19, 2013, 6:07 PM), http://www.forbes.com/sites/nigamarora/2013/06/19/microsoft-gives-in-to-gamers-on-xbox-one-used-games-connection-requirement/# 7c37025c318f (discussing when Microsoft "restricted the reselling of used games").

56   *See id.* ("In a big win for gamers, Microsoft has just announced that it is reversing the unpopular policies.").

57   *See, e.g., General Questions About eTextbooks*, RUTGERS, http://rutgers.bncollege.com/eBooks/ EBooksFAQ.html (last visited July 11, 2016) ("[A]ccess codes are good for one-time use only. Once an access code has been redeemed, it cannot be used again.").

58   *See* THOMAS J. MICELI, THE ECONOMIC APPROACH TO LAW 4 (Stanford University Press 2004) (describing "Pareto efficiency" as the "basic definition of efficiency in economics").

59   *See* PIKETTY, *supra* note 51, at 9 (discussing "the 'principle of infinite accumulation,' that is, the inexorable tendency for capital to accumulate and become concentrated in ever fewer hands, with no natural limit to the process").

that brought consumers great value in the twentieth century to atrophy in the twenty-first.

We are dependent on our property for our livelihood. Consider the farmer who is not permitted to repair his tractor under intellectual property laws. His crops wither away. He cannot earn a living if the intellectual property licensor decides to charge exorbitant fees for a mechanic to access the tractor's diagnostic software. Consider the Uber driver who derives her supplemental income from her ownership of her personal car, or the AirBnB host who derives income from her ownership (or rental, if the terms of the rental agreement permit hosting – but that's a property right, too) of her apartment or home. Consider the programmer who relies on his computer as a tool of the trade, or the lawyer who no longer has law books and relies on database services to provide her with access to case law. Imagine a construction company that is reliant on the GPS-enabled and software-controlled heavy equipment provided by Caterpillar. Imagine the owner of a plant who must shell out large sums of money to upgrade the software on his machinery, which is currently working just fine. Imagine the television repair shop around the corner that cannot repair a $300 television with a $12 part because the manufacturer has locked up information about how to repair the television, and threatens to sue technicians who do find out how to fix the TV under various copyright claims.

There are many more examples, from the doctor who is dependent on his medical equipment to practice his profession to the semitruck independent owner-operator whose entire business is her truck. Each relies on the rules of property – that they control what they own, may repair it, change it, upgrade it, or sell it if need be – to earn a living. To these, the extraction of consumer surplus isn't a mere matter of getting a better or a worse deal in an online purchase, but a matter of livelihood or unemployment, of continued economic independence.

A Market of One

There may be a strong intuition that competitive markets can resolve much of the difficulties of extraction of consumer surplus discussed thus far. That is without a doubt true. It is very difficult to extract the entire surplus if a competitor is willing to forego part of the surplus in order to get a worse but still profitable deal.

Yet the entire idea of markets and competition depends on substitutable products. A standardized product available at a standardized price is a critical component of a mass market. The idea that the consumer can in fact get a better deal somewhere else depends on a reasonably similar deal being available from another source. If only the same deal is available from every source, or a reasonably similar deal is not available from another source, the intuition that markets are all the protection we need might not hold. Recall, too, that breaking up mass markets into perfectly differentiated markets is the goal of perfect price and product differentiation. Instead of one price for a whole market (everyone buys an iPod at $100.00), you get a special price just for you (your iPod costs $199.95 because data show you can and will pay that much). Data disrupt the mass markets on which we depend. In the words of Bernasek and Mongan, the price is all we can pay.

Consider a very simple example. You are late for a meeting. (How would a seller know? Your calendar and your current GPS location as well as current traffic data.) Your car is low on gas. (How would a seller know? If you have a smart car, it can report the data. If you just have a cell phone and a credit card, an algorithm can track your miles traveled and tie that to the last time you bought gas.) The question, then, is how much a seller might charge for gas, knowing that you are late, desperate, and that its gas station is the only one in range. Having shrunk the mass market for gas to the specific conditions that currently drive your decision to buy, the seller can avoid competition in a mass market. You are a market of one.

5

Private Property

"We guard with particular zeal an individual's right to carry on private activity within the interior of a home or office, free from unreasonable government intrusion. We also recognize a high privacy interest in the 'curtilage' of a residence – that zone immediately surrounding the home where its private interior life can be expected to extend."

– People v. Cook, 41 Cal. 3d 373, 379 (1985)

In the previous chapter, I explored some basic reasons why property is important to our freedom, sense of self, and wealth. I turn now to one particularly important reason to take consumers' rights in their digital and smart property seriously: property rights can bolster privacy.

This chapter examines the constantly shifting relationship between property and privacy. It suggests that property can be used as a bulwark, a shield, a floor, and a foundation for privacy. Property law's characteristics of clarity, robustness, and default exclusion help to fortify privacy rights that are fuzzy and fragile, rights that too often operate only when the consumer has taken costly steps to protect her interests. Property law serves to shore up privacy's weakest points.

At this point, you may be wondering what I mean by privacy. I am not sure that a precise definition would help much, since we would always leave something out – and quite a lot of ink has already been spilled on the question. For purposes of this book, though, I mean the set of viable options people have for protecting their own privacy, however they define it, and however they are willing to employ their property to defend it. Privacy, for me, is not a word with a definition, it is an act with consequences. Once, when pressed on this point at a presentation, I joked: "Some dismiss privacy, saying they have nothing to hide. I don't accept that argument from anyone wearing clothes." In other words, what people do matters more than an abstract definition. And that is the point of this chapter. If our property rights define what we can do, and if privacy rights can be usefully defined by what we actually do, then property and privacy are necessarily and inextricably intertwined.

The options that property rights provide can be used to protect and bolster privacy. Privacy interests are often hazy. Property provides some bright-line rules. Privacy relies on expectations and hard-to-evaluate mental states. Property is to some degree objectively discernible. Courts are skeptical of privacy harms. Courts are not at all skeptical of real property harms, which are often very easy to prove on a simple theory of trespass. Privacy remedies may come through courts or regulators. By contrast, many of the solutions available to us to actively protect our own privacy are actually property solutions. We plant hedges. We draw the drapes. We lock the doors.

I propose a partnership between property and privacy. In a series of recent cases, the Supreme Court has stated something new: property serves as an "irreducible constitutional minimum,"[1] in Justice Sotomayor's words, a bright line below which privacy protections cannot fall. This cuts against a broad trend in which scholars think that property and privacy are at odds, and ought not be so closely connected.[2] As Charles Reich has written: "Today it is widely thought that property and liberty are separable things; that there may, in fact, be conflicts between 'property rights' and 'personal rights.'"[3] Currently, scholars celebrate legal systems that have "largely decoupled the protection of privacy from property interests and the law of trespass."[4]

Those scholars make good points, although I find them ultimately unconvincing. They are correct that there is reason for caution in re-coupling privacy and property.[5] A poorly thought-out focus on property might strengthen already overreaching intellectual property laws and intensify the very surveillance this chapter discusses, or might empower companies that hold key physical infrastructure to hold up or restrict traffic unless they are paid off.[6] Property rights

---

[1] United States v. Jones, 132 S. Ct. 945, 955 (2012) (Sotomayor, J., concurring).
[2] *See, e.g.*, Larry Lessig, *Privacy as Property*, 69 Soc. Res. 247, 258 (2002) ("Privacy and property talk is resisted, however, by many in the privacy community."); *see also* Sonia M. Suter, *Disentangling Privacy from Property: Toward a Deeper Understanding of Genetic Privacy*, 72 Geo. Wash. L. Rev. 737, 764–70 (2004) (arguing that it would be a mistake to conflate property and privacy because they are "fundamentally different concepts").
[3] Charles A. Reich, *The New Property*, 73 Yale L.J. 733, 772 (1964).
[4] Ronald Krotoszynski, Privacy Revisted 40 (Cambridge 2016); *see also id.* at 61.
[5] *Id.* at 4.
[6] For a full debate on cyberproperty, see Richard A. Epstein, *Cybertrespass*, 70 U. Chi. L. Rev. 73, 88 (2003); Patricia L. Bellia, *Defending Cyberproperty*, 79 N.Y.U. L. Rev. 2164–78 (2004); Michael A. Carrier & Greg Lastowka, *Against Cyberproperty*, 22 Berkeley Tech. L.J. 1485 (2007); Greg Lastowka, *Decoding Cyberproperty*, 40 Ind. L. Rev. 23, 23–43 (2007); Mark A. Lemley & Philip J. Weiser, *Should Property or Liability Rules Govern Information?*, 85 Tex. L. Rev. 783 (2007); Mark A. Lemley, *Terms of Use*, 91 Minn. L. Rev. 459, 470 (2006); Mark

in personal information would just package that data for sale on the market.[7] Worse, if the property–privacy connection were to become so strong that privacy could only be protected by property, those without property would be devoid of privacy.

Because of these concerns, I do *not* propose to make all data about us into our property.[8] If a key piece of information is that I am a criminal, I would obviously want to keep that fact out of other people's hands; but since that information is a part of the public record, I should not be able to do so. What I *do* propose in this chapter is much more modest. I argue that we should reinforce our control over things that most of us would consider our property – our phones, our tablets, our houses, our cars, and even fully electronic things like our bank accounts, stock portfolios, Bitcoins, and so on. Through the old connection between property and privacy, this increase in control can have some simple, solid, positive effects. The Internet of Things, by definition, involves the seeding of computing mechanisms and sensors throughout our devices and physical context.[9] It relies on gathering information about us through sensors embedded in things and walls. We used to own that environment and the things in it. But we do not stand to inherit control of these devices and sensors, and thereby we stand to lose control of our environment. Control over our environment is control over the sensors. If we can assert control over our environment by asserting ownership over things in that environment, we can seize control of the sensors, the eyes and ears of the Internet of Things.

If we think that privacy and property should be divorced as legal concepts – and this is the current trend – then we lose the power of property to provide tools and analogies to judges, journalists, and policymakers, and even to use in public discourse. As Larry Lessig has noted: "[p]roperty talk would give privacy rhetoric added support within American culture."[10] This puts the rhetorical power of property at the disposal of those who wish to use it as they always have: to secure their privacy by leveraging "[t]he different social resources available within our culture to claims that are grounded in property."[11]

A. Lemley, *Place and Cyberspace*, 91 CALIF. L. REV. 521, 521 (2003); Maureen A. O'Rourke, *Property Rights and Competition on the Internet: In Search of an Appropriate Analogy*, 16 BERKELEY TECH. L.J. 561, 586–87 (2001); Dan Hunter, *Cyberspace as Place and the Tragedy of the Digital Anticommons*, 91 CALIF. L. REV. 439, 445 (2003); Sonia K. Katyal, *The New Surveillance*, 54 CASE W. RES. L. REV. 297 (2003).

[7] *See* Pam Samuelson, *Privacy as Intellectual Property?*, 52 STAN. L. REV. 1125, 1137–38 (1999) (noting that propertization of personal data will not help because of the principle of alienation).

[8] Cf. Paul Schwartz, *Property, Privacy, and Personal Data*, 117 HARV. L. REV. 2055 (2004).

[9] Recall our discussion of the Internet of Things in Chapter 3.

[10] Larry Lessig, *Privacy as Property*, 69 SOC. RES. 247, 255 (2002).   [11] *Id.* at 254.

The fight for privacy in the modern era is a fight using symbolism and reasoning by analogy – which is, not coincidentally, how the common law works. Stories are key to our understanding about property. As property scholar Carol Rose has emphasized, narratives help us to build a consensus community around what property means.[12] We have to do this because technology has made our world unrecognizable. To make it recognizable again we have to tell familiar stories.

One familiar story about privacy is the story of property. As mentioned, if I want privacy, I grow a hedge along the side of the road that leads up to my house. I might build a fence and a gate. I shut my door. I might even lock it. I pull the curtains. Property is of course a story of economics, wealth, and independence. But it is also the story of putting distance and objects between ourselves and those who want to peer in through the windows.[13]

Property and privacy have a strange and symbiotic relationship. As I noted earlier, Mark Zuckerberg has joined the chorus of Silicon Valley giants declaring that privacy is dead.[14] Yet the Facebook cofounder purchased his Palo Alto property through a shell company in order to protect his identity.[15] Zuckerberg later purchased the four houses adjoining his Palo Alto property to protect his privacy.[16] A developer had planned to build a palatial estate next to Zuckerberg's house and market it as a chance to live next to him.[17] Zuckerberg protected himself with his wallet, spending some thirty million dollars purchasing adjacent real estate.[18] He spent millions more tearing down and rebuilding the surrounding houses. That's a lot of money for supposedly dead privacy.

[12] See Carol M. Rose, *Introduction: Approaching Property, in* Property & Persuasion: Essays on the History, Theory, and Rhetoric of Ownership 6 (Westview Press 1994); Carol M. Rose, *Property as Storytelling: Perspectives from Game Theory, Narrative Theory, Feminist Theory, in* Property & Persuasion: Essays on the History, Theory, and Rhetoric of Ownership 26 (Westview Press 1994).
[13] For an exploration of the relationship between property and personhood, see generally Margaret Jane Radin, *Property and Personhood*, 34 Stan. L. Rev. 957 (1982) ("The premise underlying the personhood perspective is that to achieve proper self-development – to be a person – an individual needs some control over resources in the external environment.").
[14] See Bobbie Johnson, *Privacy No Longer a Social Norm, Says Facebook Founder*, Guardian (Jan. 10, 2010), http://www.theguardian.com/technology/2010/jan/11/facebook-privacy.
[15] See Mark Berniker, *Zuckerberg Snatches Up Palo Alto Homes in Privacy Bid*, CNBC (Oct. 11, 2013), http://www.cnbc.com/2013/10/11/zuckerburg-snatches-up-pao-alto-homes-in-privacy-bid.html ("Zuckerberg used the tactic of forming a shell corporation to hide his identity when he purchased his main house, the $7 million house on 1456 Edgewood Drive in 2011.").
[16] See Laura Vecsey, *Facebook's Zuckerberg Buys Up Four Properties Near His Home*, Forbes (Oct. 11, 2013), http://www.forbes.com/sites/zillow/2013/10/11/facebooks-zuckerberg-buys-up-four-properties-near-his-home ("According to property records, Zuckerberg purchased three homes behind him, and the one next door.").
[17] *Id.*   [18] *Id.*

Property has for hundreds of years symbolized the ability to defend against unwanted intrusion. Without law to enforce our right to keep people off our property, that right means nothing. Our commitments to property help us come to the correct rule. A property owner has the right to set the automatic and default rule, "Do not trespass," and to enforce the law against trespassers and Peeping Toms. This is what property means in the privacy context – exclusion of intruders by default, enforceable by clear and strong rules of law. If you wish to come onto my property to hunt or fish, you must obtain my permission. Imagine if that were the rule for companies collecting your personal information from your smartphone, or controlling your house or car through a smart grid or insurance chip in the engine. It would be a useful boost to consumers' claims that they ought to be able to exclude surveilling companies from their devices.

HOW PROPERTY HELPS STOP GOVERNMENT SNOOPING

In the words of Charles Reich, "Civil liberties must have a basis in property, or bills of rights will not preserve them."[19] Privacy is a particularly strong example of a civil liberty that is tightly tied to property: the two are wound together throughout our history and law. Courts have most extensively discussed the relationship between property and privacy in the context of the Constitution's Fourth Amendment, which deals with government searches and seizures of citizens' property: their "houses, papers, and effects." There are two broad streams in Fourth Amendment case law: an older conception focused on property, and a more recent one focusing on personal privacy.[20] In early cases, privacy was property.[21] The law of trespass allowed landowners to exclude others from their land. As a practical matter, the principle protected wealthy landowners, but English law made a point of extending the principle to protect property of all kinds. As William Pitt the Elder famously stated: "The poorest man may in his cottage bid defiance to all the forces of the Crown. It may be frail – its roof may shake – the wind may blow through it – the storm may enter – the rain may enter – but the King of England cannot enter – all his

[19] Reich, *supra* note 3, at 771.
[20] *See* MARGARET JANE RADIN, REINTERPRETING PROPERTY 61 (University of Chicago Press 2009) ("Dissatisfied with what it considered the anomalous results of a musty old doctrine, the Court in Warden v. Hayden and Katz v. United States decided that privacy, not property, is the philosophical bedrock of the fourth amendment.").
[21] *See, e.g.*, Klug v. Sheriffs, 129 Wis. 468, 472, 109 N.W. 656, 657 (1906) (noting "upon examination of the cases cited as sustaining the so-called right of privacy, that many of them turn upon property rights or breach of trust, contract, or confidence").

force dares not cross the threshold of the ruined tenement!"[22] This tradition was imported into U.S. constitutional law when the Supreme Court was asked under what circumstances government may enter and search the home.

Trespass on Property and the Fourth Amendment

The home is many people's greatest property asset and most private place. For this reason, the principle of the sacrosanct home governed the first intrusive covert surveillance cases. In the 1928 case of *Olmstead v. United States*,[23] the U.S. Supreme Court asked whether the government had improperly intruded on a suspect's property in placing wiretapping devices in the basement of his building (where he maintained an office) and in the streets near his home. The *Olmstead* Court determined that property was the bedrock of the Fourth Amendment: "The well-known historical purpose of the Fourth Amendment, directed against warrants and writs of assistance, was to prevent the use of governmental force to search a man's house, his person, his papers and his effects...."[24] However, because the tapped wires themselves were not on Olmstead's property, the court took an unduly restrictive view of privacy:

> The amendment itself shows that the search is to be of material things – the person, the house, his papers, or his effects.... The language of the amendment cannot be extended and expanded to include telephone wires, reaching to the whole world from the defendant's house or office. The intervening wires are not part of his house or office, any more than are the highways along which they are stretched.[25]

In other words, once the communications of a person exited her property, they were subject to search without constitutional protection.

It was clear from the outset that a property-based rule, by itself, was not enough. Justice Brandeis (who not coincidentally coauthored the article founding the modern right to privacy) predicted in his stinging dissent to *Olmstead*:

> The progress of science in furnishing the Government with means of espionage is not likely to stop with wire-tapping. Ways may someday be developed by which the Government, without removing papers from secret drawers, can reproduce them in court, and by which it will be enabled to expose to a jury the most intimate occurrences of the home.[26]

---

[22] William Pitt, Speech on the Excise Bill, House of Commons (Mar. 1763), *in* 1 HENRY LORD BROUGHAM, HISTORICAL SKETCHES OF STATESMEN WHO FLOURISHED IN THE TIME OF GEORGE III 41–42 (Paris, A. & W. Galignani & Co. 1839).
[23] 277 U.S. 438 (1929). [24] *Id.* at 463. [25] *Id.* at 464–65. [26] *Id.* at 474.

And history has proved Brandeis right. In 2013, NSA whistleblower Edward Snowden revealed widespread warrantless government tracking of and intrusion into citizens' electronic communications. Citizens' smart property is a particular target for government surveillance. In March 2017, WikiLeaks revealed that "[t]elevisions, smartphones and even anti-virus software are all vulnerable to CIA hacking.... The capabilities described include recording the sounds, images and the private text messages of users, even when they resort to encrypted apps to communicate."[27] One such CIA hacking tool is called "Weeping Angel," which "places the target TV in a 'Fake-Off' mode, so that the owner falsely believes the TV is off when it is on. In 'Fake-Off' mode the TV operates as a bug, recording conversations in the room and sending them over the Internet to a covert CIA server."[28] It is thus abundantly clear that property protection alone is not remotely enough to secure privacy; government must also respect citizens' reasonable expectations of privacy. The question remains, though: does property protection help? This is a central question, and one to which we will return as we trace the path of privacy-related cases throughout U.S. law.

While Olmstead dealt with the home – real property – other cases dealt with "papers and effects" – personal property. *Boyd v. United States* is a particularly strongly worded example. The Supreme Court in 1886 greatly opposed the government rummaging untrammeled through citizens' papers. "The great end for which men entered into society was to secure their property," Justice Bradley trumpeted.[29] "Papers are the owner's goods and chattels; they are his dearest property."[30] Seizing a defendant's papers was deemed a particularly virulent overreach, equal to forcing a person to testify against himself. "It is not the breaking of his doors, and the rummaging of his drawers, that constitutes the essence of the offense," the Court wrote, "but it is the invasion of his indefeasible right of personal security, personal liberty, and private property."[31]

Boyd is not modern law, in the sense that it is entirely proper for investigators these days to seize our papers and use them to convict us of crimes. But there is something to *Boyd's* particular concern for seizing our recordings of our own thoughts willy-nilly. As we will see, Justice Roberts echoed this concern 128 years later in *California v. Riley*, holding that a smartphone contains too many of our thoughts to simply be rifled through during an arrest. *Boyd's*

---

[27] Craig Timberg, Elizabeth Dwoskin & Ellen Nakashima, *WikiLeaks: The CIA Is Using Popular TVs, Smartphones and Cars to Spy on Their Owners*, WASH. POST (Mar. 7, 2017), https://www.washingtonpost.com/news/the-switch/wp/2017/03/07/why-the-cia-is-using-your-tvs-smartphones-and-cars-for-spying. *Id.*

[28] *Id.*   [29] Boyd v. United States, 116 U.S. 616, 627 (1886) (citations and quotations omitted).

[30] Id. at 627–28.   [31] *Id.* at 630.

principles – the importance of personal property to personal privacy, the abhorrence of earlier generations to the unrestricted right to rummage through personal property, and the particular importance of "papers and effects" that hold our personal thoughts – seems to have fired the imagination of the court well over a century later.

Another case, *Ex Parte Jackson*, protected papers – in this case, letters – from government search even when the letters were handed off to a federal agency, the U.S. Postal Service.[32] The *Jackson* court wrote:

> Letters and sealed packages . . . are as fully guarded from examination and inspection . . . as if they were retained by the parties forwarding them in their own domiciles. The constitutional guaranty of the right of the people to be secure in their papers against unreasonable searches and seizures extends to their papers, thus closed against inspection, wherever they may be.[33]

Jackson shows that our papers and the communications they contain, even when out of our personal control, out of our sight, or even directly in government hands, still benefit from constitutional protection. Putting those papers and communications in digital form should not matter at all.

Reasonable Expectations of Privacy

In *Katz v. United States*,[34] the Supreme Court decided that protecting property was not, alone, enough to fully vindicate Fourth Amendment values. Charlie Katz was convicted for making interstate gambling phone calls from a telephone booth in Los Angeles in violation of a federal anti-gambling law. The FBI tapped the calls without a warrant. The court determined that wiretapping personal and private communications, wherever the tap was physically placed, triggered Fourth Amendment protections. Overruling *Olmstead*, the Court decided that the Fourth Amendment protected "people, not places."[35] In so doing, the *Katz* court held that property could not be the sole metric for determining privacy from government intrusion, noting that "[t]he premise that property interests control the right of the Government to search and seize has been discredited."[36] Justice Harlan, in an influential concurring opinion, went further, arguing that the critical question was whether a person had a

---

[32] *Ex Parte* Jackson, 96 U.S. 727 (1877).   [33] *Id.* at 733.
[34] Katz v. United States, 389 U.S. 347, 351 (1967) (stating also that "what he seeks to preserve as private, even in an area accessible to the public, may be constitutionally protected [by his right to privacy].").
[35] *Katz*, 389 U.S. at 351 (citations and quotations omitted).
[36] *Id.* at 353 (citations and quotations omitted).

"reasonable expectation of privacy," regardless of whether the search occurred in a place or over a device that she owned. That "reasonable expectation of privacy" test was adopted by later courts as the gold standard for determining when law enforcement would need to seek a warrant.[37]

Katz is clearly right if one reads it to understand that the Fourth Amendment does not exclusively protect property. But the question remains: can property serve as a useful guide and as a protective floor below which privacy interests may not be allowed to fall? As cases unfolded after *Katz*, it became clear that the "reasonable expectations" test had gaps. What if government could convince citizens they had no reasonable expectation of privacy? *Katz'*s protection would fail.

Moreover, although property was not always necessary to show an expectation of privacy under *Katz*, property's features provided an important signal about expectations of privacy. This was the case even in *Katz* itself. The Court stressed that Charlie Katz paid the toll to use the telephone booth for a short while and closed the doors of the booth to exclude prying ears. Katz expressed his expectation of privacy by manipulating the objects around him. Use and control of property mattered because of the signals it sent.

Finally, while the *Katz* rule was better than *Olmstead'*s trespass rule as a matter of theory, it was not easily practicable. We all keep off other people's land and away from their personal property every day. But deciding whether someone expects their conversation to be private on the basis of that person's body language and context is another matter entirely. This matters particularly in the context of police searches, because police must often make a quick decision about searching or surveilling without a warrant.

For these three reasons, the Supreme Court began to add property back into Fourth Amendment cases, this time as (1) a backstop against erosion of expectations of privacy; (2) a rich source of signals about expectations; and (3) a clearer rule instructing law enforcement to obtain a warrant in a range of easy cases.

Adding Property Back: Kyllo *and* Jardines

As noted, *Katz* was widely read to hold that persons, not property, were protected by the Fourth Amendment. But the Supreme Court has discernibly, if not always consistently, added property back into the equation. In this new formulation, trespass to property does not replace the *Katz* test, but serves as a bright-line foundation on which *Katz* can rest. The Supreme Court has used

---

[37] *See* Smith v. Maryland, 442 U.S. 735 (1979).

traditional property conceptions to defend both the home, called "first among equals" for purposes of the Fourth Amendment,[38] and personal property, like cars and cell phones.

In *Kyllo v. United States*,[39] defendant Danny Kyllo used indoor garden grow lights to grow marijuana. The U.S. Department of the Interior, without a warrant, aimed a thermal imager at his house from the street, and observed that the roof and walls of his garage were emitting an unusually higher amount of heat compared with other parts of his house. From this, law enforcement inferred that he was growing marijuana, and based primarily on their thermal scan, a magistrate issued a warrant for Kyllo's arrest. The question in the case was whether a thermal imaging camera aimed at a house was a "search" of the house under the Fourth Amendment and, if so, whether that search could be conducted without a warrant. The Court said yes, it was a search, and no, authorities could not use heat-sensing technology to reach through the walls of the home.

Justice Scalia authored the court's opinion, and addressed the basic problem with the *Katz* privacy expectation test: expectations erode, especially as new privacy-invasive technology is developed. Consider that under the *Katz* test, all a government needs to do to eliminate citizen expectations of privacy is make a single prime-time broadcast (or, these days, a Facebook advertising campaign) announcing that citizens' homes are subject to search at any time for any reason. Or, perhaps closer to real life, a government could simply deploy incrementally more intrusive surveillance techniques and thereby gradually erode citizen privacy expectations. To curb privacy erosion, Justice Scalia turned to property law. Property interests, he wrote, could help draw a "firm but also bright" line around privacy in the home, removing the need to ask whether a specific conversation or interaction involved reasonable expectations of privacy.[40] The *Kyllo* use of property as a shield for privacy helped stem the erosion of privacy expectations in the home. Fierce, clear protection of the home both creates a clean, justiciable backstop for private interactions and, moreover, lays a normative foundation on which privacy interests can be built. By saying something should be as private as it would be in the home, privacy seekers can rely on the powerful emotions home invokes.

In the more recent *Florida v. Jardines*, the police used a different sense (smell) and a different detector (a trained dog rather than a thermal imaging camera).[41] Police walked a drug-sniffing dog up to Joelis Jardines' front door without a warrant. When the dog went on alert, the police got a warrant and

[38] *See* Florida v. Jardines, 569 U.S. __, 133 S. Ct. 1409, 1414 (2013).   [39] 533 U.S. 27 (2001).
[40] *Id.* at 40.   [41] *See Jardines*, 133 S. Ct. at 1413 (discussing the background of the case).

found marijuana plants in the home. Although Jardines had no expectation of privacy, since police, delivery people, and canvassers can generally come up to the front door of a house to knock, the court found the dog sniff to be an unconstitutional search. The Court held that the police, without a warrant, had entered and searched the area immediately surrounding the home (which, since the days of outhouses, has been protected nearly as strongly as the home itself), and that constituted a Fourth Amendment search. Justice Scalia wrote in the majority: "By reason of our decision in *Katz*, property rights are not the sole measure of Fourth Amendment violations – but although *Katz* may add to the baseline, it does not subtract anything from the Amendment's protections."[42] In short: the Fourth Amendment protects *at least* our persons, houses, papers, and effects. It may also protect privacy interests above and beyond those, but it protects at least that much. Or, as Justice Kagan wrote in concurrence: "Was this activity a trespass? Yes, as the Court holds today. Was it also an invasion of privacy? Yes, that as well."[43]

Is there reason to pick between these approaches? Is protecting privacy by adding property protections better than would be the case if we protected expectations of privacy alone? Perhaps. We have an established point of comparison. Before *Jardines*, the Supreme Court decided a similar dog-sniff case in *Illinois v. Caballes*, in which it approved suspicionless use of a drug-sniffing dog at a routine traffic stop.[44] Without the backstop provided by the strong emotions evoked by house and home, *Jardines* could have gone the same way.

The *Kyllo* and *Jardines* dissents believed that gathering heat data or scent data from a house neither intruded on the home nor upset expectations of privacy. That feels shortsighted in light of current technology. MIT, for example, has developed technology that lets Wi-Fi systems track people through walls by bouncing signals off human bodies.[45] The Xbox One, the Amazon Echo, Siri, or any phone with Android Lollipop on it can hear (and often see) what goes on in a living room or bedroom. As to the casual dismissal of smells listed in *Jardines*, chemical sniffers constantly improve in accuracy and portability. In future cases, police may simply be able to detect what occurs in a house by means of a car-mounted sniffer that scans every home. Would the dissenting judges not consider this to be invasive? Their *Jardines* dissent made much of the implied license everyone has to walk up to someone's front door and knock (and, apparently, sniff). Would that logic stand up to sense-enhanced

---

[42] *Id.* at 1414.   [43] *Id.* at 1418.   [44] Illinois v. Caballes, 543 U.S. 405, 409–10 (2005).
[45] *See, e.g.*, BBC News, *How Wi-fi Can Identify and Track People Through Walls*, BBC (Nov. 4, 2015), http://www.bbc.com/news/technology-34581694.

body cameras? To drones coming up the driveway once a day and snuffling around the front door?

Here's a personal story. A childhood friend of mine was convicted of marijuana possession a few years ago. His story is the same as Kyllo's, but with a technology upgrade. The police raided his house not because of a thermal imager that reached into his home, but because of the amount of electricity he was pulling off the grid. They, like the police in Kyllo, thought he was growing marijuana. He wasn't. He was building Bitcoin mining rigs – computers that crunch a lot of numbers very fast in order to secure the Bitcoin blockchain (more about that in Chapter 7). Perfectly legal. Although he did possess a small amount of marijuana, the electrical consumption upon which the police based their search came from entirely legitimate activities – not exactly probable cause.

I wonder what the dissenters in *Kyllo* and *Jardines* would make of smart grids and smart homes. Their view was that technology that relied solely on data gathered from the surface of the home ("off the wall" they called it, as opposed to "through the wall") or, in *Jardines*, technology that could detect invisible particles carrying scent from inside the home to outside, was fine. There was no technical invasion of the interior of the home. But this fails to understand what is happening. Heat from inside the home is data. Scent particles from inside the home are data. Electricity flowing to the home is data. Sounds bouncing off the inside of the windows when I cheer on my favorite team – that's just data. Homes are leaky data boxes. With the right technology, nobody needs to go within a hundred miles of the home in order to know just about everything that happens inside. The smart home, which can do all sorts of wonderful things, like automatically dim the lights or adjust the heat in unoccupied rooms, respond to voice commands, and determine on an hourly basis the water needs of the home, also collects that intimate information and passes it off to the grid.

Smart Property and the Fourth Amendment: Jones *and* Riley

The Supreme Court brought these Fourth Amendment questions to the Internet of Things through two cases, *United States v. Jones*, concerning car geo-tracking, and *Riley v. California*, concerning police searches of smartphones. In *Jones*,[46] police had a warrant to put a GPS tracker on Antoine Jones's car, but they didn't install the tracker until after the warrant had expired. The GPS tracking data tied Jones to a house used to store drugs. At trial, Jones argued

---

[46] 565 U.S. __,132 S. Ct. 945 (2012).

that since the GPS unit was put on his car without a warrant, the evidence gathered by it could not be used against him.

The Supreme Court unanimously agreed that the search was unconstitutional, although once again with some disagreement between the justices as to why. The majority's problem was that the police intruded on Jones's personal property without a warrant.[47] Whatever Jones' expectations of privacy on public streets, the Constitution protects "papers and effects." A car is an "effect," and the government had intruded on that effect to gather information.

Four concurring justices (justices who agreed with the majority decision, but for different reasons), led by Justice Alito, were worried about the broader implications of long-term geotracking surveillance on privacy, including cases where property interests are not implicated at all. We are tracked by cameras everywhere we drive. Many police cars have cameras mounted on them. Those cameras, combined with license plate readers and traffic cameras along interstates and intersections, provide a pretty comprehensive database of who drives where.[48] Even though a police officer doesn't need a warrant to lawfully observe if and when someone drives past on a public road, the concurring justices felt it was another thing altogether to bug someone and follow every move he made for an extended time.[49]

Of particular importance in *Jones* is Justice Sotomayor's separate concurrence, in which she reconciled the privacy and property approaches. Justice Sotomayor agreed with the Alito-led concurrence that people's personal expectations of privacy must be protected under *Katz*. She wrote: "Of course, the Fourth Amendment is not concerned only with trespassory intrusions on property. Rather, even in the absence of a trespass, a Fourth Amendment search occurs when the government violates a subjective expectation of privacy that society recognizes as reasonable."[50] However, she also agreed with the majority – indeed, hers was the deciding vote for the majority – that property still plays a critical role in securing the rights of citizens against the state. She wrote: "I join the Court's opinion because I agree that a search within the meaning of the Fourth Amendment occurs, at a minimum, where, as here, the Government obtains information by physically intruding on a constitutionally protected area."[51] Thus, Justice Sotomayor joined the majority because the

[47] *Id.* at 951–52.

[48] *See* ACLU, You are Being Tracked: How License Plate Readers are Being Used to Record Americans' Movements 2 (2013), *available at* https://www.aclu.org/files/assets/071613-aclu-alprreport-opt-v05.pdf.

[49] *Jones*, 132 S. Ct. at 961–62.   [50] *Id.* at 954–55 (citations and quotations omitted).

[51] *Id.* at 954 (citations and quotations omitted).

Katz "reasonable expectation of privacy" test is subject to expectation erosion.[52] As privacy law icon Dan Solove has written, the "expectation" approach "is not merely in need of repair – it is doomed."[53] Justice Sotomayor echoed these concerns in her concurrence, writing that relying solely on the personal privacy approach would "erode[] that longstanding protection for privacy expectations inherent in items of property that people possess or control."[54]

Justice Sotomayor was very worried about the impact of big data analysis on personal privacy, which does not require any trespass on property. So why did she join the majority opinion, which focused on property, rather than the concurrence, which focused on reasonable expectations of privacy? She explained: "The trespassory test applied in the majority's opinion reflects an irreducible constitutional minimum. When the Government physically invades personal property to gather information, a search occurs. The reaffirmation of that principle suffices to decide this case."[55] She voted with the property side not to undermine privacy, but to provide a clear, bright-line rule that would set a floor below which privacy expectations cannot be allowed to fall.

In 2014, *Riley v. California*[56] extended Fourth Amendment protection to smartphones. In *Riley*, police searched an arrested suspect's smartphone without a warrant. The Supreme Court unanimously ruled that the search was unconstitutional. If police wish to search a smartphone, even at the time of arrest (where police have particularly strong powers to search a suspect for weapons and contraband), they must get a warrant.

Riley is a solid example of the power of property intuitions to limit government overreach and prevent erosion of privacy expectations. During an arrest, expectations of privacy are at their lowest. A person in custody can pretty much expect to be thoroughly searched and constantly watched. The *Katz* standard is not much help to an arrestee. So Justice Roberts, who wrote the *Riley* opinion, could not really rely on expectations of privacy (beyond stating that they weren't gone entirely, just "diminished").[57] Rather, he turned to two property analogies. First, Roberts noted that smartphones should be protected because they were like a house – an analogy repeated again and again in the decision.[58] Smartphones contain our entire lives, he wrote, including access to our communications, documents, contacts, and a record of our real-world movements. Roberts cited the famous judge Learned Hand, who wrote: "[I]t

[52] *See* Daniel J. Solove, *Fourth Amendment Pragmatism*, 51 B.C. L. Rev. 1511, 1523–24 (2012) (observing that "it is very difficult to measure society's expectations of privacy accurately" and that "[e]ven if a metric could be devised . . . the reasonable expectation of privacy test would still be flawed for several reasons").

[53] *Id.* 1521.   [54] *Jones*, 132 S. Ct. at 955.   [55] *Id.* at 955.

[56] 134 S. Ct. 2473 (2014).   [57] *Id.* at 2488.   [58] *Id.* at 2488, 2490–91.

is a totally different thing to search a man's pockets and use against him what they contain, from ransacking his house for everything which may incriminate him."[59] Smartphones, Roberts argued, are like houses, in the quantity and quality of private information they contain. And second, Roberts resurrected the old discussion of the importance of papers in *Boyd*, stating that "[m]odern cell phones are not just another technological convenience. With all they contain and all they may reveal, they hold for many Americans the 'privacies of life.'"[60] With these analogies to home and personal papers, Roberts offered smart property *more* protection than regular personal property found on a defendant during arrest. The police may, without a warrant, search your briefcase if you are arrested, but not your smartphone.

Both *Jones* and *Riley* show the Court's newfound interest in extending Fourth Amendment protections not just to our "houses" but also to our "papers and effects" – our personal property. In her groundbreaking article *The Lost "Effects" of the Fourth Amendment: Giving Personal Property Due Protection*, legal scholar Maureen Brady explores how constitutional protections apply to personal property – stuff we can move – in addition to our real property – stuff we can't move.[61]

Brady identifies three general ways courts think about constitutional protection for our effects: bright-line, locational, and contextual.[62] She summarizes: "[I]f the owner has neither physical custody of the property nor an expectation of privacy in the area in which it is located, then the personal property is without protection from examination and seizure."[63] At a slightly higher level of complexity, the *Jones* majority suggested that effects are protected against trespass just as land is. But such a bright-line rule does not come close to capturing the decisions of lower courts, which essentially have turned on where the personal property is located, whether it's in a container, whether it's been abandoned, or whether it's still within the possession and control of the owner. Brady divides lower-court decisions between those that rely purely on location and those that rely on other contextual cues that might indicate if the owner intended to come back for the property or considered what was inside to be private.

I believe it is possible to further simplify Brady's framework by noting that courts are looking for information about a piece of property that might be searched. Courts want signals. Courts treat a locked suitcase differently than

---

[59] *Id.* at 2490–91. [60] *See id.* at 2494–95 (*quoting* Boyd, *supra* note 27, at 630).

[61] Maureen Brady, *The Lost "Effects" of the Fourth Amendment: Giving Personal Property Due Protection*, 125 YALE L.J. 946 (2016).

[62] Id. at 980. [63] Id. at 950.

a coat left behind at a restaurant. The lock signals an attempt to keep the property private; the location of the coat indicates that the owner has lost it and may even prefer that someone try to ascertain the owner in order to return it. Location – even when that location is not itself the real property of the owner – can still give a lot of information about the property. A suitcase sitting outside the bathroom in a bus terminal might give a different impression from that of a suitcase at the local dump.

We will return to this point. For now, it is worth noting that smart property and digital documents can communicate signals about the owner's intentions. Both smart property and online papers can be encrypted. Smart property can be secured with fingerprint locks or passcodes. In these cases, regardless of the location or circumstances in which the property is found, the property itself can tell those who encounter it that the owner expects the contents to remain private. If courts are looking for signals about the owner's intentions for property that is not immediately in the owner's possession, smart and digital property can provide them.

Property and the Third-Party Exception

The U.S. Constitution stops the U.S. government from searching our persons and property without a warrant. But it doesn't stop third parties from doing the same.[64] The Constitution doesn't govern relationships between you and me. So we normally use very different areas of the law for each problem. If a government official searches my house without a warrant, she violates the Fourth Amendment. If my nosy neighbor does the same, we invoke the common law of trespass to property, or, if the neighbor does something bad enough, criminal sanctions like burglary.

Where the law of the Fourth Amendment leaves off, the law of property trespass is supposed to pick up. The police cannot search my house without probable cause and a warrant because of the Fourth Amendment. My neighbor cannot rummage through my house because that would be a trespass. For smart property and digital information, though, this arrangement has fallen apart. Companies search our data for their own purposes, often well beyond any reasonable expectation of the owner. A flashlight app on your smartphone might rip off your contacts list. Companies insist on being able to snoop through our communications when we send them through their service. Google scans your email to find out what you might want to buy. When companies collect or otherwise ferret out such information, government can

---

[64] *See* Kiel Brennan-Marquez, *Fourth Amendment Fiduciaries*, 84 FORDHAM L. REV. 611 (2015).

get that data without a warrant by demanding it in subpoenas or national security letters, or by using the threat of such demands to work out an ongoing arrangement between itself and a service provider to permit itself direct or facilitated access to user data.[65] The Fourth Amendment does not apply because a private, nongovernmental entity is doing the rummaging. And the law of trespass does not apply because we do not have strong property rules about digital devices and the data they contain. This Fourth Amendment loophole – closer to a sucking chest wound – is called the "third party exception." Police do not directly search our devices and communications, third parties like Google do so on their behalf.

Here's an example: assume that your friend is going to be married next weekend. You write her an email: "We're going to burn that bar down!" Unfortunately, before you get to go, the bar suffers an actual fire. Computational linguistics algorithms run by your commercial email provider notice the phrase in your email, and the email reaches the hands of law enforcement through an intelligence fusion center. The government asserts that since your service provider can see your information, you must not have meant for it to be private. And because your service provider is not bound by the Constitution – it's just a company, it's not tied to government – it can search through this data without any constitutional restrictions, and pass the results on to law enforcement. At your trial for arson, you are not told how police came into possession of the materials. You are not permitted to examine the algorithm or the chain of custody of the email. Indeed, the police are instructed by the FBI and other federal agencies to lie about where the information came from, in a process called "parallel construction."[66] (The agencies claim this is necessary to protect sources and methods.) As it happens, this hypothetical example is not so hypothetical. Cases like this have been cropping up all over the country.[67]

The Stored Communications Act is the major statute that permits law enforcement to demand our records from companies like Google (there are

[65] *See generally* Smith v. Maryland, 442 U.S. 735 (1979); United States v. Miller, 425 U.S. 435 (1976); United States v. White, 401 U.S. 745 (1971)

[66] *See* Patrick Toomey & Brett Max Kaufman, *The Notice Paradox: Secret Surveillance, Criminal Defendants and the Right to Notice*, 54 SANTA CLARA L. REV. 843, 863–64 (2014); Beryl A. Howell & Dana J. Lesemann, *FISA's Fruits in Criminal Cases: an Opportunity for Improved Accountability*, 12 UCLA J. INT'L L. & FOREIGN AFF. 145, 156–57 (2007).

[67] *See, e.g.*, John Shiffman & Kristina Cooke, *U.S. Directs Agents to Cover Up Program Used to Investigate Americans*, REUTERS (Aug. 5, 2013, 3:25 PM), http://www.reuters.com/article/us-dea-sod-idUSBRE97409R20130805 (noting how DEA agents would receive tips from intelligence agencies to make certain traffic stops, and "agents then pretended that their investigation began with the traffic stop").

other, looser standards for intelligence agencies like the NSA).[68] The SCA treats our email and other stored communications as if they were letters – personal property. The SCA uses a rule borrowed from property law to determine when police can demand records without a warrant: if property is abandoned, police can search it without a warrant. So, per the SCA, if email is "abandoned," police can search it with no warrant. But the SCA has an absurd rule for when email is considered to have been abandoned. At the time the law was passed, in 1986, people downloaded their email from a central server onto their local computers, then deleted the originals on the server. This was at a time when the Internet itself was unknown to most people – the New York Times, for example, only mentioned the Internet once before 1988.[69] By keeping the email on the server more than a certain number of days – six months, to be precise – the law believes you have abandoned it and that any law enforcement personnel who want it can simply request it from the service provider without a warrant.[70] Given that nearly all of us keep our email in the cloud, this has huge implications for us today. I don't know about you, but I have thousands of emails that have been sitting in my inbox for years. As the Sixth Circuit observed when asked if the SCA truly means that government can access almost all of our emails without a warrant: "To the extent that the SCA purports to permit the government to obtain such emails warrantlessly, the SCA is unconstitutional."[71]

The third-party exception is a considerable problem for anyone concerned about government mass surveillance enabled by sensor proliferation in the Internet of Things. Broadly speaking, there are three solutions, and the problem is bad enough that we should try them all. First, the third-party loophole could itself be closed by the Supreme Court, and statutes could be revised to comply with the Constitution. As Justice Sotomayor noted in *Jones*: "It may be necessary to reconsider the premise that an individual has no reasonable expectation of privacy in information voluntarily disclosed to third parties . . . . This approach is ill suited to the digital age, in which people reveal a great deal

---

[68] 18 U.S.C. §§ 2701–2712 (2012).

[69] *See* Roy Rosenzweig, *Wizards, Bureaucrats, Warriors, and Hackers: Writing the History of the Internet*, 103 AM. HIST. REV. 1530, 1530 (1998) (observing that the New York Times' only mention of the Internet prior to 1988 was in a brief aside).

[70] *See* David Kravets, *Aging 'Privacy' Law Leaves Cloud E-Mail Open to Cops*, WIRED (Oct. 21, 2011), http://www.wired.com/2011/10/ecpa-turns-twenty-five/ ("E-mail often remains stored on cloud servers indefinitely, in gigabytes upon gigabytes. That means the authorities may access gigs of e-mails, or other cloud-stored content, without warrants if it's older than six months. The law, believe it or not, still considers as abandoned any e-mail or other files housed on servers for more than six months.").

[71] United States v. Warshak, 631 F.3d 266, 288 (6th Cir. 2010).

of information about themselves to third parties in the course of carrying out mundane tasks."[72] A related action would be to reform the statutory framework permitting access to this data. On the intelligence side, intelligence-gathering (spy) statutes have already been slightly amended to limit some forms of bulk collection from corporate third parties (although the practice of routing the fruits of warrantless surveillance to law enforcement has only picked up steam). There is likewise some momentum for reform of the Stored Communications Act.[73] Courts have already begun the process of overhauling the statute by ensuring it conforms to constitutional standards.[74]

Second, as legal scholars Jack Balkin, Woodrow Hartzog,[75] Kiel Brennan-Marquez,[76] and others have argued, we could make information intermediaries shoulder special responsibilities toward their customers – scholars call them "information fiduciaries."[77] Like our doctors, lawyers, and religious counselors, perhaps our internet service providers should have a special status and be required to treat their customers loyally and act in their customers' best interests. The simple difficulty with this path is that there are almost no situations, other than lawyers, doctors, and priests, where law enforcement cannot make demands for records. Furthermore, an information fiduciary approach might help when companies treat customers' data badly, but it will not do much to stem the massive flow of data from third parties to government.[78]

A third path is to draw reasonable limits around the searching of our devices and our data. I believe it is possible to harness the power of property analogies to stop third parties from trespassing on our devices or opening our cloud-stored messages. To stop that from happening, we need property-like protections. If I lend you my watch to wear, you may not sell it to whomever you please. The

---

[72] *Jones*, 132 S. Ct. at 957 (2012).

[73] *See* Somini Sengupta, *Updating an E-Mail Law From the Last Century*, N.Y. TIMES (Apr. 24, 2013), http://www.nytimes.com/2013/04/25/technology/updating-an-e-mail-law-from-the-last-century.html.

[74] *See, e.g.*, Microsoft Corp. v. United States (*In re* Warrant to Search a Certain E-mail Account Controlled & Maintained by Microsoft Corp.), No. 14-2985, 2016 U.S. App. LEXIS 12926 (2d Cir. July 14, 2016).

[75] *See generally* Neil M. Richards & Woodrow Hartzog, *Taking Trust Seriously in Privacy Law*, 19 STAN. TECH. L. REV. 431, 458 ("[T]he concept of fiduciaries helpfully reorients privacy and crystalizes the concept of trust in information relationships.").

[76] *See, e.g.*, Kiel Brennan-Marquez, *Fourth Amendment Fiduciaries*, 84 FORDHAM L. REV. 611, 614 (2015) (explaining how "the Fourth Amendment should not only constrain the way law enforcement officials gather information, but it should also constrain the way that private actors – information fiduciaries – transmit it").

[77] *Id.*

[78] *Id.* at 645–49 (describing these disclosures to law enforcement as "data vigilantism").

same should be true of my email messages and my Google documents. What-ever else they are, these are the modern-day "papers and effects" mentioned in the Constitution. Wherever our communications are stored, whether on personal email servers locked in the basement or in the depths of Google's data centers, our papers and effects should be off-limits to government intrusion absent a warrant. Wherever our papers and effects go, they should keep this protection, unless we grant consent to someone to look at them. This is hardly a radical suggestion. It's just replicating the protection we have had for cen-turies when we put a letter in the mail.[79] If we don't get this right, then I think Justice Sotomayor was correct to cite in her *Jones* concurrence the words of Seventh Circuit judge Joel Flaum: the government's "unfettered discretion" to use our property and the information it produces against us may well "alter the relationship between citizen and government in a way that is inimical to democratic society."[80]

HOW PROPERTY HELPS STOP PRIVATE SNOOPING

I do not pretend that setting limits on when companies can rummage through our devices and files will be simple, but I do think we can work it out through careful experimentation. Consider the complex property interactions when a mailman delivers a package to your house. Clearly the mailman can walk up your driveway. If it is raining, may he put your package in the cab of your nearby truck to keep the rain off? (Mine does.) May the mailman enter your house and put the package on the counter? Probably not. In this area of law, it is hard to say exactly where the line is between reasonable use of property and trespass, but that's alright for our purposes; lines can be fuzzy as long as easy cases remain easy.

Courts across the country have begun to articulate standards for determining when a company has intruded onto a device or computer server, and are treating trespass on electronic assets with the default exclusionary rule that is so badly needed online. This is the law of cybertrespass.[81] The early cases involved spam. During the rise of the internet, few people thought that the current Wild West of connected computers could compete against the curated and carefully groomed enclaves of AOL, Prodigy, and CompuServe. Those companies provided a "half internet" experience, where most of their users'

---

[79] *See, e.g., Ex Parte* Jackson, 96 U.S. 727, 733, 24 L.Ed. 877 (1877).
[80] *Jones*, 132 S. Ct. at 957 (Sotomayor, J., concurring).
[81] Epstein, *supra* note 6; Bellia, *supra* note 6; Carrier & Lastowka, *supra* note 6; Ebay, Inc. v. Bidder's Edge, Inc., 100 F. Supp. 2d 1058 (N.D. Cal. 2000); Intel Corp. v. Hamidi, 30 Cal. 4th 1342, 1346 (2003).

activities happened within their own gated servers, with limited on- and off-ramps to the internet as we know it today. But CompuServe had a problem – advertisers had started to send bulk emails to CompuServe customers.[82] At that time there were not many legal theories regarding what one could and could not do on someone else's web server. CompuServe developed a new theory: someone using up server resources they weren't supposed to was akin to someone stepping on your daffodils when they weren't supposed to. In short, the law of trespass was applied to online interference with web servers.

One issue was that while daffodils do not exist to be trampled, email servers exist to have email sent to them. Web servers exist to be contacted by browsers. So it seemed nonsensical to apply the law of pure trespass online. Remember, if someone steps on your real-world daffodils, they have committed trespass whether or not they hurt the flowers. But online, the network of interconnected systems would fall apart if each electronic contact were a trespass. Electronic contact is the entire point of the internet. This requires a balancing act – but the balance is not hard. Your mailbox is indeed on your property, but it is a part of your property that others may interact with. It's the same as your driveway and your front door: it exists for that purpose. UPS does not commit trespass when it leaves a package in your mailbox. The post office does not interfere with the use and enjoyment of your mailbox if it drops off a letter. It is possible to reconcile property and interconnectivity by pointing out that just because you expose parts of your property in order to permit and encourage contact, you're not opening the door for every would-be trespasser.

This issue came to a head in *Intel Corp. v. Hamidi*, a case in which the computing giant sued a disgruntled former employee for sending mass emails to other Intel employees.[83] The courts felt torn. On the one hand, email servers are meant to accept emails. On the other, enough emails being fired at a single server can act like a denial of service attack.[84] The courts compromised. Increased server load on an internet-connected system was permissible unless it was seriously slowing down the system.[85] If the drain on server load created a serious interference with the owner's use and enjoyment of the servers, then

---

[82] *See* CompuServe v. Cyber Promotions, Inc., 962 F. Supp. 1015, 1018 (S.D. Ohio 1997) (noting that the defendant used "the Internet to distribute advertisements by sending the same unsolicited commercial message to hundreds of thousands of Internet users at once").

[83] *See Intel*, 30 Cal. 4th at 1346 ("Kourosh Kenneth Hamidi, a former Intel employee, sent e-mails criticizing Intel's employment practices to numerous current employees on Intel's electronic mail system.").

[84] *See id.* at 1381 (Brown, J., dissenting) ("Unwanted messages also drain the equipment's processing power, and slow down the transfers of electronic data.").

[85] *See id.* at 1356–58 (majority opinion) (distinguishing Hamidi's emails from those at issue in *CompuServe*).

the messages could be excluded under cybertrespass law. That let disgruntled employees have their political say, but permitted companies like Intel to manage the integrity of their systems.

Nowadays, cybertrespass serves a useful purpose in regulating decent behavior between those who contact a computer and need to run code on it and those who own those computing resources. For example, it's fine if I search eBay for new Polaroid sunglasses. But I can't search eBay for every auction by sending web-crawling programs to gather up all the information on its site. That causes server load, which gets much worse if I crawl its website often enough to keep the auctions up-to-date. The eBay website would slow down for everyone, or even lock up. That is, after all, one way to take a website offline: by barraging it with attempts to contact the server, choking it up so that legitimate users can't make headway – the aforementioned denial of service (DoS) attack.[86]

The cybertrespass rule helps in that it provides a middle position between an all-or-nothing alternative. Many companies interact with our devices only to the extent necessary to get the job done. But many others don't ask, or go well beyond the resource use necessary for the task at hand. They chew up resources. Have you noticed that your computer, even though it still works perfectly well, slowly grinds down over time? It becomes loaded with software that takes more and more of your computing resources for its own purposes. Your internet connection becomes infected with companies using your connection. Your CPU spends more time doing what a company tells it to do rather than what you, its owner, tell it to do. Many companies will use their customers' own bandwidth instead of the company's to send copies of the company's software to other customers.[87] I once found that a game my daughters bought had hijacked my very limited cell phone internet connection and uploaded an entire month's worth of data to other purchasers of the game overnight – the game company was using players' connections as its distribution network.[88] Now I religiously check my computer to find out if Pando Media Booster

[86] A denial of service attack usually consists of a barrage of contact requests for a server that has been set to accept incoming messages. This floods the server and makes it unable to process legitimate requests. It's sort of the digital equivalent of a sit-in of a restaurant: the protesters make it impossible for diners to eat.

[87] See, e.g., Brad Chacos, *How to Stop Windows 10 From Using Your PC's Bandwidth to Update Strangers' Systems*, PCWORLD (Aug. 3, 2015, 7:39 AM), http://www.pcworld.com/article/2955491/windows/how-to-stop-windows-10-from-using-your-pcs-bandwidth-to-update-strangers-systems.html (discussing the integration of peer-to-peer, or "P2P," update delivery in Windows 10).

[88] For more information about the Pando Media Booster and other P2P delivery methods, see Petter Martensson, *Setting the Record Straight: Massively's Interview With Pando Networks*,

has been installed again. It shows up every once in a while. Recently, one startup sought to use the computer chips in Internet of Things objects to mine bitcoin, and send the bitcoin back to the company.[89] In one particularly egregious example, the IT manager (and bush pilot) for an anti-poaching project in the Central African Republic reported that Windows 10 nagware hijacked their computer and downloaded six gigabytes over the organization's pay-per-megabyte satellite connection. The computer in question was used to coordinate responses to, among other things, militarized poachers and crisis situations.[90] Had there been a crisis at the time, a computer crash could have cost lives.

We should be able to invite people onto the digital equivalent of our front porches, but boot them out if they kick in the front door and rummage through the digital equivalent of our refrigerator or bedroom. Owners should be protected from entities who are given an inch, but take a mile. The law of cybertrespass, which right now permits people to use some resources from a site or service, but excludes them if they begin to make extensive or damaging use, is a pretty good place to start. The law of cybertrespass provides a common-sense property rule. Companies on our devices are guests. Once they begin impeding our use of the item, they are unwelcome guests, and ought to be subject to both technological exclusion and legal sanction.

With regards to our privacy, cybertrespass has the capability to cut off certain overreaches at the source. Recall, from earlier, that companies overuse the access they have to devices, and the fruits of that overreach are made available to government, without a warrant, under the third-party exception. Trespass law has always been the constraint on private parties. It has kept Peeping Toms out of the bushes for centuries. It can at least help keep companies from overreaching and searching off-limits parts of our phones on the off-chance that what they find will increase profits.

Cybertrespass does not solve everything. In fact, if we are not careful, cyberproperty and cybertrespass will make the internet worse. Consider the companies that own the principal data routes of the internet – Level 3 is one such internet backbone provider. Imagine if it were to apply strict

ENGADGET (Jan. 2, 2012) https://www.engadget.com/2012/01/02/setting-the-record-straight-massively-interview-with-pando-ne/.

[89] *See* Michael J. Casey, *Secretive Bitcoin Startup 21 Reveals Record Funds, Hints at Mass Consumer Play*, WALL ST. J.: BLOGS (Mar. 10, 2015), http://blogs.wsj.com/digits/2015/03/10/secretive-bitcoin-startup-21-reveals-record-funds-hints-at-mass-consumer-play/.

[90] *See* Kavita Iyer, *Forced Windows 10 upgrade could have caused fatality in remote African bush*, TECHWORM (June 5, 2016), http://www.techworm.net/2016/06/forced-windows-10-upgrade-caused-fatality-remote-african-bush.html.

exclusionary rules to its hubs.[91] For those who rely on Level 3 infrastructure –
and that is many of us[92] – it would be like living in a town with only private roads. If we mistake what property is or how it is best used, we could
end up splintering the world into small private digital fiefdoms where consumers would have to pay tolls to cross bottlenecks and digital bridges between
areas. The internet cannot live without broad connectivity.[93] This is one of
the reasons that net neutrality, the principle that all users and providers on a
network must be treated equally when their traffic crosses the network, is so
important.[94] Otherwise, internet backbone providers could extort those cross-
ing their digital bridges, raise prices, stop start-ups from being able to compete
with established companies on a level playing field, and generally disrupt traffic from one part of the internet to another unless they were paid off. These are
not new problems, however. Railroads tried to use their power over property to
extort passengers in the nineteenth century, AT&T used its monopoly position
over telephone lines to dominate telecommunications in the twentieth century, and Comcast misused its power over broadband to extort Netflix in the
twenty-first. Courts and the FCC imposed common carrier and net neutrality
requirements so that the property power these companies had over transportation and communications networks didn't balloon into further extortion.

To return to the Fourth Amendment questions of whether and when the
government may invade our property, and with it our privacy: we should not
let the electronic nature of a contact with our property bother us too much.
Under the old system, the Fourth Amendment prohibited government from
unreasonable searches, and the law of trespass prohibited private parties from
snooping on others' property. In the absence of trespass rules for electronic
assets, companies have overreached, and government has exploited that overreach to do an end-run around the Fourth Amendment. This should not be
terribly difficult to fix. The common law has already worked out cybertrespass
rules. Those rules could apply simply and by default to companies who overstay
their welcome on our property, and to governments who seek to subvert our
property to spy on us. The rules for companies who have our permission to contact our electronic mailboxes are that they may use our computing resources

[91] *See* Carrier & Lastowka, *supra* note 6, at 1486–90.
[92] *See* Ramakrishnan Durairajan et al., *InterTubes: A Study of the US Long-Haul Fiber-Optic Infrastructure*, Computer Comm. Rev., Aug. 2015, at 1, 4 tbl. 1, *available at* http://www.sigcomm.org/sites/default/files/ccr/papers/2015/August/2829988-2787499.pdf.
[93] *See* Carrier & Lastowka, *supra* note 6, at 1501.
[94] *See* Tim Wu, *Why Everyone Was Wrong About Net Neutrality*, N.Y. Times (Feb. 26, 2015), http://www.newyorker.com/business/currency/why-everyone-was-wrong-about-net-neutrality.

as long as they do not impede with our use and enjoyment of our property, and do not pry beyond the permission they have been given to accomplish a certain task. The same rules should apply with equal force to flashlight apps that covertly scrape contact lists, or apps that hijack battery power or bandwidth for their own purposes. Governments should not electronically intrude on our property and command processor cycles from our Internet of Things devices without a warrant. The law is rarely neat, but restoring the traditional restraints on government and private snoops would be an ideal opportunity to make it simpler and more elegant than it is now.

WHAT PROPERTY DOES FOR PRIVACY

Property law cannot replace privacy rights, but it can bolster them. Our privacy rights are safer with property rules than without. Privacy rights can be hard to define. Property rights are clearer; as Justice Scalia has noted: "One virtue of the Fourth Amendment's property-rights baseline is that it keeps easy cases easy."[95] Privacy rights, at least in the United States, permit intrusion by default. Property rights exclude intruders by default. Privacy rights are fragile. Property rights are robust. Privacy rights tend to fade permanently if relinquished even for a moment. Property rights are tough and sticky. Privacy rights are enforced by courts. Property rights are often in owners' hands – you do not need a court order to install a lock on your front door or to encrypt your phone. Privacy harms can be hard to prove.[96] Property harms are cheap and easy to prove: did someone trample your daffodils or not? It would be wonderful if privacy rights were clear, robust, and excluded intruders by default. We should work to make them that way. But since they are not, those seeking clear, robust, and automatic privacy protection can turn to property law.

Consider the new Microsoft Windows 10 operating system. It gathers information directly from users' desktops, everything from their keystrokes to their websites visited, and turns that information over to Microsoft.[97] Microsoft sells that information to advertisers – who use it to get a better price out of you – and also may hand the information off to the government without requiring a warrant. Cortana, the digital assistant program that comes with Windows 10,

---

[95] *See Jardines*, 133 S. Ct. at 1417.
[96] *See generally* Daniel J. Solove & Danielle Keats Citron, *Risk and Anxiety: A Theory of Data Breach Harms*, 96 TEX. L.R. __ (forthcoming 2017), *available at* https://papers.ssrn.com/sol3/papers.cfm?abstract_id=2885638.
[97] *See* David Auerbach, *Broken Windows Theory*, SLATE (Aug. 3, 2015), http://www.slate.com/articles/technology/bitwise/2015/08/windows_10_privacy_problems_here_s_how_bad_they_are_and_how_to_plug_them.html.

will "get to know you," which both trains the program to better serve you and permits her to be a better salesperson on behalf of paying advertisers.[98] Imagine if, unbeknownst to you, your real estate broker were working for the person trying to sell you a house. The agent would show you nice houses, but at the end of the day would be trying to sell you something fast to get a commission and move on to the next deal. In the same way, the better Cortana knows you, the more consumer surplus she (or the advertiser she works for) can extract from you.

On top of that, Windows 10 assigns every user a unique ID, tied to their account and email account, so that you can be tracked wherever you go, no matter what precautions you take.[99] It's like being tagged with a radio collar, the kind they use to track wild animals. It doesn't matter if you use protective software, a virtual private network, or anything else – the radio collar ID will call home and tell Microsoft, and anyone who advertises with Microsoft, who you are, where you are, and what you will pay for goods and services. The least it could do is ask if all of this was okay with you. Microsoft doesn't have to, though, because we don't have a default rule of exclusion from our smart property the way we have with our real or personal property. And worst of all, from a security perspective, Windows 10 stores the device's encryption key in Microsoft's own cloud.[100] This means that anyone who can hack the cloud the way Apple accounts were hacked in a recent celebrity photograph scandal[101] can decrypt your device. Or, Microsoft itself could decrypt it upon government request.

A default rule of exclusion – drawn from the common law of trespass – would significantly boost efforts to protect our smart property and our data privacy. The burden should not be on the owner who wants privacy. The burden should rest on the outside party to verify that she is allowed inside. An easy way to see this is to consider how the opposite rule would work if we used the online rule for offline property. If, hypothetically, we were to apply online

[98] *Id.*

[99] *See* Andrew Griffin, *Windows 10 Sends Personal Data to Microsoft, Even If Users Tell It Not To*, INDEPENDENT (Aug. 13, 2015), http://www.independent.co.uk/life-style/gadgets-and-tech/news/windows-10-sends-personal-data-to-microsoft-even-if-users-tell-it-not-to-10453549.html.

[100] *See* David Auerbach, *How Bad Is Microsoft's Data Land-Grab*, SLATE (Jan. 7, 2016, 12:25 PM), http://www.slate.com/articles/technology/bitwise/2016/01/microsoft_holds_a_copy_of_windows_10_users_drive_encryption_keys_how_scary.html.

[101] *See* Andrea Peterson et al., *Leaks of Nude Celebrity Photos Raise Concerns About the Security of the Cloud*, WASH. POST (Sept. 1, 2014), https://www.washingtonpost.com/politics/leaks-of-nude-celebrity-photos-raise-concerns-about-security-of-the-cloud/2014/09/01/59dcd37e-3219-11e4-8f02-03c644b2d7do_story.html.

rules to drones, they would be permitted to fly into your house and circle the bedroom, unless you affirmatively told the creator of the drone that this was not allowed. But assume there are thousands of companies with drones. Further assume that each company requires you to go through a different and lengthy process to contact it and tell it to stop sending drones to spy on you. Also imagine that even if you told all the companies to stop sending random drones, if you ever told one drone it could come in, say to deliver a package from Amazon (they're working on the technology as I write), then all future drones from all affiliates of that company could again send drones zipping all over your property.

Reversing the default rule would change much of the balance between citizen and company online. By shifting to a requirement that the company must ask and get affirmative permission first, we can already do most of the work of ensuring that consumers get full control of their own information. Having and following the rule of exclusion for digital property would help keep operating system designers and advertisers from tracking your desktop. And it should make perfect sense to apply the law of trespass to your physical property. When a company wants to invade your car or house to extract data, they must ask your permission first, not your forgiveness afterward.

To be sure, there would be a cost if everyone opted out, although the chance of that is low (after all, technology like Siri and Cortana, which work by using personal data, are major selling points for the iPhone and Windows 10). Services funded by targeted advertising may generate less revenue. But there are reasons to think the effects may not be dramatic. Opt-in buttons would certainly be made visible, whereas opt-out buttons these days are often hard to find, if not nearly invisible. Once companies have an incentive to secure active consent, they will.

There is a further reason to resist the argument that because certain services are worse off when they must seek permission, we must allow our devices to surveil us and pass on the data. That is looter's logic. Apply the same argument to our houses: certainly it would be beneficial if Amazon could fly package delivery drones through our windows. Yet we would not say that this benefit should remove an owner's power to exclude Amazon from her property. In other words, the institution of private property certainly imposes public costs. People may use their property irresponsibly, or even destroy it. I can paint my house a shocking shade of green. My uncle, a doctor, took his anatomy and physiology textbook out into a field after the class was finished and shot it. Yet the reasons for private property ownership far outweigh the benefits of permitting Amazon a kind of private right of eminent domain, one permitting it to take one stick out of the bundle of property rights and fly across our land without our consent. The same ought to be true for entities that lurk in our devices and extract our data.

Finally, what goes for companies should go doubly for governments. The state cannot say you have no reasonable expectation of privacy in your own property. It must get a warrant to search your cell phone. It needs a warrant to search your desktop or your laptop computer. Just as the government would need a warrant to search your non-electronically connected house, it should need a warrant to gather information from your smart house, regardless of whether it gathers that information from you directly or from the company that designed the software running your home.

PROPERTY, PRIVACY, AND THE INTERNET OF THINGS

When we put a letter in an envelope, it gains the full protection of the Fourth Amendment against the government. It doesn't matter that anyone with scissors can tear through that envelope. What matters is that the envelope serves as a persistent reminder, traveling with the message, that it is private. The same should be true of all of our "papers and effects," whether in the cloud or on smart devices. Why should it matter whether I store my documents in a locked filing cabinet in my home or in an encrypted cloud drive with Google? Why should it matter whether I send my messages wrapped in an envelope and set with a stamp or texted from me to my wife using Signal? Why should it matter whether the government searches our houses by sending an officer to fumble through our drawers or by obtaining information from companies that listen in to our living rooms through the Amazon Echo or watch for movement through the Xbox One?

There are slight shifts in perspective that make it possible to extend the strong protections of the Fourth Amendment to the Internet of Things, and the law of trespass and other analogies to property law to keep corporations from overreaching into our documents and onto our devices. The bulk of this chapter has reviewed the path of the law thus far. It turns now to the question, what now? Now that servers hold more of our papers than our desks, and smartphones hold more clues to our intimate lives than our homes, how should the law develop?

Protecting Personal Property

Despite recent victories (primarily *Jones* and *Riley*) that show a positive trend toward the protection of personal property, there remains a significant imbalance between the sturdy constitutional protections for real property and the weak constitutional protections for "papers and effects." That weakness carries over to many of our most important electronic personal effects: emails, smartphones, and IoT devices. As things are, real property is increasingly surrounded by a firm, bright line. Personal property generally gets little protection unless it is within the owner's reach or within her home.

Cases like *Jones* and *Riley* show that this "home first" view of protecting privacy is not nearly enough. Justice Roberts noted in *Riley* that smartphones contain more intimate information than homes do. *Jones* protected cars with homelike bright-line rules at least in part because of the vast amount of information that could be gathered by geotracking citizens' movement over time. As computers and sensors get smaller and more portable – miniaturization and mobility are hallmarks of the Internet of Things – more and more computerized assets will fall more naturally on the "personal property" end of the spectrum, in contrast with assets like land and houses that have been traditionally considered "real property." It seems odd that we would protect information under one standard when it is maintained on a server in a home, and the same information differently when the server is stored remotely or when the hard drive is as portable as a smartphone SD card.

The question is whether the home protects the information it contains because the home is special, or if the home is special because it has traditionally protected our most intimate information. As in *Jones* and *Riley*, I believe it is the latter.

Protecting personal smart and digital property does not have to be difficult. The basics of the legal regime are already in place. Following the Sixth Circuit's decision that warrantless searches of stored email are unconstitutional, it makes sense to require police to seek a warrant to open electronic mail just as they would to open snail mail. Following *Riley*, it makes sense to require a warrant to search computers that contain large amounts of personal, private information, whether that computer be in the form of a password-protected laptop, a smartphone, or (in the cases sure to come) a smartwatch, smart fitness band, or other wearable. If we take *Riley* seriously, it is the depth and breadth of the type of information available on a given device that renders that device especially protected under the Fourth Amendment. Fortunately, the court has given us a touchpoint of comparison: given that a smartphone is no longer subject to warrantless search, one could easily say the same of other small, portable devices that have a similar reach and depth of personal data.

To this, we can add some commonsense updates to current law. As things stand, if personal property is outside of the owner's possession or control, the property can be considered to be abandoned, at least for privacy purposes, and thus can be searched.[102] This is the "abandonment doctrine." On the other hand, property placed inside containers has historically been given much stronger protection from searches and seizures.[103] So, for example, a locked briefcase might be given greater constitutional protection against searches even if the owner is not immediately present. This is the "container doctrine." These rules need to be updated to reflect the structure and function of smart property.

First, smart objects are themselves containers. They contain and encapsulate information. "Container encryption" is the practice of encrypting the entire device, not just specific files on it. Container-encrypted devices bring new salience to the commonsense "container" cases. If a locked suitcase demonstrates the owner's ongoing privacy interest in personal property outside her immediate control, a container-encrypted smartphone surely does the same.

Second, if courts are looking for signals regarding how and whether the user intends to use the property, smart property can provide signals. It would be nearly effortless to permit smartphones to blink a specific color to signal "Police invited," which I suspect would be less commonly used than whatever color indicates "Sticky fingers off my property." In short, there may soon be no need to guess about the owner's expectation of privacy, because the property will be able to tell whoever picks it up what she is permitted to do. More seriously, however, the very use of container encryption, fingerprint locks, and other unmistakable signals can help police understand that the owner meant for the device to be kept private. There are many phones that don't employ a lockscreen, or don't have one. Perhaps those owners mean to invite intrusion. But the standard locked smartphone should leave police in no doubt, regardless of the device's location, that the owner does not want people to rummage through it.

Third, my reading of both the modern and historical cases is that courts tend to consider control over the asset as a signal of expectations of privacy. Recall Justice Sotomayor's statement in *Jones* that "privacy expectations [are] inherent in items of property that people possess or control." Conversely, courts have often looked at separation from the owner's possession and control as a sign of abandonment. Some lower courts believe that it is acceptable to search through personal property as long as it is not in the owner's immediate control. In one case, for example, a court found that a container (with marijuana inside

[102] *See* Maureen E. Brady, *The Lost "Effects" of the Fourth Amendment: Giving Personal Property Due Protection*, 125 YALE L.J. 946, 962 (2016) (discussing "*California v. Greenwood*, in which the Court held that a person could not claim Fourth Amendment rights in curbside trash").
[103] *See id.* at 962–63 (noting that "past cases from the Court rel[ied] so strongly on signals of privacy inherent in containers").

it) passed out of the owner's possession and control when the owner hid it under a rock seventy-five feet from where he was fishing.[104] One might reasonably question the court's conclusion, and indeed many of these cases look as though courts are just eager to get on with the trial.

But to the degree courts find that separation from control gives police carte blanche to search personal property without a warrant, they will need new analysis for autonomous smart property: robots, autonomous cars, drones, and the like. The very purpose of these assets is that they are away from their owners but not out of the owners' control. The rhetoric of abandonment will not work. An autonomous car that is driving from its parking lot to pick up its owner is separated from its owner by much more than seventy-five feet, but it is certainly not out of her expected control. It is even difficult to claim that a misplaced cell phone is out of the owner's control. If left undisturbed, there is every chance that the owner can use a tracking app to find out where she left it.

Protecting the Smart Home

Just as personal property must receive increased protection because of the increased amount of intimate detail it can hold, so the legal rules that contemplate the home as a last line of defense and a bastion of privacy must be updated, or risk their relevance. Homes, especially smart homes, are now less information-protective spaces and more information-generative spaces. The home will soon lose any natural ability to restrict data flows. Whereas before data could flow only out of windows and open doors, soon data will flow out of the home through every appliance, device, thermostat, console, power socket, and light fixture.

Recall the now-discredited idea in *Olmstead* that once data leaves the home, it is fair game for warrantless search. Consider the dissents in *Kyllo* – which argued that gathering heat data off the house wall was fine – or *Jardines* – which argued that sending dogs (and thereby drones) up onto citizens' front porches to sniff for drugs was not an invasion of the home. These are all the same kind of thinking: once data are "in the wild," once it leaves in any way the walls of the home, it is not protected from government or corporate rummaging. If that becomes the rule, we will live in the digital equivalent of glass-walled houses.

Home as locus-of-information-generation must trump home as means-of-information-protection. We must find rules that protect the information-generative functions of homes by protecting the information they produce,

---

[104] *See generally* Anderson v. State, 209 S.E.2d 665 (Ga. Ct. App. 1974)

and reduce our reliance on rules which imply that the ability to gather information (whether because it exits the home on wafting air particles, as heat seeping through walls, or carried by Wi-Fi signals or smartgrid wires) implies the right to gather that information.

Protecting Device-Sourced Data

A critical element for protecting both smart personal property and smart homes is, therefore, a consideration of the data's source when determining whether and to what extent the data are protected. Here I draw on the excellent work of Professor Andrew Ferguson, who says that it matters where data comes from, not just where it ends up. He proposes protecting information curtilages – those areas of protection that surround data after it leaves the actual object or the possession of the person who generated it.[105] In a recent article, Ferguson focuses on data trails leaking from constitutionally protected sources. He argues that when information originates in a constitutionally protected location, it should not lose that protection when it exits that location.[106] In his view, information that is generated by a constitutional locus and is subsequently subject to strong information-security safeguards should still benefit from constitutional protection. In the extreme, a server itself could be a constitutionally protected location, insofar as it contains documents of a scope and nature similar to those stored within the home. Consider: I put a folder in my desk drawer at home. It is constitutionally protected. I click "save" on a computer, and store the same file in my desktop computer. It is constitutionally protected. What possible logic would argue that it would lose this protection if my "save" action included – as it so often now does even without our knowledge – saving the file to a secure, encrypted cloud location?

Certainly, one caveat to Ferguson's theory is that it might be difficult for law enforcement to determine the constitutional source of data. Consider a Google doc: was it written in the home or in a public cafe? But there is something important about the source of the data, as opposed to its bare existence. We live in our homes, and they are our final information refuges. In a similar sense, we keep smartphones intimately close to us. *Riley* recognized that the problem with searching a smartphone was not just the information that it contained, but also the information to which it had access. Smart devices are talismanic: they are keys to other informational stores. If someone has my smartphone, they have not only information stored on that phone, but also access to my

---

[105] *See* Andrew G. Ferguson, *Personal Curtilage, Fourth Amendment Security in Public*, 55 Wm. & Mary L. Rev. 1283 (2014).

[106] *See* Andrew G. Ferguson, *The 'Smart' Fourth Amendment*, 102 Cornell L. Rev. 547 (2017).

work server, my Amazon purchase history (and the ability to order anything they wish with one click), my app library, my movies, my music, my photos, my reading collection (I just finished rereading *The Martian*, in case you were curious), and my progress in my meditation, fitness, and language-learning applications.

Ferguson must be right that data must be protected if it is generated in a constitutionally protected locus and thereafter protected by information-security safeguards. Similarly, governments and corporations should be limited in their ability to seize the informational trove represented by our smart devices and file storage. Learning about someone by snooping their smartphone is like shooting fish in a barrel. The cost of snooping is too low, the payout is too high, and therefore the incentive for overreach is too large. Gathering information by subverting or searching an intimate, sensor-laden general-purpose processor like a smartphone, smartwatch, smart car, or smart home is like fishing with dynamite. It works, but it's not fair to the fish.

UPGRADING PRIVACY

The historical relationship between our property and our privacy is long and fraught. The critical question is whether property rules can help privacy rights. It is clear that they can. Property's characteristics of clarity, robustness, and automatic exclusion help cover for privacy rights that are often hazy, fragile, and permit intrusion by default.

Even though property rules help, they need an update. With the advent of a major mobile revolution, we have changed how places and objects interact with private information. We no longer consume data in the privacy of our own homes, where the traditional boundaries of the house have provided some protection. Instead, our consumption of data flows through our mobile devices and out of our soon-to-be smarter homes. This should change nothing. Our interest in protecting our smartphones, our smart cars, or our smart glasses from tracking us wherever we go is as much an interest as prohibiting government or commercial entities from peering into our homes. Indeed, there are signs that courts are aware that pervasive mobile surveillance can be even more intrusive than it can be to surveil the traditionally sacrosanct home. It can be worse to bug a phone than a bedroom. So we need to add strong protections for personal property – hard drives, smartwatches, smartphones, smart cars, fitness trackers – that correspond to the enormous amount of information they now possess. We also need to protect the increasingly transparent walls of the home by considering the home as a locus of information generation, and privileging information generated through that locus.

   Linking property and privacy is a messy business. There are legitimate
concerns that mixing the two will lead to overly powerful property owners,
even to the point of increasing the strength of internet infrastructure providers.
Yet property law has much strength to lend to privacy: its solidity, resilience,
and default exclusion features are badly needed in the privacy arena. For these
reasons, I would still prefer to strengthen private ownership of personal smart
and digital property, and indeed to leverage the strong emotions that surround
personal property to create a right of privacy that travels with our property
when we leave our homes, when we entrust it to those who have promised
to keep our secrets, and even when we leave our smartphones unlocked and
sitting on a table in a restaurant.

6

Property as Information

"Property is a broad concept that includes 'every intangible benefit and prerogative susceptible of possession or disposition.'"

– Kremen v. Cohen, 337 F.3d 1024, 1030 (2003) (Kozinski, J.)

As I have noted earlier, courts have a tendency to lump everything intangible into the category of intellectual property.[1] This impulse causes us to miss many important assets.[2] Your bank account, or at least the funds it represents, is certainly your property, but it is not intellectual property, and it is also not general unowned information, to be used by anyone. It's just traditional personal property, even if you can't touch it.[3] But especially for certain kinds of assets that are partially intellectual property, like an online music collection, courts have ignored consumers' rights to their specific copies in favor of copyright owners' power over their copyrights.[4]

Courts are coming to recognize that this approach is far too narrow. Consider *Kremen v. Cohen*, which asked whether a domain name, sex.com, should be protected by the same rules as traditional personal property. Gary Kremen had obtained sex.com from domain name registrar Network Solutions. Stephen

---

[1] *See* Juliet M. Moringiello, *False Categories in Commercial Law: the (Ir)relevance of (In)tangibility*, 35 FLA. ST. U. L. REV. 119, 143 (2007) [hereinafter *False Categories*] (observing the "overbroad classification of electronic assets . . . in case law").

[2] *See* Juliet M. Moringiello, *What Virtual Worlds Can Do For Property Law*, 62 FLA. L. REV. 159, 160–63 (2010) [hereinafter *Virtual Worlds*] (examining virtual property and "discuss[ing] the ways in which the study of virtual worlds can contribute to real world law").

[3] *See, e.g., In re* Porayko, 705 F.3d 703, 705 (7th Cir. 2013) (finding that a bank "account is 'personal property' under" Illinois law and being unable to identify "any decision" in "any other state . . . concluding that a bank account is *not* personal property for the purpose of a statute similar" to the Illinois provision).

[4] *See, e.g.,* Capitol Records, LLC v. ReDigi, Inc., 934 F. Supp. 2d 640, 660–61 (S.D.N.Y. 2013) (holding a corporation in the business of selling "used MP3s" liable for copyright infringement).

Cohen stole sex.com by sending an obviously fake letter to Network Solutions, which fell for the pretty dumb con. Cohen fled the country, so Kremen sued Network Solutions for being careless with his domain name. The district court held that even though sex.com was property, it couldn't be stolen (or, in a civil case, "converted"), because it was intangible.[5]

On appeal, the Ninth Circuit Court of Appeals reversed the lower court decision, setting a strong standard for treating intangible property just like traditional personal property. Judge Kozinski wrote:

> Property is a broad concept that includes "every intangible benefit and pre-rogative susceptible of possession or disposition." We apply a three-part test to determine whether a property right exists: "First, there must be an interest capable of precise definition; second, it must be capable of exclusive pos-session or control; and third, the putative owner must have established a legitimate claim to exclusivity."[6]

In short, the district court was too worried about tangibility, when it should have been worried about what makes an intangible right a piece of property. Overfocus on tangibility causes property law to overlook large categories of consumers' assets, which we can call intangible property. Once you recognize intangible property, you start to see it everywhere. It includes not only our bank accounts and MP3 collections, but also our stock portfolios, e-book libraries, virtual items and money collected in video games, Bitcoin, games purchased and downloaded on Steam and Xbox Live, and hundreds of other assets. People justifiably feel that they own these assets, even though it is not always immediately clear where these assets fit into the law as it stands – they aren't physical, they aren't unowned general information, and they aren't purely intellectual property.[7]

The fault lies with underdeveloped traditional property law just as much as with overreaching intellectual property theory.[8] Traditional real and personal

---

5 Kremen v. Cohen, 99 F. Supp. 2d 1168, 1173–74 (N.D. Cal. 2000).
6 Kremen v. Cohen, 337 F.3d 1024, 1030 (2003) (Kozinski, J.).
7 *See, e.g.,* Bragg v. Linden Research, Inc., 487 F. Supp. 2d 593, 595 (E.D.Penn. 2007) (noting the plaintiff's argument that "many people 'are now living large portions of their lives, forming friendships with others, building and acquiring virtual property, forming contracts, substantial business relationships and forming social organizations' in virtual worlds such as Second Life"). The *Bragg* court denied the defendant's motion to dismiss, *id.* at 612, and the parties then reached a "confidential settlement." ANDREW MURRAY, INFORMATION TECHNOLOGY LAW: THE LAW AND SOCIETY 104 (Oxford University Press 2013). This, unfortunately, prevented the courts from more thoroughly addressing the issues of virtual property raised by the case.
8 *See* Moringiello, *False Categories,* supra note 1, at 119 ("Classifying property according to its tangibility or intangibility creates false categories unrelated to significant legal distinctions, and

property have historically been connected to objects or land.[9] We think of traditional property as being concerned with stuff. Stuff is physical. As discussed in earlier chapters, courts have often assumed that if something isn't physical, it can't be normal, traditional property. We need to scrap this line of thinking and find what lies underneath property as an institution. That is the project of this chapter. We will strip property down to its cogs and gears, and try to figure out what makes it tick.

In doing so, we will discover something important about the nature of property and its relationship to information. Viewing property as physical is more than underinclusive – it's wrong. Property is all about information. In fact, traditional property rights are nothing but information: information about *who* may do *what* with *which resource* over *which time period*. As famed property scholar Felix Cohen put it, a property right "is a sector of space in time and no more tangible than a song."[10] Property rules are rules that package information about property rights so that property can flow smoothly between interested parties. And property systems are just databases: stores of information meant to convey the information of property rights. "It is not *the resource* itself which is owned," write economics scholars Arman Alchian and Harold Demsetz. "In its original meaning, property referred solely to a right, title, or interest."[11] So to boil this chapter down into one thought: property is not stuff – property is information.

And this is where things get exciting. If traditional property rights are just information, traditional property rules will work just fine in information environments. And if property is just a list of who owns what, we can easily do that with digital and smart property. You own your house and your car because of an entry in a database: the county land records for your house and the title registration for your car. Computers are great at databases. There is nothing particularly hard about keeping track of who owns what MP3 or online movie or e-book or cell phone or smart car or smart home in exactly the same way. We should be able to own digital and smart property the same way we own houses or cars. If we see property as information, rather than as stuff,

---

these false categories hinder the ability of commercial law to expand to adequately accommodate electronic assets.").

[9] *See* Henry E. Smith, *Property as the Law of Things*, 125 HARV. L. REV. 1691, 1703 (2012) ("Property clusters complementary attributes – land's soil nutrients, moisture, building support, or parts of everyday objects like chairs – into the parcels of real estate or tangible and intangible objects of personal property").

[10] *See* Felix S. Cohen, *Dialogue on Private Property*, 9 RUTGERS L. REV. 357, 361 (1954) [hereinafter *Dialogue on Private Property*].

[11] Armen Alchian & Harold Demsetz. *The Property Rights Paradigm*, 33 J. OF ECON. HIST. 16, 17 (1973).

we can make huge strides in bringing traditional rules of property to information environments like the internet. Property becomes a matter of keeping good databases of who owns what. And we can do that.

REBOOTING PROPERTY

Imagine you walk into a room and see a table. On that table is a plate of cookies and a cell phone. Would you feel comfortable taking a cookie? Would you feel comfortable taking the cell phone? What are the property rights in the cookie and phone? Do they include you?

You would need more information before making a decision. Let's say the table is in a relative's house during the holiday season. You'd suddenly feel comfortable taking a cookie, but not the phone. You don't know whose phone it is, but you know it's not yours. On the other hand, let's say the table is in an acquaintance's house. You would feel uncomfortable taking a cookie, and certainly would not touch the cell phone. Unless you were a guest at a party, in which case cookies may be back on the menu.

Let's try another thought experiment, this one dealing with that most traditional of property interests: land. Land is the most "real" and tangible property interest we can have. But our ownership interests in land are pure information. Imagine a house on the side of the hill. Who owns it? We need the information in the county land registry. How much land around the house goes with it? We need the information on the deed. The land itself has very nearly nothing to do with the ownership interest, which is pure information. As Felix Cohen has written: "[L]et's take the simplest case of tangible property, a piece of real estate.... [I]f you cut down the trees and sell them for firewood, the real property is still there ... [a]nd if you cut the sod and sell that, and dig up the top soil and sand and gravel and rock and sell that, the real property is still there."[12]

Sure, the rocks and trees that serve as the borders of the land exist and are tangible, but their meaning, the significance accorded to them as a boundary – that is pure information. Why do those particular rocks and trees and streams matter, and not other ones? They matter only because we have attached critical information to those particular features of the landscape and called them a boundary. On family trips, I have often driven across state lines, or from one country to another. I often notice there is no difference in the land on one side of the border or the other. The boundary is purely a line on a map. Change that information, and you change property rights, without touching the physical

---

[12] Cohen, *Dialogue on Private Property, supra* note 10, at 360.

asset at all. At the end of 2015, Belgium and the Netherlands agreed to move their borders to swap land between them.[13] The land wouldn't change; the information pertaining to it would.

The traditional definition of property is that it is the relationship of actors to assets and to each other.[14] That's not bad, but it doesn't go far enough. A relationship is just one kind of information. The relationship between you and your family members is information. But the fact that you have been invited to a holiday party is also information. As is the fact that you are not the owner of the cell phone.

One important ramification of this theory is that property isn't about physical things, at least not without a real change in our understanding of what a "thing" is. Think about it: the existence of the cell phone, or its presence on a table, tells us next to nothing. What matters is additional information: the cell phone is mine, the cell phone is yours, or the cell phone is not mine or yours, which means that both of us are unwilling to pick it up (unless we're thieves). If the cell phone is on a table in my family's house, maybe I might answer it for a sibling. If the cell phone is sitting on a table in a restaurant, I wouldn't. Information is everything.

Property and Information

To arrive at a new theory of property as information, it is helpful to look at some of the thinking that has gone before. In the past several decades, there has been a resurgent interest in property theory.[15] What was once the dustiest of legal subjects has become the source of much legal reasoning about why we choose to allocate resources the way that we do. But even in some of the oldest rules in property law, property and the rules that govern it have always been about information.

---

[13] *See Belgium, Netherlands to Exchange Territory – Without a Fight*, ASSOCIATED PRESS (Dec. 30, 2015, 10:43 AM), http://bigstory.ap.org/article/bfa0fa64233d4d19b6ff1b614e1693cd/belgium-netherlands-exchange-territory-without-fight (reporting that "the two nations' parliaments should be able to complete a deal sometime in 2016").

[14] *See* JOSEPH WILLIAM SINGER, INTRODUCTION TO PROPERTY 1.1.1 (2d ed. Aspen Publishers 2005) (arguing that "it is preferable to define property as the relations among people with respect to valuable resources").

[15] *See, e.g.,* Craig Anthony Arnold, *The Reconstitution of Property: Property as a Web of Interests*, 26 HARV. ENVTL. L. REV. 281, 282 (2002) (advocating for "a new understanding of property as a web of interests" as opposed to "a bundle of rights"); Abraham Bell & Gideon Parchomovsky, *A Theory of Property*, 90 CORNELL L. REV. 531, 531 (2005) (proposing "a unified theory of property predicated on the insight that property law is organized around creating and defending the value inherent in stable ownership").

Horizontal Information: Who Gets It Now?
Good property rules identify who can do what, when, with which resources. The most basic problem in property systems is how to resolve conflicts between people who want to use a resource at the same time. To solve that problem, property law needs to make it easy for people to pass information back and forth to each other "horizontally" – information about what they intend to do and are permitted to do with resources they encounter. There are a lot of people out there. Imagine trying to inform each of them individually what rights they have with your property – or even that you claim a given resource as your property in the first place! Imagine sitting on your porch and trying to negotiate with each person who passes your house to not walk on your lawn and trample your daffodils.[16] You'd soon give up.

So we need something else, a way of conveying information to people without the need for individualized negotiation or massive amounts of signage. Property law does the work of a billion contracts or signs by creating a simple default rule of property. People can't use or trespass on someone else's property unless they work something out with the owner. The institution of property therefore conveys the information of a billion signs just by existing. And it applies not just to people with whom you have negotiated, or people who see the sign, but also to people who have never met you and have encountered something – say, your cell phone sitting alone and lonely on the table – that doesn't or can't have a sign on it. Or, as Cohen writes, property rights consist largely of the following information, conveyed to all who encounter an owned thing:

> *To the world:*
> *Keep off X unless you have my permission, which I may grant or withhold.*
> *Signed: Private citizen*
> *Endorsed: The state*[17]

The very existence of a property regime conveys enormous amounts of information to everyone who encounters every resource. It immediately divides information flows between the majority of people who only need to know to stay away from a given resource and those few who desire to use the property and thus know they must seek out the owner for further information exchange. So when I say that property rights are information, I do not mean merely that

---

[16] *See* Joshua A.T. Fairfield, *Anti-Social Contracts: The Contractual Governance of Virtual Worlds*, 53 McGill L.J. 427, 443–44 (2007) ("There is no law of nature that prohibits contracts from governing one-to-many relationships – but there is a law of mathematics that makes contracts decreasingly useful as the number of negotiating parties grows.").

[17] Cohen, *Dialogue on Private Property*, *supra* note 10, at 374.

they convey information about something else. They certainly do that. But in addition, they directly convey information by their existence.

The Information of Possession

One really easy way to tell others that you claim something is to pick it up – to possess it. That's why possession plays such a strong role in traditional property law. Possession signals to all others who encounter the resource that it is already claimed. Carol Rose, examining the perennially fascinating case *Pierson v. Post*, which asked whether pursuit or possession of a fox during the course of a fox hunt created an ownership right,[18] writes that "possession thus means a clear act, whereby all the world understands that the pursuer 'has an unequivocal intention of appropriating the animal to his individual use.'"[19] Possession is communication of information: "The clear-act principle suggests that the common law defines acts of possession as some kind of *statement*."[20] Thus, "[p]ossession now begins to look even more like something that requires a kind of communication, and the original claim to the property looks like a kind of speech, with the audience composed of all others who might be interested in claiming the object in question . . . . What 'possession' means is acts that apprise the community[,] . . . arrest attention, and put others claiming title upon inquiry."[21]

The court in *Pierson v. Post* applied the same rule for the "law of capture" that my daughters apply when they shout "Shotgun!" as we head to the car. An unmistakable act of appropriation communicates to others the intent to take the resource, which helps the community organize who gets what. Just as a warning turn signal in the parking lot tells other drivers that you claim that rare parking space, the act of possession means that the possessor lays claim to a resource that was previously unowned.

Possession is not, of course, all of ownership. Possession is only important to the extent it conveys good information. It is enough when the resource was previously unowned, perhaps, but when the resource has a history, or provenance, then possession is only valuable if it confirms and conveys information about that history. When the best available information (for example, a land record or title registry) indicates that a given person's possession is illegitimate, property law goes with the better information. As Rose puts it, provenance is the critical informational element needed to supplement possession, that is,

---

[18] Pierson v. Post, 3 Cai. R. 175, 2 Am. Dec. 264 (1805).

[19] CAROL M. ROSE, PROPERTY AND PERSUASION: ESSAYS ON THE HISTORY, THEORY, AND RHETORIC OF OWNERSHIP 12 (Westview Press 1994) [hereinafter PROPERTY AND PERSUASION] (quoting Pierson v. Post, 3 Cai. R. 175, 2 Am. Dec. 264 (1805)).

[20] *Id.* at 13.   [21] *Id.* at 14–15 (citations and quotations omitted).

whether possession was "derive[d] from a voluntary transfer."[22] In fact, most of the property rules we come up with deal with how to store the information created by the physical separation of owner and owned. Or, as one commentator wrote: "legitimate claims are based on history, beginning with just first possession and succeeded by voluntary transactions from just claimant to just claimant all the way to the present."[23] Writing down every transaction works for land, but for personal property, logging every owner and every transaction has historically been "too informationally demanding."[24] Thus, for personal property, possession acts as a cheap way to convey information about ownership. Present possession is history's compression algorithm.

Possession is by no means a perfect proxy for the history of provenance, but it is a great balance of cheap and clear. People can always subvert the information function of possession by possessing things they don't own without permission. That's theft. But, in general, possession provides reasonably good and really cheap information in situations where a full provenance record is not available. In short, possession is good information. Where it is trumped by better information – in a registry, for example – that better information governs. But where possession is the best indication of ownership that we can find, such as when the property has been lost or abandoned and we cannot determine who the true owner is, then possession restarts the physical chain of title under various flavors of whether the finder or another party – say, the proprietor of a restaurant where the item was found – is better positioned to restore the item to the original owner.

Vertical Information: Who Gets It Next?

So property rules help convey important information horizontally to people who may want to use a resource at the same time. They also help package important information for people who want to use property sequentially, one after another. Usually this is in the context of buying and selling. If I want to use your car after you are done with it, I can buy it from you. To do that, I need to know what I am getting when I buy the car. I need to know that you have not made my life complicated by promising anyone else that they can use the car too. I need to know that you haven't already sold it to someone else. Sequential provenance can also be in the context of inheritance. Who gets the family farm after someone dies – the nephew who got a secret deed

---

[22] Carol M. Rose, *The Law Is Nine-tenths of Possession: An Adage Turned on Its Head*, in LAW AND ECONOMICS OF POSSESSION 44 (Yun-chien Chang, ed. Cambridge University Press 2015) [hereinafter *Nine-Tenths*].

[23] *See id.* at 44.　　[24] *See id.* at 44 n.13.

during the testator's life or the niece who is named in the testator's will? These are questions of vertical information flow. The critical question is, who gets it next?

Problems of vertical information propagation are all over the law. Consider chain of title for land. Typically, a piece of land passes from person A to B to C by recording deeds in the local land registry. That works well, but what if A gives a deed to *both* B and C, and both claim ownership? What if C sells her interest in the land to D, who sells to E, who sells to F, only to find that B has passed his deed along to X, who sold to Y, and then to Z? Suddenly F and Z are in litigation over who owns the land. This scenario is pretty common, often as a result of poorly thought-out estate planning. A grandparent might provide a deed to a favored grandchild, but instruct that the deed not be recorded in the registry until after the grandparent passes away. But in the will, the land goes to another grandchild. If one grandchild sells the farm in good faith, and the other grandchild sells to another buyer, then the two buyers, both having paid good money in good faith for the farm, suddenly find themselves in conflict.

These "wild deed" dilemmas are purely ones of information. If a deed is not on file, third parties lack the information they need to determine their rights to the property. Recording statutes therefore provide incentives for parties to tell everyone else that they own the property by getting that claim on file. Often, the first person to file a record in the property registry stating her ownership claim to the rest of the world owns the property despite other subsequent or less-public claims. It's not a perfect system by any stretch of the imagination, but we can see that its goal is to transmit information about property to third parties.

Deed problems show us how information carries property interests with it. Imagine a land transaction. At first, just the buyer and seller know about the deal. Later, word about the deal spreads, either person-to-person or to everyone by a filing in the land records. Just as a stone thrown into a pond makes ripples, information about a property transaction alters the property rights of the people the information reaches as it spreads. Consider the case of a grandparent and grandchild in which the grandparent hands a land deed to the grandchild. As between those two, the grandchild takes the land. The conveyance of the deed is effective. But what if the grandparent provides two separate deeds to the family farm to two different grandchildren? Laws for recording interests vary, but the core of the matter is that the grandchild who publicly declares her ownership first by filing with a public ledger of land records is usually protected, as long as neither child knows about the other. Things get interesting, though, if one child knows about the conveyance to the other. If grandchild 2 knows about the conveyance to grandchild 1, then in some jurisdictions she cannot take away the interest of grandchild 1 simply by filing first.[25] The property interests shift purely as a function of the spread of information about the deal.

Let's take an example from a different area of law. Suppose I take my watch to a jewelry shop to have it cleaned. The jeweler sells it to a customer. Under the law of sales, the person who bought it can keep it.[26] Why? Normally, I can't just sell someone else your property. The answer lies in the information inherent in buying something in a shop. Property's position and context carry information. When a consumer sees the watch in the jeweler's case, she has every reason to believe, given the information in front of her, that the watch is for sale. It may seem crazy that the information available to the consumer would trump my ownership of the watch. Law uses this rule because if we could not be certain of settled property rights in our purchases, we would need to conduct expensive investigations into the true ownership of everything that we bought. Better that a few property interests be unfairly terminated (I'd be pretty mad about the watch, and I'd certainly expect the jeweler to make it right!) than everyone have to conduct some sort of title search on every television or watch that they purchase.

Consider adverse possession, an old and famous rule of property. If one person uses another person's property, openly and obviously, in a way that clearly indicates that the possessor is holding herself out as the true owner, then property law will eventually, after many years, treat the possessor as the owner. Again, we might reasonably ask, why? Adverse possession laws are unpopular: one view is that adverse possession rewards the theft of another's property as long as the possessor gets away with it for long enough.

A major rationale for adverse possession again has to do with information.[27] There are two ways to find out who owns what. You might look at the land records, or you might talk to the people who live on the property. When those two conflict, the land records are the traditional trump card, because they usually represent better information. However, the context of property and the information the context conveys has meaning. The information created by actively possessing and using the land over a long period can eventually come

[25] *See, e.g.,* CAL. CIV. CODE § 1214 (2016) (granting a recorded conveyance priority over a prior unrecorded conveyance only if done "in good faith").

[26] *See* U.C.C. § 2-403(2) (2002) ("Any entrusting of possession of goods to a merchant who deals in goods of that kind gives him power to transfer all rights of the entruster to a buyer in ordinary course of business.").

[27] *See* Rose, *Nine-Tenths, supra* note 22, at 53 (arguing that "the numerous cases of adverse possession reinforce the idea that for purposes of the law, "possession" does not mean the rule of the stronger, but rather simply acting like a legal owner").

to trump the information recorded in the land record. Adverse possession isn't really a fight between an owner and a possessor – it's a conflict between two methods of storing information about ownership. One person is proclaiming ownership through the land record system, and the other is proclaiming ownership by actual, obvious, adverse, and exclusive possession and use of the land.

Some scholars think adverse possession rules are mostly about getting land into productive use. If I am not going to develop my farm, perhaps some squatter will – so I had better get to plowing and building, or sell it to someone else who will. But I am bearish on this theory. Adverse possession is a pretty lousy way to incentivize productivity. It takes years, and pretty much anything can interrupt the period of adverse possession. Adverse possession takes too long to incentivize either owners or squatters to really develop the property.

The overwhelming majority of adverse possession cases clarify boundary disputes between neighbors. If I build my garage one foot over onto your property and we only discover the mistake when you go to sell your land twenty years later, must I tear down my garage? The rule clarifies who owns what by harmonizing the information encoded by physical use of the land with the information encoded in the title database. So I don't think adverse possession is mostly about incentives. We don't want to incentivize people to just take others' property anyway. Instead, adverse possession is about information.

The idea once again is that possession can act as a crude proxy for chain of title.[28] In one sense, possession broadcasts information horizontally: the neighbors think that a person in possession of land is the true owner. But in another sense, if that possession continues uninterrupted and for a long time, it begins to convey information about the vertical provenance of the claim. As Rose notes, "[p]ossession itself does give *evidence* of title. Indeed, it gives a quite powerful kind of evidence."[29] After all, if a person uses the property as if she were the owner for a very long, uninterrupted time, there is some evidence that her claim may be free of conflict because in all that time no one has come along to challenge her ownership.

So while property law acts to convey information through title and possession, it also seeks to simplify and streamline information by removing complicating claims that can shift property interests years or even decades after a transaction. Some of the more feudal forms of property, such as the "fee tail male," which kept property of the English nobility firmly in the hands of

---

[28] *See id.* at 45 (observing that "judges . . . treat possession only as evidence of the more important issue" of "title").

[29] *Id.* at 47.

the male heirs, have been eradicated. Other rules, like the infamously thorny rule against perpetuities, may themselves be complicated, but act to simplify property enormously. Briefly, the rule against perpetuities blocks a property owner from attaching certain kinds of conditions to her property that would cause interests to shift long after she and everyone she was thinking about in her estate planning was dead. It's a way of simplifying ownership interests over time. It does so by eliminating the offending interest, and returning ownership to simple "I just own it" status.

As these examples show, a major function of property law is to package information about property rights so that the property can be neatly passed from one person to another. All of these traditional property rules demonstrate that where a "true" ownership interest (that is, the first-in-time interest in the property that was legally recognized and enforceable) conflicts with an informational interest (such as a consumer who buys my watch from the jeweler, or a buyer of land who files first without notice of a first conveyance), the informational interest prevails.

Information and Physicality

We tend to separate the physical world from a supposedly distinct informational world.[30] One example would be our separation of the "real world" from "cyberspace."[31] This separation of information from physicality is a recent and wrong invention. We have always recorded information physically. Street signs are physical, and they convey information. Many people can tell the make and model of an F-150 truck just by looking at it. Property's physical characteristics, whether color, size, styling, make, model, version, edition, or anything else, convey information. If we examine the information that physical objects have always conveyed, we will see that physical property systems, by extension, have always been about information. So it will not be hard to replicate those characteristics in information environments like the internet or its more recent incarnation, the Internet of Things.

The Information of Physicality
Physicality has been consistently important for property law not because it is itself important, but because physicality conveys certain information cheaply and obviously. This is well understood by children squabbling over a toy. They

---

[30] *See generally* Joshua A.T. Fairfield, *The Magic Circle*, 11 VAND. J. ENT. & TECH. L. 823 (2009).
[31] Dan Hunter, *Cyberspace as Place and the Tragedy of the Digital Anticommons*, 91 CAL. L. REV. 439 (2003); Mark A. Lemley, *Place and Cyberspace*, 91 CAL. L. REV. 521 (2003).

understand that the physicality of the toy means there is only one of it. The person with physical possession has enormous advantages in enjoying the toy.

Consider the old case of *Haslem v. Lockwood.*[32] The dispute was over manure: the plaintiff's servants had scooped the manure up into piles, intending to cart it off later. The defendant, without knowing of the plaintiff's actions, came and got the manure first. The court said the fact that the manure had been moved into piles should have conveyed information to the defendant. Even though the defendant did not actually know the plaintiff wanted the manure, he was on notice because the piles conveyed – or should have conveyed – that information. The court therefore gave ownership of the manure piles to the plaintiff. It's a down-to-earth case, but one that we invoke every time we save seats at a theater by draping coats over chairbacks.[33] We use physical markers to indicate that we intend to possess and use a given resource, allowing others to coordinate by looking elsewhere for their own resources. A sign on a tree that says "No trespass" is both very physical and also the basic statement of property exclusion.

Physicality was never the opposite of intangible information, nor is it now. Information is always carried on a physical medium that represents it. Today, the actual mechanisms of computing are hidden away in silicon chips and behind the smooth surfaces of servers. It is easy to forget that physicality is a way of recording information. Think about writing something down. The paper, the pencil, and the marks are all physical, and the marks record information. When we more closely examine those physical elements of property that matter for property law, we find that they are precisely those features that convey information. That is your decaf soy latte – your name is on it.

In particular, the position, context, and physical attributes of property are information. Consider the board game Chutes and Ladders (or Snakes and Ladders, depending on where you lived growing up). Players roll dice and move their figure up the game board. The figures slide down chutes and climb up ladders in an attempt to reach the end. What is interesting is that the physical game figures serve as a very simple way of recording a state that is the combined information of the game thus far.

We can think of all property as a giant game of Chutes and Ladders. As an experiment, look around the room in which you are reading this book. Pick an object. Consider how the current placement and position of that object is the end result of that object's entire history. Perhaps the object is another book, printed, transported across the country, stored in a bookstore, purchased by someone, driven home in a car (or, more likely, delivered via Amazon Prime,

---

[32] 37 Conn. 500 (1871).   [33] *See* Rose, *Nine-Tenths, supra* note 22, at 50.

but you get the point), brought into the home, placed on the bookshelf, and
taken down to read. The book's physical location sums up that information. (It
does not encapsulate all of it, of course.) The book's pages may bear the marks
of hard reading – lines underlined and highlighted, pages folded, sticky notes
appended. Even the reader's progress in the book can be recorded physically,
via a bookmark.

The information-recording attributes of property are not to be taken lightly.
Cash, for instance, is undoubtedly physical, but its physical attributes are not
the point, other than the number printed on the bills.[34] Rather, cash serves
as a recording mechanism for resource allocation in a community. We could
remember who owes who what by writing everything down in a big ledger,
but it is easier to simply have bits of paper that record the state of allocation in
a huge, distributed, and physical database. Or, as one article puts it, money is
society's memory.[35]

In summary, to the extent property law has focused on the physical features
of objects or land, it has not done so for the sake of those features, but for
the sake of the information those features encode. A tree marking the edge of
my property is not important because it is beautiful, or because it produces
apples, but because it marks an intangible, informational boundary between
my land and my neighbor's. Once we notice this, we are freed from needing
any physicality in property systems. The boundary between my land and my
neighbor's can be marked by GPS coordinates just as well (or better) than
by the old apple tree. All we need to run a good property system is good
information.

The Information of "Thing"-ness

One valuable thing physicality does is communicate the extent of property
to everyone who comes into contact with the asset, without the need for the
owner to inform everyone personally. Borders between countries need not
follow geographical features, but they might, because the terrain can serve as
a useful referent for third parties. Similarly, the idea of "thing-ness" contains
important information as to the extent of property rights. Imagine that you
owned a "handful of sand" out of an entire sandbox. It would be hard to
determine where your property rights began or ended. But if you owned one
brick out of a stack of bricks, you would know your rights with much more

---

[34] *See* Narayana R. Kocherlakota, Federal Reserve Bank of Minneapolis Research
Department Staff Report 218: Money is Memory 2 (1996), https://www.minneapolisfed
.org/research/sr/sr218.pdf (noting that "money itself is intrisically useless").
[35] *Id.*

certainty. The hard delineation of the physical form makes the determination of rights much easier. Or, imagine that you rent a car with a built-in GPS. There is little chance you would think you couldn't use the GPS as part of your rental. However, if the GPS is rented separately from the car, you understand that you will need to enter a separate transaction to have right to use the separate module.

Merging physical forms changes the informational nature of the object. Vanilla ice cream plus root beer makes a root beer float: a different informational "thing." If you buy a furnace, it is personal property. If you install the furnace in your home, it becomes part of the house (this is aptly termed a "fixture").[36] The reason it does so is that we generally think that things joined to the home are part of it. Things not joined to the home (say, your furniture) remain personal property, not real estate. The physical fact of joining is important for its informational content. Physical joining determines which "thing" we are talking about when we discuss a property interest.

I owned a house in Indiana when I first became an academic. It had a porch swing and a large brass dinner bell mounted on the front of the house. When it came time to sell the house, there was some back-and-forth between our family and the buyer: did the bell and the swing come with the house or not? The reason we had to discuss those two things out of everything in the house was because, while they were attached to the house, they could have been unbolted or unhooked with relatively little effort. And conceptually, the bell and the swing fit less easily within the concept of a "house." Although windows and doors can be removed, they are certainly part of what we think of when we think of the "house" object. As a result, while additional information needed to be exchanged about the bell and swing (we finally decided to leave them both), there were thousands of parts that had been incorporated into the house that needed no discussion. Windows, doors, handles, switches, and wiring all went with the house without discussion. Their physical bond to the house meant they became part of the house "thing." On the other hand, even though the buyer viewed the house with all our furniture in it, there was never any question about whether desks, beds, pictures, chairs, silverware, or our dog, Jack, would go with the house when sold. Those remained separate "things." The carpets went with the house, the rugs came with us, and no questions needed to be asked. That is the informational power of a "thing."

Finally, physicality is important for purposes of bounding complexity. Consider a desktop computer tower. If you have ever taken the case off one, you are aware that the case is just a shell. It creates a neat package surrounding the

---

[36] U.C.C. § 9-102(a)(41) (Am. Law Inst. & Unif. Law Comm'n 2016).

complexity inside the box. The case defines the limit of what the computer is, never mind that more, fewer, or different components might be included within. The idea of buying "a computer" and not "a collection of linked memory, wires, a fan, and processors" has more to do with the case than any component inside.

"Thing"-ness is about information. A "thing" is a conceptual shorthand for a collection of components and processes, grouped together for informational convenience. So if "property is the law of things,"[37] that is not because things are physical or important in their own right, but because of the information conveyed by their "thing"-ness. Once we understand the informational importance of "things," we can begin to replicate them online, to create digital objects and things that encapsulate a neat box of resources and processes.

Rivalrousness and Scarcity
Physical property encodes information about the number of people who can use it through the physical characteristic of rivalrousness. Rivalrousness means that if I have a thing, you don't. Imagine a vinyl record. If I give it to you, I don't have it any more. We are rivals for its possession, hence the term. If an asset is non-rivalrous, both you and I can have it at the same time. Consider the same recording, but as an MP3. I can give you an identical copy of the MP3 without giving up my own copy. The MP3 is non-rivalrous. Rivalrousness has always been the dividing line between traditional and intellectual property. As Judge Richard Posner has written, the key distinguishing feature of intellectual property is that others can copy it at near-zero cost.[38] Physicality has been traditionally connected to rivalrousness, because it has traditionally cost more to make physical copies than to make digital copies. We have tended to sort products into one camp or the other on the basis of physicality, when what we are really interested in is whether the product is rivalrous.

The fact of rivalrousness is critical information for product manufacturers. If property is largely an exercise in managing information about who owns what, rivalrousness is property's way of leveraging physicality to limit *how many whos* own each *what*, with the default being one *who* to one *what*. The maker of a CD knows that the physical CD is one copy, one sale, generally to one person. Physicality isn't important, but that limitation is. Without that limitation, a manufacturer creates a competitor every time she sells a

---

[37] *See supra* note 9.
[38] *See* Richard Posner, *Antitrust in the New Economy*, 68 ANTITRUST L.J. 925 (2001) (observing that "it is only a slight overstatement to speak of marginal cost [of copying intellectual property] as zero").

product. The buyer could make infinite copies and go into business for herself selling those copies. This is the basic problem with online ownership. Online ownership has therefore been marked by a quest for digital rivalrousness.

Rivalrousness becomes profitable through the mechanism of scarcity. The two characteristics are closely related. If an asset is rivalrous, then its scarcity can be managed. I cannot easily make another copy of the vinyl record. That means the vinyl record can be rare, which in turn increases its value. So, for example, the Wu-Tang Clan auctioned off a single copy of their album *Once Upon a Time in Shaolin*. The scarcity of the album was intentional – limiting it to a single copy – and was a bit of a publicity stunt. The price rose accordingly: the album was purchased for $2 million by rap fanatic and pharmaceutical price gouger Martin Shkreli.[39]

Rivalrousness creates the possibility of managed scarcity. There have always been rivalrous objects that are not truly scarce in the hands of the manufacturer. Take the most valuable baseball cards, or Magic cards, or Beanie Babies, or whatever fad your generation suffered from. The manufacturer can make as many of the supposedly scarce and valuable Peanut the Royal Blue Elephant dolls (price tag around $3,000),[40] "Black Lotus" Magic cards (one sold on eBay for close to $27,000),[41] or Mickey Mantle baseball cards as it wants, but by destroying the managed scarcity, it would destroy the value of the items. By managing scarcity, the manufacturer can ensure that it profits from its creation.

The key to creating scarcity for manufacturers is managing rivalrousness once the goods reach consumers. Scarcity permits manufacturers to extract value from different market segments. Where rivalrousness and scarcity don't naturally occur – say in full intellectual property – then we need strong rules against copying in order to stop the market for the MP3 from being destroyed by digital pirates. Yet, notice that digital piracy doesn't really have much to do with *Once Upon a Time in Shaolin*. Physicality provides a form of natural copy protection.

---

[39] See Christine Hauser, *Martin Shkreli Bought Sole Wu-Tang Clan Album, Report Says*, N.Y. TIMES (Dec. 9, 2015), http://www.nytimes.com/2015/12/10/business/media/martin-shkreli-wu-tang-clan-album.html?_r=0.

[40] *See* Alyson Shontell, *TY WARNER: How to Create Mass Hysteria and Pocket $2.4 Billion Dollars*, BUS. INSIDER (June 1, 2011, 9:00 AM), http://www.businessinsider.com/how-to-create-a-ravenous-fad-and-pocket-6-billion-dollars-2011-5 ("The most expensive Beanie Baby, Peanut the royal blue elephant, was sold for over $3,000 on eBay in 2000.").

[41] Amanda Kooser, *Guy Opens Old Magic: The Gathering Deck, Stumbles on $27,000 Card*, CNET (Oct. 14, 2014, 10:13 AM), http://www.cnet.com/news/guy-opens-old-magic-the-gathering-deck-stumbles-on-27000-card.

But physicality is not the only way to create rivalrousness and scarcity. We can recreate the rules of physicality through code. Doing so is especially easy, since we do not need all of the characteristics of physicality. We just need rivalrousness, and through rivalrousness, scarcity. Consider baseball trading cards. They work because the cards are physically rivalrous, and some cards are scarce and valuable. Yet as anyone with a smartphone knows, collectible trading card apps and games are knocking it out of the park. Trading cards and collectible card games work just as well electronically as they do physically. All we have to do is mimic the rules of trade, rivalrousness, and scarcity that made cards collectible offline. We can code the rules of scarcity and rivalrousness into electronic objects so that they appear and act, to a human, like a regular piece of property. I will look at some of these systems in depth in the next chapter, but for now it is important to note that the most critical element of these systems is maintaining information: who owns which cards, or bitcoins, or whatever the resource might be.

The Information of Property

Scholars have already done some excellent work on the informational characteristics of property rules. Their arguments aren't quite the same as those raised here, but they are worth discussing. They argue that property law makes it easier to get information about property, which reduces transaction costs. So, for example, if you own land in what lawyers call "fee simple absolute" – where you are the true owner uncomplicated by other interests – you don't have to ask a lot of questions about who else could claim the land. It's yours, plain and simple. That "plain and simple" is a matter of information costs. It doesn't cost you much to find out what you can do with your land, because the property forms – the limited available types of legal ownership – keep it simple for you.

This is not quite the same as the arguments in this book. The information-cost literature treats information as a costly byproduct of property transactions that needs to be streamlined by property rules. Henry Smith writes: "I argue that the baselines that property furnishes, as well as their refinements and equitable safety valves, are shaped by information costs."[42] That is true, but it does not go far enough. I do not propose that property law is shaped by information costs; I think that property is pure information. If I say, "There is a cow," we know nothing. If I tell you *who* may do *what* under *which*

---

[42] Smith, *supra* note 9, at 1691.

circumstances and in *which time frame* with the cow, we know who owns it. Without that information, the cow is not property. With it, it is.

There is nevertheless a close relationship between property-as-information and the literature of property information costs. Both explore how information about property can be streamlined and communicated. Both identify ways to neatly package information about resources and relationships between users in a way that improves information flow. A lot of my thinking about property-as-information was inspired by the information-cost literature, and I believe its arguments about simplicity and modularity are well worth exploring as a foundation for where the law of digital and smart property might go from here.

Numerus Clausus: Movie Night

When I was growing up in Virginia in the 1980s, our family didn't have a television. My friend James had only one movie on VHS: *Return of the Jedi*. So when I spent the night and we watched a movie, we knew which movie we were going to watch. Not a lot of information needed to change hands. Our choices were constrained, but that constraint made choosing what to watch cheap, quick, and easy. Plus, Luke Skywalker's green lightsaber was cool.

On the other hand, anyone who has tried to decide what movie to watch on Netflix with a group of friends or family knows what an exercise in discussion, negotiation, and frustration that can become. The more movies we have, the harder it is to decide what to watch; more time may be spent negotiating than watching the movie! Psychologist Barry Schwartz lays this out in his book, *The Paradox of Choice*: the more choices we have, the more cognitive load we must bear.[43] Extreme choice may lead to choice paralysis. If a person can do anything, she may well do nothing. That is supposedly why Steve Jobs wore the same black turtleneck and jeans every day. It reduced "decision fatigue."[44]

That's the basic tension between contract law and property law. With contract law you can get exactly what you want out of a deal. All you have to do is write it out in the contract and get the other party to agree. That takes a lot of information exchange. With property law, you can only get one of a very few choices. You can own a lot of different kinds of property, but you can only own it in one of a very few ways. And even among those different ways, there is a strong gravitational pull toward the simplicity of outright ownership. No complications. This pull reduces the need to exchange information, because the range of choices is constrained.

---

[43] Barry Schwartz, The Paradox of Choice: Why More is Less 2 (Harper Perennial 2014).
[44] *See* John Tierney, *Do You Suffer From Decision Fatigue*, N.Y. Times (Aug. 17, 2011), http://www.nytimes.com/2011/08/21/magazine/do-you-suffer-from-decision-fatigue.html?_r=0

Simplicity is important for property because property rules do not just affect the two people who trade a piece of property. They shift the rights of everyone else, too, even of people not involved in the deal. Consider what would happen if, for example, a town sold a public park to a private buyer. Before the sale, citizens of the town could use the park. After the sale, they cannot. The citizens weren't directly part of the sale, but their ability to use the park shifted. So property rules both keep short our list of ways we can hold property and favor the simplest forms.

Tom Merrill and Henry Smith theorize that property rules reduce information costs.[45] They tell a simple story. Imagine that you own a bicycle, and that I would like to use it on Tuesdays to get to work. You and I can certainly enter into a contractual agreement to let me do that. That agreement will bind the two of us, but no one else. But let's say you wanted to sell me a property right in the bicycle for Tuesday mornings. I would have the right to use the bicycle on Tuesday mornings even if you sold the bicycle to someone else. That's a different matter. Property law generally excludes such rights. They complicate the property. If someone were to want to buy the bicycle, they would have to check around and make sure that someone like me wouldn't come and take it unexpectedly on Tuesday mornings.

Merrill and Smith use the term *Numerus Clausus*, Latin for "the number is closed," to describe this simplicity function of property law.[46] The idea is the same as my *Return of the Jedi* movie selection. Property law imposes a strong gravitational pull toward simplicity precisely because property rules control third parties. If a property rule is going to affect a third party, it had best be as simple as possible so that the third party can understand if she may use the property, or if she can buy it without worrying about complicating interests.

Numerus Clausus is very important for our project of protecting digital and smart property. If you were to sell me the Tuesday morning bicycle right, Merrill and Smith would object because that arrangement complicates matters for other, potential buyers. Buyers do not know what they are getting when they buy, and don't know what they are permitted to do with what they bought. This sounds remarkably like the terms of agreement for the smartphone I just bought.

Every carve-out right, like the Tuesday morning right, increases the costs of buying and using property. An analogy may help here. You may recall from high school physics that the unit of resistance for electrical current is called

---

45 Thomas W. Merrill & Henry E. Smith, *Optimal Standardization in the Law of Property: The Numerus Clausus Principle*, 110 YALE L.J. 1, 8 (2000).
46 *Id.* at 4.

an "ohm." By analogy, let us define the unit of resistance and hassle for a property owner as a "shenanigan." Our Tuesday morning bicycle right would be a textbook "shenanigan." The owner's life would be complicated by my right to use the bicycle on Tuesday mornings. (By the way, the legal term for "shenanigan" is "servitude," a right held in the property of another, but I like my term better.)

The more shenanigans that glom onto a piece of property, the more hassle people face in trying to buy, use, or sell it. It would not take too many shenanigans before the piece of property loses its value entirely and no one wants to buy it. This is why the law of personal property usually does not permit shenanigans.[47] Real property, like houses and land, does permit some shenanigans. But personal property tends to be lower in value than houses and land, so it doesn't take as many shenanigans to bog it down.[48]

The problem with digital and smart property is that they are currently riddled with shenanigans. In legal speak, property law generally does not permit personal property servitudes, but companies have recreated these servitudes through the End User License Agreements for software embedded in the devices.[49] Our smartphones are swarming with use restrictions, and our digital media accounts are so bound up in contractual shenanigans that we are back to step one: no one knows what she is getting when she buys a piece of smart or digital property. Companies' shenanigans are significantly impeding our ability to control, use, and sell our own property. Merrill and Smith's *Numerus Clausus* theory helps us understand why we shouldn't have to put up with all of these shenanigans.

Modularity: A Lesson from Legos

There is another way property rules help to clarify and simplify the flow of information resources. Henry Smith calls the concept "modularity."[50] A module is a part that can be fitted into a whole without requiring extensive restructuring. Think of Lego bricks. A single Lego is a module. Imagine that you built a toy car out of dozens of Lego. You could take one Lego brick out of the car and substitute another one without having to rebuild the entire car. But you could not do that with a standard plastic toy car. There, if you broke off the plastic door, you would need to get a new toy car.

---

[47] *See* Christina M. Mulligan, *Personal Property Servitudes on the Internet of Things*, 50 Ga. L. Rev. 1121, 1227 (2016) (noting that "as a general matter, chattels cannot be burdened with servitudes").

[48] *Id.*   [49] *See generally id.* (analogizing license EULAs to servitudes).

[50] *See* Smith, *supra* note 9, at 1700.

Modules contain and encapsulate complexity. If you have ever worked on your own computer, you know that RAM comes in modules. It is not hard to change the RAM on your computer because you can simply pull one module out and swap another module in. The RAM itself is of course incredibly complicated. The motherboard is complicated. But the module of RAM is easy to swap in and out of the motherboard.

Here we must be careful. Lots of physical objects are modular. The water pump in my car is modular: it can be swapped out without having to change every other component under the hood. But that is not all that Smith means when he says that property is modular. What he means is that property rules help us swap property between us simply, and help pieces of property fit together smoothly. They keep the interface between people simple and uncomplicated. Single-person fee simple absolute ownership is, when you think about it, an odd way to hold property. I own a car. But other people borrow it all the time. My children benefit from it and ride in the back. Why would law say that I own it in fee simple absolute?

Simple ownership preserves a tidy interface between me and anyone else who wants to buy my property. If someone wishes to buy my car, they just need to talk to me, not my brother who regularly borrows the car, or my children who ride to school in the back. The fiction of single-person fee simple absolute ownership keeps the property interest modular. It means that all the complicated side deals and relationships that may affect a given piece of property (like the fact that I use the car to drive my third daughter to cello lessons on Thursday nights) do not affect third parties. When someone comes to buy the car from me, it transfers smoothly, like a Lego brick detached from one Lego creation and attached to another.

Physicality isn't entirely out of the picture, however. Remember, physical traits have informational content. As Smith observes, the law gives a "special respect . . . to physical objects [because] the objects themselves provide an excellent form of fixed rule. The contours of an object . . . establish a boundary that is highly resistant to revision in a particular dispute."[51] Think of the concept of a "part" in a car. The part is made with tidy inputs and outputs so that it can be swapped out modularly, but also so that it can be built into a greater whole. Property becomes, quite literally, building blocks for more complicated forms of property. This would cause an impenetrable muddle of rights if the legal rights were not carefully aligned with the boundaries of the part. So we finally get to the root of property's obsession with physicality. Property relies on physicality not for its own sake, but because physicality conveys information.

[51] *Id.*

When we recreate the informational rules of physicality, and maybe improve on them, we can make digital things that feel to humans like property.

Creating Digital Things

It is relatively easy to talk about property claims in smart property. Smart property – your Fitbit, for one – is at least partially physical. Digital property is harder. What is the digital thing we are talking about when the consumer's experience is often an amalgam of a local client application that interprets data, a remote server that contains at least some of the data, and perhaps many other computing processes, some local and some remote? Consider a movie you have purchased on Google Play. You might download the movie remotely through your account, you might stream it if you can't wait to watch it, and there is likely some combination of the two. The movie is likely buffered locally even if it is supposed to be streamed, and it is likely downloaded while you are watching if you select the download option. You can even delete the movie to free up space on a tablet, then re-stream or download it when you watch it the next time. How can this series of distributed technologies be made to fit into the category of a "thing"?

For the purpose of this discussion, a thing is a thing when it is designed to appear that way to a human. It is a thing when it has been specifically identified, packaged, and delineated as a thing. Remember, "thing"-ness is information. It is a communication between people. It is the answer to the consumer's question "What am I buying here?" There is a reason Amazon sells us "e-books" and not "temporary access to electronic words." The word "e-book" calls on the long-standing thing-ness of books. Even though there is no technological difference between an e-book and a webpage, humans respond very differently to the perceived thing-ness of an e-book.

As Michael Madison has explained in his exhaustive discussion of thing-ness in law, things can be found (a pebble) or designed (a bank account).[52] There is an extensive literature regarding what thing-ness means in law and in culture, and I don't want to reinvent that particular wheel. What is important to me is how things appear, who designed them to appear that way, and why that design decision was made. People pay more for things they buy than for things they rent. When a company designs a digital object to trigger people to pay more by using "buy" language, I think we shouldn't care what the technology underlying the "thing" is. We should instead look to the impact on the buyer.

---

[52] Michael Madison, *Law as Design: Objects, Concepts, and Digital Things*, 56 CASE W. RES. L. REV. 381 (2005).

What information does the supposed form of the property and the form of the transaction transmit to a buyer?

The boundaries of things are fuzzy, especially when there is no physical form to set commonsense limits on the thing. Consider a copyrighted "work." It starts as an idea, not a thing, and passes through manuscripts and drafts, which might be things, and ends up as a book on a shelf in a bookstore, where it is definitely a thing. I don't care where it becomes a thing in that process. That's a question that has occupied a lot of scholars' time, but we don't need to go into it here. What interests me is that it has, at some point, become a thing.

We can make an immaterial thing by defining the thing with particularity, by defining boundaries to the thing that mimic the distinctness and boundaries of a physical object, and by making it distinguishable from other things. A thing must be particular. Digital property can be made particular by assigning each of them a separate identification number. That's what license servers do. A thing must have boundaries. Again, not a problem: boundaries are part of the modularity we have been talking about. One can think of thing-ness as wrapping up complexity in a neat package, kind of like a holiday present. Finally, we must be able to tell one thing from another. Things are things if they can be differentiated from one another. Consider a wool sweater. The yarn is so woven together that we perceive the sweater as a thing, rather than its individual threads. If those threads were neatly separated and wound on spools, we would see them as separate things.

Thingness is about perception. My father is a computer scientist, now retired. The early focus in his career was machine vision – how to get computers to see the way we do. Consider a person sitting behind a desk. The desk appears to cut the person in half. A machine might view "torso" as one thing, while seeing the "legs" as a separate thing, because the desk is in the way. Yet we perceive the person to be whole. The desk does not interfere with the informational integrity of the person. We just see a person and a desk. Two separate things. How we see is defined by the contours of the objects we encounter. We know it's a desk and a person because we are informed by knowledge of those objects.

I am less interested in whether or not digital things exist, since we can design digital objects that we perceive to exist, and can back up that perception with technology. I am more interested in boundaries of things as communicated, especially as communicated to consumers under conditions of information asymmetry. The seller knows all of the technological complexity that goes on under the surface. The user simply sees "Buy now!" and sees an object downloaded onto their computer. Thing-ness is a powerful legal and cultural move. When a company creates an intentionally bounded, distinct, and differentiable object with the purpose of packaging a resource for sale, we shouldn't engage in sweaty metaphysics to undo the thing-ness of the resulting digital object.

In summary, property rights are information. Traditional property rules, including the oldest and most venerated, are about packaging and conveying information. To the extent property law has focused on physical features of objects or land, it has focused on those features that convey information. To the extent property law focuses on things, it is because "thing"-ness carries information. We can replicate the information that property law has traditionally needed using electronic systems, which are better at handling information anyway. And when we do, we can create digital things: fully intangible informational objects that trigger the same responses in humans that physical objects do. Once we understand the nature of property as information, we can build fully intangible information-based property systems. As the next chapter shows, we have already started.

CHALLENGES TO PROPERTY-AS-INFORMATION

Defining property as information raises some valid and valuable questions, which I briefly address here. These questions can be grouped into two broad categories. First, can property be reduced to information if property rules must be enforced in the real world? Second, does a theory of property-as-information mean that all information is property?

Enforcing Property

How can property be purely information when real police with real guns are necessary to enforce property rights? And if the fact that a property right will be enforced is just more information, then what *isn't* information? Wouldn't all laws, including complicated areas of law like constitutional civil rights, be just more information?

Property is a particularly good area for using information theory. Unlike constitutional rights, which are muddy and not susceptible to neat categorization, property's project is the delineation of clear rights to promote the use and sale of resources. That's property's purpose, its central point. Property has always been about metes and bounds, about geolocation coordinates, about recording who owns what in lists and ledgers. Property has always focused on the information connecting people to resources. Civil liberties aren't like that: they're imprecise negotiations between groups of people and the government.

Sure, they could be reduced to information too, but the math is fuzzier, less defined. We don't record civil liberties on a register – and when we do, for example, with No Fly, No Vote, or No Work lists, the results are pretty ugly.[53] Now, if you pressed me, I would agree that everything is in fact information. Life is information coded on a DNA helix. But we don't need to go that far here. Property is an area of law that is particularly focused on information, and is therefore ripe for applying basic principles of information theory. In fact, I'd make an even stronger claim. It's not just that all law is information to some extent and more so with property. Property reduces nearly entirely to information. In other words, information is necessary in all areas of law, but in property, it's practically sufficient.

The other question is how property can be information when it requires physical enforcement. Enforcement is not particularly special to property. People with guns have to enforce all laws. As Hernando de Soto writes in *The Mystery of Capital*: "Formal property's contribution to mankind is not the protection of ownership; squatters, housing organizations, mafias, and even primitive tribes manage to protect their assets quite efficiently. Property's real breakthrough is that it radically improved the flow of communications about assets and their potential."[54] I'm more interested in the flow of information that makes de Soto's property revolution possible. And as a practical aside, if police with guns are going to be enforcing laws, then we want them to be doing so using the very best information.

Further, at the risk of chasing a sacred cow of property theory, I am not certain that state enforcement is absolutely central to the core idea of property. A lot of property theory gets worked out by my children arguing over toys, and the state (c'est moi) rarely gets involved. Do we consider only property arrangements specifically created and enforced by the state to be property? Ask the "owners" of parking spaces in Chicago who have dug their spot out of a snow bank and reserved it with a parking chair.[55] Ask ranchers in the West, who work out their own rules for grazing and enforce those rules without asking government to intervene.[56] Sure, government enforces some property arrangements, and knowing government is standing guard in the background

---

53 *See* Margaret Hu, *Big Data Blacklisting*, 67 FLA. L. REV. 1735, 1738 (2015) ("Big data blacklisting harms result from the mediation of and interference with fundamental liberty interests.").
54 HERNANDO DE SOTO, THE MYSTERY OF CAPITAL 59 (Basic Books 2000).
55 *See* Susan S. Silbey, *Invocations of Law on Snowy Streets*, 5 J. COMP. L. 66, 66 (2010), *available at* http://anthropology.mit.edu/sites/default/files/documents/silbey_jlocke_pub.pdf (detailing the practice of claiming parking spots in northern American cities).
56 *See* ROBERT ELLICKSON, ORDER WITHOUT LAW 72 (Harvard University Press 1992) (discussing "customs" among ranchers that "everybody understands")

gives force to property deals. But the majority of property activity doesn't directly call on government to enforce it. The point of private property is that it implies that the owners can make certain uses and transfers of property without asking the government for permission. It's easy for us to get caught up in enforcement, and perhaps in some systems government is the sole source of property. But that's not our system. In our system, the very point of property is that we've divorced a lot of the decision making about resource use from the sole control of government. It's important that the government, after the fact, comes along and enforces property arrangements between owners once they've been concluded, but that enforcement doesn't change what the property rights are.

Information Is Not Property

I want to be clear that although all property is information, all information is not property. That would be a tempting route to take. Consider the benefits to our personal privacy, for example, in asserting a property right in information about us.[57] That's a tempting proposition, because it makes our information something that businesses would have to negotiate with us for before they could take it. Some theorists speculate that property interests would help us control downstream uses of our information.[58] So if I own the information that I have a rare genetic disorder, I might be able to reach out and stop third-party advertisers from advertising to me on that basis.

As tempting as that view of the world is, I think we'll have to let it go. First, propertizing information is hard. Can I own the fact that the sky is blue? Can I sue anyone who uses the fact that the sky is blue? This is a real question in law. Everyone can see that the sky is blue, but some facts take a lot of work to uncover. Or, at least, it takes a lot of work to organize simple facts into a useful database. Even so, law in the United States has not recognized the right of someone who researches or gathers and organizes facts to sue anyone else for using those facts.[59] Facts are just too important. We need to be able to use them freely to function in the world. So creating a property interest in facts,

---

[57] *See generally* Paul Schwartz, *Property, Privacy, and Personal Data*, 117 Harv. L. Rev. 2055 (2004) (discussing personal information as a commodity); *cf.* Pam Samuelson, *Privacy as Intellectual Property?*, 52 Stan. L. Rev. 1125, 1137–38 (1999) ("Achieving information privacy goals through a property rights system may be difficult for reasons other than market complexities. Chief among them is the difficulty with alienability of personal information.").

[58] *See* Schwartz, *supra* note 56, at 2096 (discussing "how a variety of devices and systems that commodify information lead to downstream uses and onward transfers").

[59] *See* Feist Publications, Inc. v. Rural Telephone Service Co., 499 U.S. 340, 364 (1991) (rejecting a copyright claim for a "white pages" compilation of phone numbers).

even if they are facts about me (like my receding hairline) that I would prefer not be publicized, is perhaps not a wise move.

Second, propertizing personal information may not promote privacy. It may well do the opposite.[60] Propertizing personal information just packages it for sale.[61] If I sell a record, the value to the buyer is that she may do what she wishes with it. She may destroy it, sell it to someone else, play it, or use it as a Frisbee. That freedom is precisely what this book is about. So if information about me is my property, and I transfer that property in exchange for the use of a site, service, or device, then the information is forever out of my control and is packaged cleanly for low-cost resale to advertisers or aggregators in the stream of commerce.[62]

Third, using property to provide additional downstream control for data – that is, control of data once it leaves the ostensible owner's hands and is being used by someone else – is dangerous. Consider the argument: because Jill owned the information on Monday, Jack should be restricted in how he uses the information on Friday because he came into possession of property with trailing rights leading back to Jill. In one British case, for example, horseracing information printed in public newspapers could not be reported by other news sources because of where the information had originated.[63] (If you're wondering, the property right came from a European Union law giving creators a property interest in their non-copyrightable databases, which we don't do in the United States.) No matter who had the information, it was still owned by the originating company. That's the opposite of how property should work. If someone sells you a car, you should be free to use it how you wish despite the wishes of the person who owned it three sales ago. As I have discussed in earlier chapters, the entire problem of smart and digital property ownership arose because of efforts to leverage intellectual property licenses to create this kind of downstream control. But property's project has been to promote free use and alienability by eliminating these sorts of trailing rights.

If, then, all property is information, but not all information is property, how do we tell the difference? A pragmatic answer is easier than a theoretical one. Property is the subset of information that has been designed with attributes that evoke the intuition of property in a buyer. Words are information; an e-book sold to a user and downloaded onto a Kindle as a separately defined,

---

[60] *See* Samuelson, *supra* note 56, at 1137 (discussing the difficulties in moving "from where we are today to a thriving market in personal data under a property rights regime in which individuals would have a right to control market transactions in data about themselves").

[61] Id.   [62] Id.

[63] British Horseracing Board Ltd and Others v. William Hill Organisation [2005] EWCA (Civ) 863; [2005] RPC 35 (Eng.)

identified, and persistent unit is, to my mind, closer to property. A technical definition follows from this pragmatic intuition: property is information that has been made rivalrous, persistent, modular, and transferable in a way that reminds humans of the attributes they commonly associate with physical objects. In its rivalrousness, the information cannot merely be duplicated, and is (as Judge Kozinski noted in *Kremen v. Cohen*) susceptible of unique possession. In its persistence, the information gains value for the long haul. In its modularity, the information is separated from other like information and given digital metes and bounds. In its transferability, it gains economic value beyond the value of mere possession and enjoyment of the asset. Of course, not all of these characteristics appear in all smart and digital property. Currently, a common practice is to suggest property by making an information object rivalrous, persistent, and modular, but to technologically block transfer, permitting the asset's creator, not its buyer, to capture secondary markets. But merely removing one attribute or another does not change the goal of the property's packaging: to evoke the intuition of property in the buyer. Once that happens, I am confident we can say that an information asset is a good candidate for being considered property.

THE INFORMATIONAL HEART OF PROPERTY

A theory of property-as-information frees property from its obsession with phys-icality. Instead, property interests are pure information; property rules set up systems and processes for packaging and conveying that information. To the extent property has been obsessed with physicality, it is because tangible objects convey certain informational advantages. If I give you "one piece of pizza," it is hard for you to revise that and claim that I really meant "two pieces of pizza." You might take the biggest piece, but the physical boundary of "a piece" conveys very clear information between the two of us. I propose that property law has always focused on the informational aspects of these physical characteristics, rather than valuing physicality for its own sake.

Property's heart, its substance, is not physical stuff. It is information. Property interests answer the informational questions: Who? What? When? Where? Some property information is about physical stuff, but other information is about your bank account, or a bank's security interests, or a consumer's interest in her specific copy of her favorite music or e-book.

Once we see that property is information, then it ought to be clear that online, or electronic, or digital, or smart property interests pose no problem for property law. All we need is a way to keep track of who owns what. Preferably, we need a way to keep track of who owns what that does not rely on any one person or entity to keep the list. That is because there is always a chance that whatever entity has the list will change it without the owners' permission (as Amazon did when it revoked Kindle users' rights in 1984), or even engage in out-and-out self-dealing. There are a number of ways to keep track of property rights, some traditional (land registries), and some new. In particular, there are some new developments in how we keep lists and ledgers, such that it may be possible to create a list of who owns what without having any one entity in charge of the list, and without making it easy to hack or subvert that list. We can create fully digital, rivalrous property. We can keep track of your MP3s on the Bitcoin blockchain.

7

The Future of Property

In her landmark 1998 article *The Several Futures of Property*, Yale professor Carol Rose attempted to predict the future of property at a time when online assets and the communities that rely on them were just beginning to bloom.[1] Her argument was very simple. Property systems are not free, or even cheap.[2] "It costs something to define rights, to monitor trespasses, and to expel intruders," she wrote.[3] As property rights became more complex and harder to define, property systems cost even more.[4] The difference in expense is why we currently have title registries for big items like houses, cars, boats, and airplanes, but not for smaller pieces of personal property. So when we look for the future of property, Rose predicted that "when there are changes in the technological or administrative costs of establishing, monitoring and trading property, there may well be changes in property regimes as well."[5] Her advice: look for drops in those costs.[6] There we will find the future of property.

She was right. Running a database to determine who owns every Barbie doll used to be too expensive to contemplate. But the entire internet has been an exercise in reducing information costs. We now move information in ways and on a scale that even twenty years ago were unthinkable. Near-zero information costs proved the fuel of rampant internet scalability. Lots

---

[1] Carol M. Rose, *The Several Futures of Property: Of Cyberspace and Folk Tales, Emission Trades and Ecosystems*, 83 MINN. L. REV. 129 (1998).

[2] *See id.* at 133 (observing that "economists point out that, for all their benefits, property regimes are not to be had for free").

[3] *Id.*

[4] *See id.* ("It costs vastly more to establish, track, and enforce property rights in body parts, reproductive material, or air pollution emission rights, particularly when those rights are transferable.").

[5] *Id.* at 139.

[6] *See id.* (noting that "lower costs are likely to lead to a proliferation of propertization").

of areas of law benefited from reduced information costs. Contract law was revolutionized.[7] It costs nothing to send a forty-page contract to a consumer for every little online purchase, and the contracts can contain all kinds of provisions beneficial to companies, so that is what companies do. That was not feasible before the internet. Imagine receiving a forty-page contract with your purchase of a gallon of milk. Similarly, the cost of transferring intellectual property dropped radically, spurring rightsholders to seek ways to protect their interests. As a result, intellectual property law was changed forever, turning from a quiet spot on the side of the road of the law to one of its most bustling hubs of activity.

But traditional property was left behind. The early internet seemed more of a threat to intellectual property than a potential solution for traditional property. It was easier to use computing technologies to copy assets than it was to track them, to break digital rivalrousness than to make it. The early days of the internet were a pirate's dream. In the Napster era, almost all music was available for simple download. The decentralized nature of the internet meant that it was very hard to determine when someone had made an illicit copy and stored it somewhere on her computer.

Early attempts to create property-like systems for the internet were more concerned with protecting intellectual property rights than with creating the features and leveraging the strengths of traditional property. Through digital rights management ("DRM") software, companies tried to get consumers to download programs that would ensure that all copies were legitimately bought and paid for. A company kept a list of which accounts had purchased access to which movies, music, and books. It placed a "watermark," a digital fingerprint, inside each file that it sold. When a user wished to access the work, the company compared the list against the watermark to find out whether that copy was legitimately purchased by that user. If the watermark checked out, the music, or the game, or the movie, would play. Otherwise, it would not.

Consumers hated these systems. They were clunky, and often got in the way of the consumers' legal uses. Companies could not resist the urge to control more than whether a person had legitimately purchased the assets. In one well-known case, Sony was so bent on controlling the use of illicit copies that its CDs installed dangerous software deep within consumers' computers,

---

7 For an in-depth look at how contract law has changed in modern times, see generally MARGARET JANE RADIN, BOILERPLATE: THE FINE PRINT, VANISHING RIGHTS, AND THE RULE OF LAW (Princeton University Press 2012).

causing large security flaws.[8] Companies tried to control the transfer and use of consumer purchases. For instance, they tried to control sales of used music and what devices would play music. Apple did not want to merely sell music – it wanted to sell iPods as well. Trusting companies to continue controlling what they had already sold to consumers did not work. Imagine buying a shirt at Target, only to have a company representative show up and check your closet every fifteen minutes. Not only that, but he replaces the locks on your house (so he can be sure to check your closet any time) and is careless with the new house keys, dropping them where criminals can find them.

That was the state of affairs for many years. Companies legitimately wanted the security of DRM registry systems to ensure that digital assets were legally purchased and not copied, but consumers resisted the extra restrictions and invasive surveillance that companies bundled with purchases. A middle-ground solution would be to have a list of who owns what, but to keep that list away from the hands of any one company to avoid knock-on restrictions. There have been two big obstacles to this approach. For one, no company will pay for a registry it cannot control and that other companies could benefit from. For another, the registry must be trustworthy even though no one company audits and verifies it. Until recently, these challenges were insurmountable.

Nowadays, decentralized and cryptographically secured public ledgers, called blockchains, can track both online and offline property with low costs, immense precision, and reasonable security. Moreover, blockchains function without a central authority, such as a company or the government, which might impose underhanded restrictions on what consumers can do with their property. Most importantly, blockchains permit information about property and property-like resources to be exchanged at significantly reduced cost. So per Rose's recommendation to look for drops in cost, decentralized public ledgers, like the Bitcoin blockchain, are good places to look for the future of property.

THE BITCOIN BLOCKCHAIN

A blockchain is a public list of who owns what, maintained by a decentralized network of computers. In the case of the bitcoin blockchain, it is a public list of

---

[8] *See* Dan Mitchell, *The Rootkit of All Evil*, N.Y. TIMES (Nov. 19, 2005), http://www.nytimes.com/2005/11/19/business/media/the-rootkit-of-all-evil.html?_r=0 (discussing an incident where Sony installed rootkits on devices, which "are often used by malicious hackers to disguise spyware, malware and other nasty stuff"). Sony's response, incredibly, was that since most people "don't even know what a rootkit is," they should not care about it. *Id.*

who owns which bitcoins. But the technology could be used to track anything: houses, MP3s, smart cars. The fact that it is an online list is no big deal. Apple keeps a list of your iTunes purchases, and Amazon keeps a list of your Kindle purchases. The difficulty is that Amazon does not recognize your ownership of songs you purchased through iTunes, and Apple does not recognize your ownership of Kindle e-books, and both of them impose sneaky restrictions on what you may do with your purchases. That is where the blockchain comes in. The blockchain is not maintained by Apple, Amazon, or any one single entity. It is maintained by a network of computers, called miners, that work to keep the network decentralized and cryptographically secure.

The blockchain permits the creation and tracking of rivalrous, intangible property. It is cheap, compared to other ways of verifying transfers of property.[9] It is more secure than other methods of keeping track of property – dusty land records especially.[10] Finally, because it is not controlled by any one entity, companies cannot easily misuse the ledger to extend control over how consumers use their purchases.[11] Just as I can hand my friend a dollar bill without the intermediary of a bank, she can hand me a bitcoin without using anyone as an intermediary.[12] Transferring a bitcoin is a matter of telling the blockchain that bitcoin #4 now belongs to my friend, not me. Everyone can see that bitcoin #4 is now my friend's. If I gave her a bitcoin, even though it is fully intangible, I no longer have it – she does, and everyone knows it. This is just like personal property in real life.

One caveat: I am not a bitcoin evangelist. I do not particularly care about bitcoin. Bitcoin may not even survive to see this book published. That is not the point. Gauging the future of blockchain technologies by looking at bitcoin is like gauging the future of the internet by looking at AOL. There are lots of uses for the blockchain technology that have nothing to do with magical internet money. Banks are eagerly exploring blockchain-based settlement

---

9   *See* Fairfield, *BitProperty*, 88 S. Cal. L. Rev. 805, 813–17 (2015) [hereinafter *BitProperty*] (comparing the costs of trustless public ledgers such as the bitcoin blockchain with traditional forms of recording property interests).

10 *See id.* at 815, 819–24 (observing that current property registries are "sometimes insecure" and that blockchain technology "result[s]" in "a distributed public ledger of interests that is difficult to falsify").

11 *See* Pete Rizzo, *VC Fred Wilson: Block Chain Could Be Bigger Opportunity Than Bitcoin*, Coinbank (May 5, 2014, 4:58 PM), http://www.coindesk.com/vc-fred-wilson-block-chain-bigger-opportunity-bitcoin (quoting Fred Wilson, founder of Union Square Ventures, as stating that "with a block-chain architecture . . . there is no third party, there is no clearinghouse of identity information").

12 *See generally How Does Bitcoin Work?*, Bitcoin, http://bitcoin.org/en/how-it-works; Ritchie King et al., *By Reading This Article, You're Mining Bitcoins*, Quartz (Dec. 17, 2013), http://qz .com/154877/by-reading-this-page-you-are-mining-bitcoins/.

systems.[13] Mortgage companies, stockbrokers, investors, entrepreneurs, and online speculators are all using this technology to recreate what we have always known to be property, but fully online and without any physical component.[14] One financial analyst noted that blockchain technology "has massive implications for really any kind of asset – and the ability to transfer ownership of digital goods. It's hard to see a world where blockchain technology doesn't end up changing the way we think about asset ownership."[15] "The consequences of this breakthrough are hard to overstate," wrote entrepreneur and venture capitalist Marc Andreessen for the *New York Times*. "Bitcoin gives us, for the first time, a way for one Internet user to transfer a unique piece of digital property to another Internet user, such that the transfer is guaranteed to be safe and secure, everyone knows that the transfer has taken place, and nobody can challenge the legitimacy of the transfer."[16]

The following pages explore the bitcoin blockchain, not as a way to convince anyone to invest in bitcoin, but as a proof of concept for how everyday property rights can be stored, tracked, and transferred online. If property rights are just information, then we can store them on ledgers like the blockchain. If we do, we will finally achieve the holy grail of internet property: smart and digital property that we can trade, track, and transfer with at least as much freedom and certainty, and probably more, as we have when we hand each other property in everyday life.

WHY BLOCKCHAIN TECH MATTERS

"Property is the law of lists and ledgers."[17] If, as Carol Rose puts it, "property . . . identifies who has what,"[18] then it ought to be possible to write down

[13] *See* Jemima Kelly, *Eleven Big Banks Test Blockchain-Based Trading System*, REUTERS (Jan. 20, 2016, 8:13 AM), http://uk.reuters.com/article/uk-banking-trading-blockchain-idUKKCN0UY28W (reporting that eleven major banks tested "using the technology that underpins crypto-currency bitcoin").

[14] *See* Jonathan Chester, *Why Innovative Companies Are Using the Blockchain*, FORBES (Jan. 11, 2016, 1:07 PM), http://www.forbes.com/sites/jonathanchester/2016/01/11/why-innovative-companies-are-using-the-blockchain/#398ca8212d93 ("Every financial institution in the world has some sort of internal R&D effort aimed at understanding how the Blockchain will affect their business.").

[15] *Exchanges at Goldman Sachs: The Future of Finance*, GOLDMAN SACHS (June 3, 2015), http://www.goldmansachs.com/our-thinking/podcasts/episodes/7-30-2015-terry-nash.html (featuring Heath Terry, an analyst in Global Investment Research for Goldman Sachs, discussing how blockchain technology will impact the financial sector).

[16] Marc Andreeson, *Why Bitcoin Matters*, N.Y. TIMES (Jan. 21, 2014), http://dealbook.nytimes.com/2014/01/21/why-bitcoin-matters/.

[17] Fairfield, *BitProperty*, *supra* note 9, at 807.   [18] Rose, *supra* note 1, at 131.

who owns what in a ledger. That is how we determine who owns land,[19] how we track who owns cars, airplanes, boats, stocks, bank accounts, and much more.[20] The only obstacles that have kept us from using ledgers to track who owns many more things, like smartphones or MP3s, are the twin problems of cost and control.

Why Johnny Can't Sell His MP3s

In 2011, an ambitious technology startup called ReDigi wanted to help consumers do something simple: sell their used MP3s.[21] The problem, according to one court, was that this constituted copyright infringement.[22] How so? To answer that we must first back up a bit. Consider CDs. If someone buys a CD and gets tired of it, or moves, or downsizes, she can sell it. eBay works well. She gets some money and someone else gets a gently used CD. Everybody benefits.

Well, not quite everybody. The company that pressed the CD would prefer that it be able to sell that music to the eBay buyer, at a higher price than the used CD. This is why we shop on eBay – it is cheaper than paying full price. The company wants to sell at full price, and so it considers the used market to be a threat. Companies attempt to limit consumers' ability to sell digital and smart property so that they can sell to secondhand buyers instead. The ability to resell threatens the primary seller's profit model.

So one of the first things that companies did once computer use exploded was claim that every unauthorized use of a CD was copyright infringement. As you may recall from earlier chapters, under the RAM copy doctrine, every time a CD was inserted into a drive, a copy was made into active memory in order to actually play it. And while the CD purchaser was a licensed user of the CD content, that new copy was considered unlicensed. Beyond that, every time music was moved from one place to another, the computer made another illegal copy. Computers do not move information physically, they move it by copying it from one location to another. This meant that any use of computer

---

[19] *See* Christopher L. Peterson, *Foreclosure, Subprime Mortgage Lending, and the Mortgage Electronic Registration System*, 78 U. CIN. L. REV. 1359, 1363 (2010) ("Public land title records have been a fundamental feature of American law since before the founding of the Republic . . . .").

[20] *See* Fairfield, *BitProperty, supra* note 9, at 873 (observing that ledgers "keep track of millions of transactions worth trillions of dollars").

[21] *See* Capitol Records, LLC v. ReDigi, Inc., 934 F. Supp. 2d 640, 644 (S.D.N.Y. 2013) ("ReDigi Inc . . . . touts itself as a 'virtual' marketplace for 'pre-owned' digital music.").

[22] *See id.* at 648, 660–61 (holding that "the unauthorized transfer of a digital music file over the Internet – where only one file exists before and after the transfer – constitutes reproduction within the meaning of the Copyright Act").

software to do almost anything with intellectual property involved the making of an illegal copy.

All this was a mistaken interpretation of the law. When an owner sells a CD, of course it gives the buyer the right to make quick, ephemeral copies necessary to play the CD on a computer. Further, as the use of MP3s evolved, other rights were necessarily added to the license. Most of us now play music from our phones or iPods. This requires copying the music we have purchased onto the device. A CD that we could only play but not move onto the devices we most commonly use would be useless. The act of moving the MP3 to an iPod is technically copyright infringement, but it is infringement that is so widespread and so necessary to playing the music that the music companies have given up enforcing it. In fact, most of the mainstream music players – think Apple's iTunes or Microsoft's Windows Media Player – include this ripping function as a core part of their functionality.[23] Why do they not get sued for copyright infringement? Because this is an important part of owning the music.

This is such a core part of the right of ownership that Section 117 of the Copyright Act permits the owner of software to make copies that are necessary to make use of that software.[24] This includes copies necessary to run the software from RAM. But it should also include copies necessary to make the property useful and *practical*. It is necessary to copy data briefly from a CD in order to play it on the devices we most often use, and so it follows that such copies are necessary to make effective use of our property.

That is not how things turned out. Companies argued successfully to courts that "licensing" is not "selling." (Never mind that we have always done both: a CD purchase includes both the physical CD *and* a license to play the music.) Courts fell for this false distinction, and held that if a customer licensed the software or the music or any other intellectual property, she must not own it.[25]

---

[23] *See, e.g., iTunes 12 for Windows: Import songs from CDs*, APPLE INC. (last modified May 27, 2016), https://support.apple.com/kb/ph20501?locale=en_US ("You can import songs from CDs into your iTunes library. Once you import songs, you can listen to them without having the original CD in the disc drive.").

[24] Copyright Act, 17 U.S.C. § 117 (2012) (providing that making a copy of a computer program is not infringement if "such a new copy or adaptation is created as an essential step in the utilization of the computer program in conjunction with a machine and that it is used in no other manner...").

[25] *See* Vernor v. Autodesk, 621 F.3d 1102, 1111 (2010) ("We hold today that a software user is a licensee rather than an owner of a copy where the copyright owner (1) specifies that the user is granted a license; (2) significantly restricts the user's ability to transfer the software; and (3) imposes notable use restrictions.").

This leads back to the *Capitol Records v. ReDigi* case. The creators of ReDigi wanted to enable people to exercise a core function of ownership: to sell their property when they were done with it. If a user sold music to someone through ReDigi, the file was uploaded to the ReDigi cloud service and simultaneously deleted from her computer.[26] So there was only ever one copy of the music in existence at a time. (Note: ReDigi didn't allow for selling MP3s ripped from CD – the company agreed that would be illegal, since owners would still have the physical CD.) When a purchaser bought the used MP3, the same process occurred. As the music was copied to the purchaser's computer, it was deleted from ReDigi's cloud. Again, only one copy of the music was ever in existence at any one time.

But the music companies wanted to shut down the used market and force everyone to buy new copies, at full price, from them. Capitol Records, for one, sued ReDigi, arguing that because computers must make copies in order to move the purchased music, ReDigi was inevitably making illegal copies of the music.[27] Notice that Capitol Records was not arguing that it was losing a sale – the company knew that argument was a losing one, since it was not entitled to take a cut of all future sales once it had sold the music the first time. The company argued copyright protection instead: the owner was simply not entitled to sell her music without selling the entire computer on which the original copy of the music was located.[28]

The court agreed. It found that any use of computer equipment to transfer the music must inevitably involve copying.[29] That is like saying any use of computer equipment to transfer money must inevitably involve counterfeiting. Perhaps a more charitable reading of the court's decision is that it was not convinced ReDigi's anti-copying technology would work. After all, the court noted, it was possible to fool ReDigi's system by first moving the song onto a USB stick, then selling the copy on the computer.[30] There is some evidence that this is what was truly bothering the court. The decision relied

---

[26] *See ReDigi*, 934 F. Supp. 2d at 645 (describing the mechanics of Redigi's "Media Manager" software).

[27] *See id.* at 647 ("Capitol alleges . . . direct copyright infringement, inducement of copyright infringement, contributory and vicarious copyright infringement, and common law copyright infringement.").

[28] *See id.* at 656 (finding that Section 109(a) of the Copyright Act, which "protects a lawful owner's sale of her 'particular' phonorecord, be it a computer hard disk, iPod, or other memory device onto which the file was originally downloaded," does not apply to ReDigi's MP3 transfer model).

[29] *See id.* at 650 (rejecting ReDigi's argument "that it 'migrates' a file" and instead ruling that "a reproduction has occurred")

[30] *See id.* at 645 (observing that ReDigi "cannot detect copies stored in other locations").

on a 2001 Copyright Office report expressing doubt as to whether true "forward and delete" technology of the kind adopted by ReDigi could ever really function.[31] So if we read the *ReDigi* decision in the best possible light, we find a court sympathetic to the problems of customers who own digital property, but constrained because no technology existed that could stop people from using the system to copy music, or, worse, from using the system to sell the same music to multiple people.

Double Spending, Copying, and Counterfeiting

The issue the ReDigi court faced is one shared by all property systems that use lists to remember who owns what. The problem is that someone may try to use the same property multiple times, sell the same property multiple times, or copy the property, leaving two copies (or many) where there was just one. Consider examples from three different contexts. With the rise of the internet, intellectual property holders were appalled by the speed with which the internet permitted people to duplicate music and movies. In the context of real property deeds, there is a very real problem when Grandmother secretly deeds her property to Cousin Fred, but also conveys it in her will to Cousin Jessica. Finally, the game developer Sony Online Entertainment created a Star Wars game in which the game money – called "credits" – were hacked by people who were able to generate huge amounts of it for free. This practice was called "duping," or duplicating, and it destroyed the value of the game money.[32]

These three scenarios have something critical in common. If there is one of a thing, or just a few of a thing, the thing has value. That's good old scarcity. But if someone can simply make more of a thing by pushing a button, why would she buy it from you? If someone can sell the same piece of property to multiple people at once, why would anyone buy it? This is the problem of double spending, copying, or counterfeiting (however you phrase it). Double spending, or copying, breaks the technological condition of rivalrousness, destroying property's scarcity and its value. Double spending, duping, and copying all involve taking something that is limited in a specific way and making it unlimited. If that happens, the music producer cannot make money from the music, because anyone can make a copy at no cost. The realtor

---

[31] *See* USCO, Library of Cong., DMCA Section 104 Report, 84–85 (2001) (reporting that "no one has offered evidence that this technology is viable at this time").

[32] *See* TIM GUEST, SECOND LIVES: A JOURNEY THROUGH VIRTUAL WORLDS 164–65 (Random House 2008).

cannot sell land because no one can be sure it has not already been sold to someone else. The user of electronic currency cannot trust that her currency is worth anything, because someone might come along and dupe it. One hundred credits may buy her something of value today, but if someone dupes the currency, one million credits might not be able to buy her anything of value tomorrow. We see this problem in real economies: when the government of Zimbabwe hyperinflated its currency between the mid-1990s and 2009, a loaf of bread cost $550 million Zimbabwean dollars, and notes as large as $100 trillion Zimbabwean dollars were printed. In November 2008 alone, the Zimbabwean dollar suffered 79.6 billion percent inflation. In 2015, Zimbabwe was offering to pay $5 USD in exchange for $175 quadrillion Zimbabwean dollars.[33]

If we want to destroy something's value as private property, it's easy to do – remove its rivalrousness. If we removed all rivalrousness from music, anyone could download it and listen to it: a boon for music fans, but hard on the musicians. If we remove rivalrousness from land, it stops being my land or your land, and becomes a public park – or, if strip-mining companies can use it too, a wasteland. If we remove rivalrousness from money, whether by runaway government inflation or private counterfeiting, we undermine the value of the currency. This problem of how to create and defend rivalrousness for intangible things has haunted attempts to build true online property systems. Until recently, computer scientists did not have a strong, tested way to create decentralized digital rivalrousness. That made online property hard to create. But now we can.

CRYPTOLEDGERS

To show that true decentralized digital rivalrousness – and thus, true decentralized intangible property – is possible, this subpart explores how decentralized, public, encrypted lists, of which the bitcoin blockchain is just one example, function. A quick reminder of some terms before we get into the details. A ledger is just a list. In the context of cryptoledgers, when we say something is encrypted, we mean that it is hard to falsify, not that it is unreadable like a spy message. A blockchain is just one version of a cryptoledger, which is maintained and protected from intruders by loosely coordinated groups rather than by any one central entity. There are many blockchains, but the biggest and best known is the blockchain that keeps track of bitcoins.

---

[33] *See* Matt O'Brien, *Zimbabwe Is Paying People $5 for 175 Quadrillion Zimbabwe Dollars*, WASH. POST (June 12, 2015), https://www.washingtonpost.com/news/wonk/wp/2015/06/12/zimbabwe-is-paying-people-5-for-175-quadrillion-zimbabwe-dollars/.

A blockchain creates fully electronic, intangible rivalrousness without the need for a centralized, trusted company or other authority to maintain the ledger of property interests and mediate disputes. For the first time, we can give each other bits and bytes in the same way that we can hand each other dollar bills or gold bars. This makes the institution of property possible online. Bitcoin accomplishes this through the expedient of a publicly available electronic list – the blockchain.[34] The ledger is available to anyone. Anyone can write down that they are moving a bitcoin from themselves to someone else. Everyone can see the ledger and check who owns what.

So far, so good. But what if somebody tries to falsify the ledger? What if they claim to move a bitcoin that does not belong to them? Or worse, what happens if somebody writes a different ledger – perhaps a ledger in which they own all the bitcoins – and tries to pass that ledger off to the rest of the world as the real one? What if Aaron gives Beth a bitcoin, and then takes back the transaction and publishes to the rest of the world a ledger in which Carla received that bitcoin instead? That would be classic double spending, and unless bitcoin had solved that problem, it could not work as a list of who owns what. So ledgers have to solve the problem of making sure that only authenticated owners can move bitcoins on the ledger, and that nobody can duplicate the ledger.

Encryption and Authentication

The first issue, authentication, is the easiest to solve. A public ledger only permits Aaron to move assets to Beth securely if everyone can trust that Aaron is Aaron and Beth is Beth, and that no one can intercept or change the transaction in the middle. So imagine that a public ledger exists to track property interests. Perhaps Aaron owns asset A, Beth owns asset B, and Carla owns asset C. The ledger can record those original interests. If owners wish to trade, the ledger needs a way to secure the identities of the trading partners so that no one can fake the trade on their behalf.

This is done through routine asymmetric key encryption, the same encryption that ensures that your email has not been tampered with in transit or that you are actually talking to Amazon.com when you type that address into your browser (that is what the little "lock" icon next to the URL means).[35] Asymmetric key encryption creates a pair of numbers that have a unique mathematical

[34] You can see the bitcoin blockchain in action at https://blockchain.info/.

[35] *See* Christof Paar & Jan Pelzl, Understanding Cryptography: A Textbook for Students and Practitioners 149–74 (Springer 2010) (discussing public-key cryptography).

relationship.[36] If a message is encrypted using one number, it can only be read with the other. Most importantly, even if you know one number, you cannot guess the other.[37] So it's safe to release one of the numbers to the public. Think of an address to a post office box: anyone can send mail to it, but only the person holding the key can open the box and get the mail.[38] These keys, one public, one private, permit parties to send each other information of any kind, including property interests, without concern that a person in the middle might intercept and change the transaction.

So if Aaron wishes to transfer his property interest to Beth, he encrypts the message with her public key and sends it. Only Beth can open it with her private key. Aaron can also encrypt the message with his private key too. That means only he could have sent it. So Aaron knows Beth will get the information securely, because only she can decrypt what he encrypted with her public key, and Beth knows Aaron sent it, because only he could have encrypted the message with his private key, which she decrypted with his public key. Moreover, when the change in asset is recorded to the public ledger, everyone else knows that Aaron sent the property interest to Beth. Beth is now the owner of asset A.

Mining and Preventing Falsification

Let us add a new character to our example: Joker. Joker wants to defraud people who use this ledger. It ought to be simple, he thinks. Even if he cannot claim to be Aaron, he can claim to own asset A. He examines the public ledger. He notices that transactions come in blocks, or sets. Every ten minutes, a new block of transactions is published to the ledger. So, in Joker's mind, all he has to do is tell the ledger that, in the next block, he is the owner of asset A, and can sell it to Beth instead of Aaron.

Joker soon discovers that life is not so simple. His first attack fails. The problem is that the ledger has been distributed to many different computers. Nearly all of those computers have a record indicating that Aaron owns asset A, not Joker. So Joker gets voted off the island, so to speak, and his claim of ownership is invalid. But even if Joker were to get more computers to believe he owns the asset, he would have another problem. The chain of transactions, reaching back to the very beginning of the existence of the ledger, shows the

---

[36] *See* J.P. & G.T., *Virtual Currency: Bits and Bob*, ECONOMIST (June 13, 2011, 8:30 PM), http://www.economist.com/blogs/babbage/2011/06/virtual-currency (describing public-key encryption in the context of a bitcoin transaction).

[37] *See* Nikolei M. Kaplanov, *Nerdy Money: Bitcoin, the Private Digital Currency, and the Case Against Its Regulation*, 25 LOY. CONSUMER L. REV. 111, 116 (2012).

[38] *See* BRUCE SCHNEIER, APPLIED CRYPTOGRAPHY 31–32 (Wiley 1996).

provenance, the record of ownership, of the transaction. Maybe Aaron got asset A from Abernathy, who got it from Allen, who got it from Aethelwulf. Each transaction block is bound to the transaction blocks that come earlier by the same cryptographic relationship that we discussed above. So the transaction blocks form a chain (hence "blockchain") going back to the beginning. That chain makes false claims of origin quite difficult to fabricate.

But Joker is persistent. If he can't break the chain, he might try to fake the chain. So he tries to get his computer to fake a provenance such that he is now the owner of asset A, and he publishes this fake ledger to the other computers in the network. He is confident that at least some of the computers will accept his ownership of asset A.

The fake ledger, however, does not look like the real one. All someone has to do to determine which ledger is the correct one is look at which ledger takes more work. The longest and the strongest ledger is the true ledger. This is because the true ledger has more computers doing more work on that ledger than any other ledger. And while it takes an enormous amount of work to create the longest and the strongest ledger, it takes almost no work at all to realize which chain is the longest and required the most work to make.

Imagine the construction of the Great Pyramid. Thousands of workers are hauling blocks up the side of the pyramid and setting them in place, layer after layer after layer. Imagine one particular block being put in place. It is dragged into position by many workers, its position is corrected by the architects and squared off by the stonemasons, and then more blocks are layered on top of it so that it becomes an integral and immutable part of the pyramid.

Now, imagine that Joker is next door, attempting to build a rival pyramid to convince visitors and tourists that his is the true Great Pyramid. But Joker does not have an army of workers to build his pyramid; he has to get all the stones into place himself. It simply would not work. Joker would move one large block into place, nearly break his back getting it into position, and then turn and try to get another block. In the time that he added four or five blocks to his tourist trap, the Great Pyramid across the way would have added hundreds of blocks.

The problem for Joker is that while pyramids are very, very hard to build, requiring an enormous amount of work, it is easy for anyone passing by to see which pyramid is bigger. Furthermore, imagine trying to steal a block from one of those big pyramids. While it might be possible with a pickup truck and some logging chain to steal one of the blocks from Joker's tourist trap, it's simply not possible to steal a block from the Great Pyramid. There are too many other blocks cemented in place around it, and too many overseers and stonemasons and architects watching.

That is how the blockchain uses work – raw computer processor cycles – to protect itself from fakers. The computers that do this work are called miners.[39] Mining consists of guessing numbers by feeding a starting number into an algorithm and crunching numbers to see what pops out. By way of analogy, think of it like rolling a twenty-sided die.[40] When the die lands on a 5 or below, the roller gets a reward. If the die is rolled every minute, then it would take an average of four minutes to get a 5, 4, 3, 2, or 1. Sometimes the roller would get a lot of hits in a row, sometimes she would get it only after ten minutes, but on average, she would get the roll she was looking for every four minutes. If she wanted to get a hit every ten minutes (which is the actual period of the bitcoin blockchain), the system would need to adjust the numbers. Let's say they were adjusted so that only a 1 or 2 on the twenty-sided die was successful. That would mean that, if the die was rolled once a minute, on average it would take ten minutes to get a 1 or a 2. Sometimes they would come faster, sometimes much slower, but on average the roller would get a success every ten minutes.

Now say that someone else starts rolling dice too, or that the first die-roller (read: computer) gets faster, able to roll dice more quickly than once a minute. The system could still adjust to keep the number of successes to a single success about once every ten minutes. It might demand three 1 rolls in a row. Or, if millions of computers could roll the dice thousands of times a second, it might demand twenty 1 rolls in a row.

That is more or less how the blockchain protocol works. It adjusts the difficulty of guessing numbers by taking a number that represents the current state of the blockchain, adding a random "salt" to it, which is just a random number that represents the guess, and then running the result through an encryption algorithm called Secure Hash Algorithm 256, or SHA-256, which outputs a very long and nearly unique string: the hash. The effective number of sides on the "die" that SHA-256 represents is greater than the number of atoms in the universe.[41] Just for fun, I ran a few numbers through an SHA-256 calculator. The number "12" hashes to 6b51d431df5d7f141cbececcf79edf3dd861-c3b4069f0b11661a3eefacbba918. The number "13" hashes to 3fdba35f04dc8c-462986c992bcf8755462571307243909c162f7e470e581e278 – completely, utterly different.

Hashing is a one-way function; there is no way to start with the desired result and work backward to the input that generates that response. The only way to

39 See *Virtual Currency Schemes*, Eur. Cent. Bank 21–25 (Oct. 19, 2012), http://www.ecb.europa
    .eu/pub/pdf/other/virtualcurrencyschemes201210en.pdf
40 Many thanks to Google engineer Mike Shick for this analogy.
41 See Alex Gorale, *Explaining the Math Behind Bitcoin*, Cryptocoinsnews (Oct. 18, 2014, 11:44
    AM), http://www.cryptocoinsnews.com/explaining-the-math-behind-bitcoin/.

see what number SHA-256 will output is to actually do the work of running the starting number through the hashing algorithm. There are no shortcuts, and no way to predict in advance what the output will be.[42] So when I say that miners "guess" by running SHA-256, I mean that they have no way to know in advance what output they will get from the hash algorithm, given their input. They just have to feed the input in, crunch the numbers, and roll the dice, so to speak.

How does the blockchain protocol decide who wins? Some numbers hash to strings that start with one or more zeroes. The blockchain protocol adjusts to require a hash string that has an arbitrary number of zeroes at the front. The first person to get a hash with the requisite number of zeroes wins. There is no reason to favor zeroes. Numbers starting with a string of zeroes are not particularly useful. It's just a way to determine who wins the jackpot. Requiring guessers to find more and more zeroes at the beginning of a hash is an easy way to ramp up the difficulty of the guess.

Hashes with one zero at the beginning aren't all that rare. Hashes with many zeroes at the beginning are much harder to find, and because the only way to find one is to crank numbers through SHA-256, the only way to find one of those rarer hashes is to just crunch the numbers, over and over. Getting three zeroes at the beginning of the hash gets a hit once every 4,096 attempts (like rolling a 4,096-sided die). For example, the number 1,039 hashes to 00037f39cf870-a1f49129f9c82d935665d352ffd25ea3296208f6f7b16fd654f. But getting more and more zeroes at the start of the hash means more and more guessing. The number 88,484 hashes to 0000a456e7b5a5eb059e721fb431436883143101275c4077-f83fe70298f5623d, which starts with four zeroes; that result occurs once every 65,536 attempts.[43] As of the time of this writing, the actual bitcoin difficulty was 1 in 144,116,447,847.

As more computers join the network, the guessing gets harder because the bitcoin protocol compensates by adjusting the number of zeroes required to win. If computers were to leave the network, guessing would get easier. The result is that there is a "win," paid out in bitcoin, given out every ten minutes, on average.

Finding these hashes with zeroes at the front is pure work for the computers, which is why the blockchain is called a "proof-of-work" system.[44] There is no

[42] *See* Kaplanov, *supra* note 37, at 118 n.49 (describing the "cryptographic hash function").

[43] *See* Chris Moore, Comment to *Where Can I See an Input That Will Hash to a Solution?*, STACK EXCH.: BITCOIN BETA (June 17, 2012) http://bitcoin.stackexchange.com/questions/3946/where-can-i-see-an-input-that-will-hash-to-a-solution.

[44] Kelsey L. Penrose, *Banking on Bitcoin: Applying Anti-Money Laundering and Money Transmitter Laws*, 18 N.C. BANKING INST. 529, 532 (2014).

value in discovering these numbers in and of themselves. Why go to all that trouble? The answer goes back to our example of the Great Pyramid. The Great Pyramid has two features that make it very hard to fake. First, it takes a huge amount of work to make. Second, it is easy to verify how tall it is relative to any other pyramids. A tourist can simply glance at the pyramid, and at Joker's fake pyramid, and know that the puny one is a fake. The same is true of SHA-256 hashes. It takes a significant amount of computing power to find a number with, say, twenty zeroes at the beginning of the hash. But it is trivial to verify that that is the case once someone else has found the number.

What's more, it is easy to see that the top block in the Great Pyramid rests on all the blocks underneath. In the same way, each block in the blockchain is connected to the next, because the guesses all start from a hash that sums up that block. Computers guess hashes starting from the hash of the prior block. So the blocks are not just guessed individually; each one has to link to the ones before it, like links in a chain. While it is very, very hard to put all of those blocks in place – intentionally hard – there is no difficulty at all in verifying how much work has gone into making the chain as big as it is. And, what's more, the "strength" of the links is different between a fake blockchain and the real thing. That's because a chain made out of very rare hashes (say, the bitcoin protocol rewards only a hash with twenty initial zeroes) is much harder to calculate than a chain made out of relatively easy ones (say, three zeroes). So both the number of blocks and the difficulty of generating those blocks gives a very easy way to verify which blockchain needed more work to create. People who want to know whether they are talking to the true ledger, the right ledger, the ledger that contains a list of what everyone really owns, need only to look at which blockchain contains the most work. A bitcoin wallet (a program light enough to reside on a customer's phone and let them store and spend bitcoin), like the tourist in Egypt, need only glance at the blockchain to know that it is the longest and the strongest.

Joker is thus going to have a very bad day trying to fake this ledger. It's possible, of course. Almost anything is, but we should not overestimate his chances. Joker would have to find a way to create a longer and stronger blockchain. That means he would have to pour more processing power into the network than all the other computers in the network put together. That's the famed "51%" attack that people talk about in relation to bitcoin.[45] An entity could fake the blockchain if it controlled 51 percent of the processing power in the network (or it could just disrupt the network if it controlled 50 percent,

[45] *See* Kaplanov, *supra* note 37, at 120 n.57 (stating that an "attacker would require fifty percent of the processing power to disrupt the bitcoin network, an unlikely event").

making it impossible to distinguish between the true and false ledgers). Using some tricks and strategies to throw the rest of the network into confusion, the percentage could be brought lower, in the same way that some stockholders can control a corporation when they only own about 30 percent of the stock.[46] But, in general, it is cost-prohibitive to hijack a blockchain.

Even when such a thing could happen, some interesting incentives come into play. For example, mining consortia are companies that control big blocks of computers. These computers work together to find hash solutions and share the bitcoin rewards among participants. One mining consortium briefly held over 51 percent of the processing network.[47] But in doing so, the consortium threatened their own holdings. Remember that bitcoin stored on the blockchain are only as valuable as trust in the system. So by taking their share of processing power over 51 percent, the consortium undermined the value of a system in which it had heavily invested. They quickly pulled back and made many public promises not to undermine the system. So *even if* Joker were able to pull together enough processing power to subvert the blockchain, he is likely to find that it is far more profitable for him to use that processing power to participate in the blockchain than it is for him to damage it. After all, all that processing power can earn him a lot of bitcoin!

The result is a ledger that is open to anyone and everyone at very low cost, controlled by no one in particular, yet still extraordinarily difficult to hack. I do not want to give the impression that the blockchain is impregnable, because as a matter of math it is not. However, it is certainly better than the security we have now. All that it takes to hack the land registry system (at least as far as double-spending is concerned) is to draft a wild deed. The celebrated hardened systems of companies do not fare better. The news is full of data breaches. Home Depot lost fifty-six million credit card numbers to malware installed on its registers.[48] Another breach involved companies as ostensibly secure as NASDAQ, resulting in 160 million credit and debit card numbers, stolen over a seven-year period.[49] The U.S. Office of Personnel Management

[46] *See* Samuel Gibbs, *Bitcoin Could Be Hijacked by "Selfish" Groups Causing Currency Collapse*, GUARDIAN (Nov. 5, 2013, 7:26 AM), http://www.theguardian.com/technology/2013/nov/05/bitcoin-hijack-research-mining.

[47] *See* Alex Wilhelm, *'51%' Fears Rattle The Bitcoin Community*, TECHCRUNCH (June 15, 2014), http://techcrunch.com/2014/06/15/51-fears-rattle-the-bitcoin-community/.

[48] *See* Jim Finkle & Nandita Bose, *Home Depot Breach Bigger Than Target at 56 Million Cards*, REUTERS (Sept. 18, 2014, 7:16 PM), http://www.reuters.com/article/2014/09/18/us-home-depot-dataprotection-idUSKBN0HD2J420140918.

[49] *See* Daniel Beekman, *Hackers Hit Companies Like Nasdaq, 7-Eleven for $300 Million, Prosecutors Say*, N.Y. DAILY NEWS (July 26, 2013, 12:41 PM), http://www.nydailynews.com/news/national/russians-ukrainian-charged-largest-hacking-spree-u-s-history-article-1.1408948.

suffered a hack of the personal and financial data of four million government employees and sixteen million contractors and applicants for government positions.[50] In comparison to the relatively out-of-date and insecure systems we currently use to track property interests, distributed ledgers offer significant comparative advantages.

WHAT THIS MEANS

Using the blockchain, we can recreate the power of everyday property in the online context. Remember, property interests are simply information: who owns what. We can record those property interests in a public, decentralized blockchain. Transferring MP3s, games, smartphones, even cars and land, can become as simple and low-cost as the transfer of slots on a blockchain.

Tying Assets to the Blockchain

For some assets, like bitcoins themselves, this process is nearly effortless. The asset *is* the slot on the blockchain. So changing the entry in the database automatically shifts the asset itself. Other assets might be tied to the blockchain. Consider ReDigi. It would not be difficult to store all the music in one place, and merely trade the ability to access the music where it resides on the cloud. ReDigi was in fact developing such technology when it was shut down by the music industry lawsuit. An updated version of that technology would permit transfer of the access tokens on a blockchain. The access would be an encryption key tied to a specific token or slot on a public ledger. Trading the token would trade the encryption key, which means that only one person could access that particular copy of the music at a time.

Other assets might exist off the blockchain, but title to them could be tied to the blockchain through a process called tokenization. Instead of having a bitcoin stand for a unit of value, it would not be hard to have that particular coin act as a token for ownership for something else. Smart property could then be programmed to respond to the owner of the token. Imagine a car that "knows" it is owned by a specific token on a blockchain. The software inside the car is tied to the token. When it is in the presence of someone who owns the token (perhaps communicated by an RFID chip in that person's smartphone), the car door opens and the car starts. When not, it stays locked.

---

[50] *See* Brian Naylor, *One Year After OPM Data Breach, What Has The Government Learned?*, NPR (June 6, 2016, 6:08 PM), http://www.npr.org/sections/alltechconsidered/2016/06/06/480968999/one-year-after-opm-data-breach-what-has-the-government-learned.

In this way, it is possible to link off-chain assets to blockchain tokens, making the shifting of the token the effective shifting of ownership rights in the asset.

Even assets without a software link to the blockchain could still be productively transferred via distributed public ledgers. Australia is already very close to such a system.[51] Land is described by plot number, and the plot number is transferrable by digital deed.[52] Possession of the digital deed is deemed ownership. The ledger indicates the owner of the plot, and a shift in the entry in the ledger is a shift in the ownership interest in the plot. The Australian digital land registry system is maintained by the government, but it would be simple to move that system to a publicly accessible distributed ledger. Indeed, some national governments have explored developing a blockchain-based land registry.[53] In some systems, many claims go unrecorded because of costly bureaucracy, corruption, and the difficulty of accessing land records. A blockchain solution could stop bureaucratic theft of land during the transfer process (a real concern in some areas), and democratize access to the land registry. Perhaps most importantly, a public and cheaply accessible registry could allow disenfranchised groups or individuals easy access to their claims to prove what they own. Or put plainly, Honduran farmers might be able to resist a land grab if their titles were clearly registered and openly available.

Public and Accessible Property

A public, distributed ledger is open to everyone. Unlike dusty land records, anyone with computer access can verify interests, and applications can be coded to do this without the user even needing to be aware of the process. The ledger is completely public in the sense that anyone can see the shifting of interests, and can know that a given asset is legitimately owned, yet private in the sense that the real-world identity of an owner need not be disclosed in the process.

Today's property interests are scattered across many different ledgers. A distributed public ledger provides a single version of the truth. Title battles, a

---

[51] See AUSTL. REGISTRARS NAT'L ELECTRONIC CONVEYANCING COUNCIL, STRATEGIC STATEMENT (Jan. 2016), https://www.arnecc.gov.au/__data/assets/pdf_file/0007/698452/ARNECC_Strategic_Statement_January_2016.pdf.

[52] See, e.g., Su-Lin Tan, *Paperless Apartment Sale in Sydney Suburb Makes History*, FIN. REV. (June 9, 2016, 5:57 PM), http://www.afr.com/real-estate/paperless-apartment-sale-in-sydney-suburb-makes-history-20160530-gp7kr2 (discussing a paperless property transfer using Australia's e-conveyance system).

[53] See Gertrude Chavez-Dreyfuss, *Honduras to Build Land Title Registry Using Bitcoin Technology*, REUTERS (May 15, 2015), http://in.reuters.com/article/usa-honduras-technology-idINKBN0O01V720150515.

long-standing cost of property transactions, can be a thing of the past. There would be no "wild deed" problems, where two people claim the same asset. A single, public version of the truth resolves an even worse problem: conflicts between different ledgers. For example, the federal Copyright and Patent Offices control national ledgers of who owns which copyrights, patents, and trademarks. But individual states control statewide ledgers of interests in personal property, which includes intellectual property and other intangibles. So when a bank lets a business borrow money on the basis of the business's patents or copyrights, there is a tremendous degree of uncertainty about what ledger should have the ultimate say: the state or the federal one. A single version of the truth would eliminate conflicts between ledgers maintained by separate entities.

Cost and Trust

If Carol Rose's prediction is right, we will see a shift in how property rights are stored and transferred when there is a change in the cost and locus of control of property systems. Blockchain technology and other related publicly distributed ledgers provide one such opportunity. If we think about Rose's hypothetical registry for personal property, a tokenized blockchain could fit the bill. Consider a registry for cellphone ownership. According to the Pew Research Center, 90% of U.S. adults owned a cellphone in 2014, putting the number of cellphone users at roughly 221 million.[54] A single bitcoin can be divided into one hundred million distinct and trackable "satoshis" (named after the pseudonymous founder of bitcoin).[55] Each satoshi could be marked as a token for a separate cell phone. So two and a half bitcoins could be split into the number of satoshis necessary to record ownership of cellphones in the United States. This is not to say I advocate putting cellphone ownership on the bitcoin blockchain. It might be better to use a different or faster chain. But the idea is not implausible. Electronic registries have the granularity to track tiny movements of tiny assets in a public manner.

A highly accessible secure single record of truth that is capable of extreme granularity and is a perfect record of provenance is not entirely free. Proof-of-work systems cost money. Those processor cycles require computers and electricity, sometimes large amounts of it. And, as described, the system becomes

---

[54] *See Mobile Technology Fact Sheet*, PEW RES. CTR., http://www.pewinternet.org/fact-sheets/mobile-technology-fact-sheet/ (last updated Oct. 2014).

[55] *See* Andreas Adriano & Hunter Monroe, *The Internet of Trust*, IMF FIN. & DEV., June 2016, at 44, *available at* https://www.imf.org/external/pubs/ft/fandd/2016/06/pdf/adriano.pdf.

more secure as more processor cycles secure the blockchain through pure work. The current bitcoin network is paid for by bitcoin speculators, who invest in mining in the hopes that the bitcoin they earn through mining will appreciate in value. That is, the bitcoin blockchain is paid for by a perception among miners that bitcoin is deflationary. There is some irony in this, since the mining process itself is inflationary. When new bitcoins are awarded to miners, the value of each bitcoin held by everyone in the system drops slightly.

A number of innovations address the challenges of trust and cost. Trust and cost are tradeoffs within distributed networks. The more a system trusts its counterparties, the less the system must pay to secure its version of truth. In a recent white paper, one financial services company has considered a lower-cost settlement network operated between trusted entities, stock purchasers, broker-dealers, banks, and the like.[56] By vetting who enters the network, the system can run without the expense of a proof-of-work system. Of course, this revives the twin problems of control and access. No one party to the network controls it; the industry as a whole does. And ensuring that only trusted entities access the ledger also removes the public nature of a distributed ledger. Another innovation relies more on game theory than on technology to secure the ledger. "Proof of stake" systems are an intensification of the dilemma that the mining consortium had when it found itself in possession of a dangerous amount of the computing power of the bitcoin blockchain. The mining consortium had to backpedal to defend the system. They had too much stake in the system to want to harm it. Thus, some concepts for how to run distributed ledgers without the cost of proof of work replace miners with entities that have a stake in the system. Those entities verify transactions by choosing the chain that they believe best represents reality. If they are wrong, they lose their stake, so absent certain events they can be trusted to verify the correct chain of transactions.

But all in all, it is not possible to wholly eliminate cost from property systems. Perhaps an analogy would be to the price, or lack thereof, of many internet goods and services. The internet costs an enormous amount to run, yet many applications are free because of economies of massive scale and the near-zero costs of providing services to the marginal consumer. In the same way, it is clear that distributed public ledger property systems will still cost something. The cost might be paid through inflationary tokens, as bitcoin, or by selecting a middle point on the cost/trust continuum, or even by taxes, if the government

---

[56] *See* Depository Trust & Clearing Corp., Embracing Disruption: Tapping the Potential of Distributed Ledgers to Improve the Post-Trade Landscape (2016), http://www.dtcc.com/~/media/Files/PDFs/DTCC-Embracing-Disruption.pdf.

were to decide to run its own nationwide blockchain registry. The question is whether the system could do significantly more for significantly less than do our current options for property rights databases. The prospects for doing so seem promising.

Decentralization

This book is about recovering our property from the hands of companies that have added a series of riders and constraints on our ability to control, fix, use, or transfer our property. Recall the clumsy attempts by companies to create single-company registries of interests through DRM, license servers, and even invasive surveillance software. One big payoff of distributed public ledgers is that they are not controlled by intellectual property rightsholders, but are controlled by the owners of the assets. Unlike company-maintained license servers, which use the license model to constrain users' ability to transfer ownership of their assets, distributed ledgers recreate how personal property and real property work in everyday life. If I wish to give away my Chewbacca coffee mug, I hand it to someone in a peer-to-peer transfer that does not require the mug manufacturer's assent. If I wish to give away my copy of Britney Spears's "Toxic," I can hand over the CD, and Britney need not assent. In the same way, it is possible to track and transfer fully intangible rights. With a distributed ledger, I can hand someone the keys to my MP3 copy of "Toxic," and, again, the rightsholder need not assent. Imagine a world in which we can transfer money, stocks, movies, music, smart cars, land, houses, or anything else to another person, securely and without going hat-in-hand to a company or government entity to ask permission. This is not a description of how things are, but of how they could be. Given the sudden drop in administration, control, and verification costs of electronic interests in databases, perhaps this is a description of how they *should* be.

DECENTRALIZING ELECTRONIC OWNERSHIP

Property is information. Information is stored in databases. Databases have suffered a traditional tradeoff between access and security. The more people who can access and post changes to a database, the less secure it has traditionally been. This means that, traditionally, intangible property databases have been very centralized. One entity must maintain the database. But advances in database technology, like the blockchain, demonstrate that it is possible to run decentralized property systems of a kind, and at a cost and scale that we have not previously contemplated.

Although this chapter has focused on the bitcoin blockchain, that technology serves only as an example. It is entirely possible that bitcoin in its current version will not last. But the idea that it is now possible to create a single version of a ledger containing a list of who owns what, without turning the list over to a single company or government agency to manage, is a compelling part of freeing digital and smart property from the entities that seek to undermine the powers of traditional ownership.

Property has always represented the power of the owner to act to some greater or lesser degree free of the interference of others. It is never complete freedom, of course, but we can measure degrees of ownership by the degree to which we can make decisions without having to ask, "Mother, may I?" It is not really yours if you cannot do anything with it, sell it, or tinker with it. Digital and smart property have been dogged by the license server model. That model recognizes the power of lists and ledgers to create online property systems, but has only worked if one trusted entity keeps the ledger, manages inputs and outputs, and fends off all interlopers. The idea that it is possible to run a system of online property without a central curating entity brings us one step closer to realizing the essential freedom of property in the hands of the owner. It permits lists of who owns what without managers. It creates digital property without digital feudal masters.

8

Jailbreaking Ownership

"Anytime someone puts a lock on something you own, against your wishes, and doesn't give you the key, they're not doing it for your benefit."

– Doctorow's Law[1]

Imagine you buy a house that has an extra room with a full-time salesman living there, and this guy is relentless. When you read the paper in the morning he suggests products based on the articles you read. When you watch TV he offers to sell you anything that appears on the screen. When you are on the phone he listens in. When you get letters in the mail he reads them first. He follows you to the grocery store, where he offers to sell you a competing brand of anything you pick out. He sees everything you do and buy, and uses that information to sell you things you did not know you wanted (because you don't want them). You hate this guy, at first. Then, as you get used to him, you think maybe he is not so bad. Maybe he is just trying to make a living. But what you do not know is that every day that you lock the door on your way out of the house, he unlocks it and props it wide open. He sits there and lets anybody walk in and take anything they want. He does not care if your stuff gets taken – after all, he can just sell you new stuff. Would you buy that house? If you bought a Lenovo computer in 2014, you already did.

For four months in 2014, new Lenovo computers shipped with software called Superfish preinstalled.[2] Superfish was an adware program that inserted

---

[1] Cory Doctorow, *Doctorow's First Law*, PUB. WKLY. (Aug. 2, 2010), http://www.publishersweekly .com/pw/by-topic/columns-and-blogs/cory-doctorow/article/44012-doctorow-s-first-law.html.

[2] *See* Thomas Fox-Brewster, *How Lenovo's Superfish 'Malware' Works and What You Can Do to Kill It*, FORBES (Feb. 19, 2015), http://www.forbes.com/sites/thomasbrewster/2015/02/ 19/superfish-need-to-know (discussing how Lenovo shipped PCs preinstalled with Superfish, which "has been described as a piece of malware," during "a four month gap in [2014], when Lenovo shipped a total of 16 million PCs").

its own ads into websites and search results. Lenovo claimed that Super-fish helped consumers "find and discover products visually."[3] The company claimed to have created the "most advanced and scalable visual search tech-nology in the world."[4] In reality, it created a significant security failure.

Superfish intercepted users' encrypted web traffic in order to advertise to them. That's called a man-in-the-middle attack – a user thinks she is commu-nicating with a trusted source, but her communications are being intercepted by a third party.[5] Superfish did this by making itself the root certificate author-ity, in effect subverting the user's ability to secure her communications with the rest of the internet. To make matters worse, the encryption key for the root certificate authority and the password needed to access that key were the same for every computer. Using relatively rudimentary techniques, security experts discovered the password, which was the name of the company that wrote the software: "komodia."[6] Armed with this password, a malicious third party could easily and surreptitiously access all the information that a Superfish-bundled computer sent over the internet.

Even without the security flaw, Superfish cost the owners of the computer by subverting their property to take advantage of them in online deals. It is one thing to present clearly marked advertisements in exchange for providing content. It is quite another to embed advertisements without users' knowledge, and to subvert their own property to gather information about how much individual consumers are willing to pay, reducing their ability to get good deals.

Programs like Superfish are dangerous and increasingly common. Compe-tition to exploit consumer information is growing fiercer. Consumers' digital and smart property is the battleground. The previous chapters discussed how intellectual property interests have taken over traditional property, and have demonstrated that this is no longer necessary. We have pretty good systems now for tracking interests in even completely intangible digital property. The old system is creaking. It is time to jailbreak ownership.

Jailbreaking ownership will be challenging, but not impossible. We can do it by accomplishing four tasks. First, we must restore ownership rights

---

[3] *Id.*   [4] *Id.*

[5] For an overview of man-in-the-middle attacks, see generally Dennis Fisher, *What Is a Man-in-the-Middle Attack?*, KASPERSKY DAILY (Apr. 10, 2013), http://blog.kaspersky.com/man-in-the-middle-attack/1613.

[6] *See* Dan Goodin, *"SSL Hijacker" Behind Superfish Debacle Imperils Large Number of Users*, ARS TECHNICA (Feb. 20, 2015), http://arstechnica.com/security/2015/02/ssl-hijacker-behind-superfish-debacle-imperils-big-number-of-users (describing the Superfish security measure as "laughably easy to bypass").

to individual property owners and update property rights for the digital age. Second, we must constrain the reach of contracts and make it clear that intellectual property licenses have limits. Third, we must make some limited adjustments to laws governing owner modification of smart property, and to the means by which consumer disputes are handled by the judicial system. And fourth, we must advance and develop technology that makes decentralized property systems not just possible, but practical. No single element will work alone, but together they can snap the chains restricting modern forms of ownership.

TASK 1: UPDATE SMART AND DIGITAL PROPERTY OWNERSHIP

Property owners have traditionally enjoyed a range of rights over their own property. Gone are the days of absolute dominion, in which a property owner could do anything she wanted (or perhaps such days never were). Try erecting an enormous ugly statue on your city lot and you will find out that the town council has some control over what you can and cannot build. But within those constraints, there are certain rights – gathered together in the proverbial "bundle of sticks" – that have been traditionally associated with owning property.[7] An owner may control her property. She may fix it when it is broken, and modify it to suit her purposes. She may use and enjoy her property. She may transfer it to others free and clear when she is done with it. And she may exclude others from entering or using her property against her wishes.

Property law prevents outside parties from interfering with owners' powers. For example, someone who takes away the owner's right to use and enjoy her property might be liable for theft, conversion, or trespass to chattels. Someone who enters real property without permission of the owner might be sued for trespass. And contracts that prohibit owners from selling their land are void as unreasonable restraints on "alienation," or conveyance.[8]

These traditional rights need to find new expression in the digital landscape. The digital right to fix, tinker with, and improve property is the right to hack. The right to alienate, or transfer, property becomes the right to sell digital and smart property. The digital right to use and enjoy property free from the interference of others is the right to run code and hardware – the right to run. The digital right to exclude others from property is the right to block intrusive code from running on one's own devices – the right to ban. These four basic

---

[7] *See, e.g.,* 2A-6 JULIUS A. SACKMAN, NICHOLS ON EMINENT DOMAIN § 6.01 (M. Bender 2015).

[8] *See* 3–29 DAVID A. THOMAS, THOMPSON ON REAL PROPERTY § 29.03 (David A. Thomas ed. 2015) (noting that "the common law developed to the point that any absolute restraint on alienation was as repugnant to the fee [simple], wholly void").

rights – the rights to hack, sell, run, and ban – frame the discussion about what modern owners must be able to do with their digital and smart property.

Right 1: The Right to Hack

"Any customer can have a car painted any colour that he wants so long as it is black."

– Henry Ford[9]

The right to hack is an extension of the traditional property rights to fix, modify, and improve property. These are rights long taken for granted: when a person buys a car, she may paint it any color she wishes (Henry Ford notwithstanding). She may buy dice to hang from the rear view mirror, or a cover for the steering wheel. She can rip out the engine and replace it, if she wants to. She can crash it, as long as no one else gets hurt, and afterwards take it to a repair shop or fix it herself. She can even express her political views with bumper stickers.

Many of us rely on this feature of property ownership to secure our independence and our livelihoods. We use our cars, for example, to drive, to eat, to do business. In the United States, the car is the quintessential modern-day symbol of American freedom. But as technology increasingly enables incursions into our private property, even our cars are not exempt. As Ford executive Jim Farley stated: "We know everyone who breaks the law. We know when you're doing it. We have GPS in your car, so we know what you're doing."[10] Our cars are increasingly embedded with digitally active software and devices, and those devices do what other people tell them to.

At the very least, we have the right to remove these tracking devices from our cars, don't we? But what if, in the same agreement that we signed to purchase the car, we signed away our right to modify or repair our own vehicles? Automobile and equipment manufacturers have begun to argue precisely that. John Deere has argued to the Copyright Office that farmers do not own their own tractors free and clear.[11] John Deere claimed that because the copyrighted software inside the tractor was merely licensed to the farmer, it could prevent

9 HENRY FORD, MY LIFE AND WORK 72 (Doubleday 1923).
10 Benjamin Preston, *Wheelies: The Ford Is Watching Edition*, N.Y. TIMES (Jan. 10, 2014), http://www.nytimes.com/2014/01/11/automobiles/wheelies-the-ford-is-watching-edition.html.
11 *See* Darin Bartholomew, Long Comment Regarding a Proposed Exemption Under 17 U.S.C. 1201, at 5 (2015), *available at* http://copyright.gov/1201/2015/comments-032715/class%2021/John_Deere_Class21_1201_2014.pdf ("A vehicle owner does not acquire copyrights for software in the vehicle, and cannot properly be considered an 'owner' of the vehicle software.").

farmers from modifying or even repairing their own equipment.[12] "It's official," reported one news article. "John Deere and General Motors want to eviscerate the notion of ownership."[13] The same report noted that a local farmer could not fix his expensive transplanter because he could not afford to pay for access to the expensive diagnostic software approved by John Deere.[14]

Cars are no different. One trade publication reported that the Auto Alliance is working to make it illegal for owners to work on their own cars.[15] The argument is the same – working on your own car is a non-permitted use of the software embedded in the vehicle. If the owner modifies the car, she infringes copyright, because she is making use of the software to do something the manufacturer does not want its customers to do. And if she changes or accesses the software to run the diagnostics now needed to fix modern cars, per section 1201 of the Digital Millennium Copyright Act (the 2008 amendment to U.S. copyright law), that supposedly constitutes illegal circumvention of copyright protections. That's right: by fixing your own car, you may be a copyright infringer at best, and a criminal at worst.

There is hope, however. In 2014, after the passage of an influential law in Massachusetts, two of the major autobuilder organizations agreed to let independent repair shops have access to their diagnostic codes.[16] And in October 2015, the Library of Congress granted a temporary exemption to the Copyright Act, permitting vehicle owners to "tinker with automobile software without incurring US copyright liability."[17] Unfortunately, the auto builders deal required repair shops to stop lobbying for laws that would enshrine the right to repair, and exemptions to the Copyright Act only last for three years.[18] So in a few years we might be right back where we started. We need to stop messing

---

[12] *See* Laura Sydell, *DIY Tractor Repair Runs Afoul of Copyright Law*, NPR (Aug. 17, 2015), http://www.npr.org/sections/alltechconsidered/2015/08/17/432601480/diy-tractor-repair-runs-afoul-of-copyright-law ("[John Deere] said ownership does not include the right to modify computer code embedded in that equipment.").

[13] Kyle Wiens, *We Can't Let John Deere Destroy the Very Idea of Ownership*, WIRED (Apr. 21, 2015, 9:00 AM), http://www.wired.com/2015/04/dmca-ownership-john-deere.

[14] *Id.*

[15] *See* Jason Torchinsky, *Carmakers Want to Use Copyright Law to Make Working on Your Car Illegal*, JALOPNIK (Apr. 21, 2015, 12:05 PM), http://jalopnik.com/carmakers-want-to-make-working-on-your-car-illegal-beca-1699132210 ("Automakers are considering cars 'mobile computing devices' and as such would fall under the DMCA's pretty draconian protections.").

[16] *See* Kyle Wiens, *You Gotta Fight for Your Right to Repair Your Car*, ATLANTIC (Feb. 13, 2014), http://www.theatlantic.com/technology/archive/2014/02/you-gotta-fight-for-your-right-to-repair-your-car/283791.

[17] *It's OK to Hack Your Own Car, US Copyright Authorities Rule*, GUARDIAN (Oct. 27, 2015, 8:42 PM), https://www.theguardian.com/business/2015/oct/28/its-ok-to-hack-your-own-car-us-copyright-authorities-rule.

[18] *Id.*

around with stopgap measures and temporary solutions, and state definitively that the owner of property has the right to repair it.

Restoring the Right to Repair

In 2016, news broke about the attempt by smartphone manufacturer Apple to lock out independent repair shops, and owners who might wish to work on their own phones, by means of the iPhone 6 fingerprint lock.[19] Only Apple could authorize the installation of a new fingerprint pad; if the pad was installed by a repair shop not licensed by Apple, the phone would cease to open, displaying instead the infamous Error 53 and freezing the owner out of her own property.[20] This is part of a well-established pattern. Just a few years earlier, Apple had "order[ed] its Apple Store Geniuses to replace" the standard, Phillips-head screws that originally shipped with the iPhone 4 "with pentalobe ones on any iPhone 4 devices that were brought in for repair.... [E]mployees were instructed not to tell customers that they had made the switch." A prominent repair blog observed, "[t]he switch should have, in theory, made it impossible for anyone except for Apple to open the device."[21]

Apple is by no means the only company seeking to limit owners' right to repair their property. When *Wall Street Journal* reporter Geoffrey Fowler tried to repair a friend's broken television, he found it nearly impossible to get good information about where to buy a $12 part.[22] The manufacturer, Samsung, went out of its way to remove information that would permit owners to simply fix this well-known problem.[23] If the owner of the TV wanted it repaired, a Samsung-authorized repair shop said it would charge $90 for an estimate and at least $125 for a repair.[24] Given that a new television cost $380, Fowler's friend was almost tempted to buy a new TV.[25]

---

[19] *See* Hiawatha Bray, *Apple's Error 53 Fueling a 'Right to Repair' Backlash*, Bos. GLOBE (Feb. 10, 2016), http://www.betaboston.com/news/2016/02/10/apples-error-53-fueling-a-right-to-repair-backlash (noting that "if the shop isn't officially authorized by Apple, it won't have the ability to sync the phone with the new fingerprint sensor").

[20] *See id.* ("If you break your phone, and have it fixed at the wrong repair shop, it might be lost to you permanently.")

[21] *See* Jason Koebler, *How to Fix Everything*, VICE: MOTHERBOARD (Nov. 24, 2015), http://motherboard.vice.com/read/how-to-fix-everything.

[22] *See* Geoffrey A. Fowler, *We Need the Right to Repair Our Gadgets*, WALL ST. J. (Sept. 8, 2015, 3:04 PM), http://www.wsj.com/articles/we-need-the-right-to-repair-our-gadgets-1441737868 (reporting the author's arduous efforts to repair a 2008 Samsung TV).

[23] *See id.* (noting that " Samsung [had been] taken to court about this exact issue, caused by a busted component called a capacitor").

[24] *Id.*

[25] *See id.* ("Why wouldn't [the friend] just buy a new TV? She felt guilty. Even recycled e-waste can end up in toxic dumps in the developing world."). Fowler was eventually able to fix the

To fix the television, Fowler needed access to parts and knowledge. Perhaps it is unsurprising that both are under attack. Companies have attempted to restrict sales of parts through distribution channels, which, if successful, would stop people like Fowler from being able to purchase replacements.[26] Other smart property manufacturers do more than just restrict parts sales – they pursue anyone who provides information on how to modify or repair devices.[27] When hacker George Hotz posted instructions and keys allowing users to hack their PlayStation 3 consoles, manufacturer Sony sued him to take them down.[28] But Sony didn't stop there. It considered the threat of consumers getting information about their own property to be so critical that it then sent subpoenas to YouTube, Twitter, Google, and Bluehost, the company that hosted Hotz's webpage, asking them to hand over the IP addresses and account information of everyone who visited and posted comments on Hotz's blog or watched his YouTube videos.[29] A federal magistrate granted Sony's request.[30] Why did Sony go to all this trouble? In a word, intimidation: consumers saw that they could be threatened with lawsuits for simply learning about how their property works or for helping others do the same.

"F – You, Windows 10!"

Another element of the Right to Hack is the right to keep property working, specifically by controlling or stopping forced updates. Users are often forced to update their phones' operating systems, only to find that the updated version doesn't work. Apple's rollout of iOS 9 was, for example, plagued with problems. Users were prompted to download it, but found that the new operating system wouldn't install. But even when operating systems are functional, they may override earlier iterations and features. Earlier versions often have features that users truly enjoy, but that manufacturers either do not wish to continue supporting or actively oppose because those features are too effective

---

television using a $20 deluxe repair kit, sold on eBay, a link to a YouTube video showing how to solder capacitors, and the assistance of a toddler. *Id.*

[26] *See id.* ("Manufacturers stop us by controlling repair plans and limiting access to parts.").

[27] *See id.* ("Some companies treat repair guides and schematics as intellectual property, and send takedown notices to people who post them online.")

[28] *See* Sony Computer Entm't Am. LLC v. Hotz, No. CV11 0167, 2011 U.S. Dist. LEXIS 13253 (N.D. Cal. Jan. 26, 2011) ("SCEA has alleged that each Defendant, individually and in concert with the other Defendants, has .... enable[d] unauthorized access to and/or copying of PS3 Systems and other copyrighted works.").

[29] *See* David Kravets, *Judge Lets Sony Unmask Visitors to PS3-Jailbreaking Site,* WIRED (Mar. 4, 2011), http://www.wired.com/2011/03/geohot-site-unmasking.

[30] *Id.*

in protecting user information from advertisers. Advertisers, after all, provide a significant revenue stream to device manufacturers.

Forced updates also result in early and unwelcome retirement for older technology. This is a particularly critical issue in regions or countries that rely on older or secondhand technology. The original iPad 1, for instance, still works just fine. But Apple stopped updating the iPad 1 operating system, and all the app providers did the same. Apple is not required to support out-of-date devices, of course, but it also has no legitimate reason to keep those devices locked to the iTunes software distribution system so that the owners cannot get software that will work. Because the iPad is locked to the iTunes store, there is no way to download, purchase, or otherwise obtain versions of software that do work on the iPad 1 without jailbreaking the device – overriding Apple's so-called security measures to run unapproved software.[31] This is not planned obsolescence, this is forced obsolescence. Jailbreaking is the only way for these owners to keep their devices working.

To be clear: regular, consensual updates are critical for device and network security. Unpatched exploits lead to turnkey hacking, where less-skilled hackers use older, developed scripts to penetrate unpatched systems. But forced updates, and updates prompted through persistent, nagging software (aptly termed "nagware"), are something different. Nagware takes the real and necessary strategy of reminders too far by bombarding the user with requests to update, updating unless the user quickly says no, and in the worst cases, initiating updates when it is the last thing a user wants.

In one particularly hilarious episode, professional gamer turned streamer Erik Flom was interrupted mid-match in front of an audience of 130,000 viewers by a non-consensual Windows 10 update. Flom's reaction perhaps sums up the experience of all of those who have been force-updated: "What. What!? . . . How did this happen! F – you, Windows 10! . . . Oh my God! You had one job, PC. We turned off everything . . . . Update faster, you f – !"[32] In Microsoft's zeal to get hesitant Windows 7 and 8 users to upgrade, it offered aggressive download options, including already-checked boxes and, in some

---

[31] *See* Alex Heath, *Unlocking a New iPhone Is Now Illegal, but Jailbreaking Is Still Safe – What It All Means for You*, CULT OF MAC (Jan. 29, 2013), http://www.cultofmac.com/213144/ unlocking-a-new-iphone-is-now-illegal-but-jailbreaking-is-still-safe-what-it-all-means-for-you (noting that jailbreaking allows an iPhone user to "circumvent[] Apple's security measures in iOS to install tweaks, hacks, and mods that aren't allowed in the App Store.").

[32] HAL 90210, *Windows 10 Updates Are Now Ruining Pro-gaming Streams*, GUARDIAN (May 4, 2016 10:13 AM), https://www.theguardian.com/technology/2016/may/04/windows-10-updates-ruining-pro-gaming-streams.

reports, the inability to refuse the upgrade.[33] Other users reported that the multi-gigabyte files for Windows 10 were downloaded onto their computers without their knowledge, even before being offered the option to upgrade.[34] And, after adopting Windows 10 upgrades, users found that certain data were transferred to Microsoft no matter what they themselves dictated. The computer responded to the commands of the operating system designer, not the owner.

Forced updates are more than an inconvenience – they are a disturbing security and privacy loophole. For example, encryption is the backbone of modern security and privacy. Encryption ensures the attribution, integrity, and security of an encrypted message or device: that a communication came from the right person, was not altered in transit, and cannot be read without the recipient's private key. When done properly, there is no known way to break encryption to read the contents of an encrypted device or message. But rather than break the encryption, companies and governments can just go around it with a force-update process – companies can, on behalf of themselves or others, force the device to accept software that circumvents the encryption. A well-publicized example is that of the iPhone 5 that belonged to one of the attackers in the mass shooting in San Bernardino, California.[35] The phone was locked and encrypted, and the FBI wanted access. But the phone was programmed to erase itself after a specific number of password attempts, so the FBI could not use powerful software to quickly guess an enormous number of passwords. The FBI asked a court to order Apple to create a software tool that would use Apple's firmware update process to force the iPhone to accept new software. That new software would then eliminate the limited number of password attempts, permitting the FBI to unlock the phone fairly quickly.

Apple resisted the order, and the FBI eventually accessed the phone using a method that did not subvert the force-update process. Still, the FBI's proposal was troubling. Although the bureau was certainly entitled to open the phone pursuant to a judicially issued search warrant, the idea that encryption, the most powerful tool in an owner's security arsenal, could be circumvented

---

[33] *See* Tom Brant, *Microsoft Gives Woman $10,000 for Forced Windows 10 Upgrade*, PC Mag. (June 27, 2016 6:59 PM), http://www.pcmag.com/news/345656/microsoft-gives-woman-10-000-for-forced-windows-10-upgrade.

[34] *See* Kavita Iyer, *Forced Windows 10 Upgrade Could Have Caused Fatality in Remote African Bush*, TechWorm (June 5, 2016), http://www.techworm.net/2016/06/forced-windows-10-upgrade-caused-fatality-remote-african-bush.html.

[35] *See, e.g.*, Evan Perez & Tim Hume, *Apple Opposes Judge's Order to Hack San Bernardino Shooter's iPhone*, CNN (Feb. 18, 2016), http://www.cnn.com/2016/02/16/us/san-bernardino-shooter-phone-apple (discussing "a judge's order to help the FBI break into the iPhone of one of the San Bernardino, California, shooters").

just by asking (or ordering) a manufacturer to load malicious software onto a device, years after that device has been sold, shows that we have a problem. For all the talk of opposing software "backdoors," the pundits have overlooked that there is already such a door – the force-update process – built into almost every internet-connected device. FBI director James Comey, in urging Apple to comply, argued that it was simply a onetime request for a single phone. But that is not how software works. What would work on one phone could work on many, creating a widespread security vulnerability.

If we oppose government backdoors because they are security flaws, why should we think that corporate backdoors are a good idea? Our devices are programmed to be hackable at the will of the company that made them, through forced software updates. What was once merely a software distribution method that helped owners patch problems or get the latest operating system updates has become a method for circumventing a device's protections and changing its features without the owner's knowledge or consent. This problem exists for all devices. Business laptops may be highly secured to protect trade secrets, and rooms of a building can be set to open only upon biometric verification. But all that protection means nothing if the manufacturer can simply load onto the device new software that removes or undermines the protections the owner put in place. Hacking the device to close these backdoors may be a responsible owner's only recourse.

Hacking Software Monoculture
Tech companies state, not without reason, that they need to control what software owners may use in order to preserve smooth operation of their networks.[36] They argue that it becomes harder to manage a network of computers when each one is different. The argument goes, if each customer has a different configuration on their cell phone, tablet, smartwatch, or, eventually, smart car, network services vendors will have a hard time supporting all of those variations. They make a good point. Imagine that you were a customer service representative tasked with handling phone calls from people who had installed many different combinations and constellations of programs and operating systems. The more combinations, the harder the work.

But it is not all that hard. Consider that the internet was built on a system of wildly different computers made by different companies and running

---

[36] *See, e.g., Unauthorized Modification of iOS Can Cause Security Vulnerabilities, Instability, Shortened Battery Life, and Other Issues*, APPLE INC., http://support.apple.com/en-us/HT201954 (last updated June 14, 2016) ("Apple strongly cautions against installing any software that hacks iOS.").

completely different operating systems. In fact, the diversity created by tinkerers who hack and meddle with their devices helps to preserve the connectivity of the internet. Think about the browser, arguably the greatest interconnectivity platform ever created. The browser connected computers that had nearly nothing in common. Diversity among nodes in a network creates a demand for simple points of connectivity, like the internet browser. Internet diversity may create short-term challenges for interoperability, but it creates enduring demand for long-term, stable interoperability standards.

While companies are correct that to have everyone run the latest, identical, fully-patched version of the software is an important way to close serious security flaws, they overlook the danger of software monoculture. It is downright dangerous to have most, or even many, of the computers in a network run the same software. Where I live, in rural Virginia, American Chestnuts once predominated. But after the introduction of the Chestnut blight fungus in 1904, American chestnuts were nearly destroyed. One pathogen wiped out billions of trees. It's the same for software. When I was a child, Macintosh computers suffered fewer viruses not because they were more secure, but because it was more valuable to program viruses that worked on PCs. Now, with Apple's rise to cell phone ascendancy, the shoe is on the other foot. Apple resisted building a virus for the FBI because it knew that such a virus could compromise millions of phones. The more of a technological monoculture we become, the more valuable an exploit that works on that monoculture is. Nobody would care about an exploit that could hack one individual computer. iPhone exploits are worth millions precisely because one exploit can unlock so many identical devices.

Some hackers may use their skills to exploit others, but many are beneficial to a networked society as innovators. They provide healthy diversity to networks by altering the configurations of the computers on which they work. They provide services that people want. Many people are driven to root their phones; an Android phone that is "rooted" permits the user to access certain core functions normally kept away from the owners' hands.[37] Cellphone owners do this because the service that they want is not provided by the manufacturer or the operator. Here's a simple illustration: we all know that a longer password is better. The encryption password to your phone – the one you have to enter when you turn it on – is one of your most important passwords. It should be long, and hard for a computer capable of 348 billion guesses per second to crack. But Samsung's popular Galaxy phones, to take one example, use the

---

[37] Thomas J. Fitzgerald, *Breaking Into the Smartphone (Risks Included)*, N.Y. Times (Nov. 24, 2010), http://www.nytimes.com/2010/11/25/technology/personaltech/25basics.html.

same PIN for the encryption password as they do for the screen lock. So if a consumer has a good encryption password, she must enter a huge and long password every time she opens the lock screen. Or, more likely, the user will enter a short PIN and therefore have a short, four-digit numerical password for their encryption. This renders encryption utterly useless. A computer can guess a four-digit numerical PIN almost instantaneously. Further, even if a user were to enter a long password and laboriously enter it every time she wished to unlock the screen, Samsung's passwords are limited to sixteen characters, which is not particularly strong either. So users turned to the hacking community. If a phone is rooted (allowing the user to control it, not the company), it is a trivial matter to download a program called Cryptfs Password that allows the user to set a long and powerful password for encryption, and keep a short and handy password for Samsung's lock screen.[38]

Hacking and modding – altering hardware or software to execute a function not original to the product – provide critical services to a networked society. There is only one way to foster the needed skills: Give people the freedom to tinker with their own devices. Hacking starts at home. Kids learn by taking things apart. Most good coders begin by hacking what is around them, by modifying it to do something that the budding coder really wants it to do. My brother, now a Google engineer, always had several disassembled computers in his room growing up. Can we really imagine producing NBA-quality players if we banned street ball? We won't produce world-class hackers, with the benefits of innovation and diversity they bring, if we ban hacking the devices that are closest to us and matter the most.

Hacking a Path Forward
So if it is that important to get our devices to do what we tell them to, why don't we just go ahead and hack them? Part of the answer is that companies lock us out of the operating software of our own devices, and we don't know how to get past their roadblocks. But if it were merely a matter of technical know-how, this section would be called "How to Hack," and the discussion would point readers to the many online forums dedicated to finding and spreading exploits that permit owners to gain full access to their devices.

Oh that it were so simple. As discussed earlier in this book, owners are blocked from modifying their property by an arcane and anachronistic cocktail of contract and copyright law. Overreaching contract law allows companies

[38] *See* Nikolay Elenkov, *Cryptfs Password*, GOOGLE PLAY STORE (Apr. 17, 2016), http:// play.google.com/store/apps/details?id=org.nick.cryptfs.passwdmanager&hl=en (providing an overview and opportunity to download the app).

to hold users to license agreements users have no choice but to sign if they want to access their device or property. Copyright law prevents users from circumnavigating controls to copyrighted programs, even if the end goal of that circumnavigation is legal. The right to hack is trapped in a double bind. And without the *legal* right to hack our own devices, so are we.

Law must recognize, grow, and expand the right to hack one's own digital and smart property to repair it, modify it, improve it, sell it, back it up, switch formats or devices, or simply have it accept the owner's commands over those of the manufacturer or rightsholder. This is not merely my proposed solution – the right to hack is picking up political steam. As mentioned earlier, the auto industry appears to be bowing to pressure from independent repair shops to permit access to diagnostic codes. Multiple states are considering "right to repair" bills. At the federal level, in 2014 President Obama signed the Unlocking Consumer Choice and Wireless Competition Act (UCCWA), a law that made it legal to hack a cell phone to unlock it for other carriers. The Obama administration was inspired in part by a petition, signed by over 114,000 citizens, requesting that cell phone unlocking be made legal.[39]

The right to unlock phones increases competition between carriers, who like to lock devices to their networks. But the law does not expressly permit users to hack their phones in order to gain root access and run programs on their own devices without approval of the manufacturer or operating system designer. It is possible that the Librarian of Congress could make an exception to the DMCA to permit users to modify their own devices, but few people are accomplished coders. Just as in the real world we would hire a mechanic to modify our car or a professional to paint our house, smartphone users need the ability to use solutions developed by experts to modify their smart property. This provision does not exist for DMCA: even where owners might benefit from an exception, that exception does not extend to experts. So if and when the Librarian of Congress were to say it's legal for users to tinker with their smart cars or smartphones, we would have to do the hacking ourselves. That is an empty right.

While there has been progress on the right to hack, the right needs to be expanded and grown. The UCCWA addresses unlocking smartphones, but leaves the question of unlocking or jailbreaking other smart property to the Librarian of Congress. Farmers still cannot repair their tractors without going to a licensed repair shop. Historically, the Librarian of Congress has taken a narrow view of owner's rights in smart property. Few exemptions have

---

[39] *See* Unlocking Consumer Choice and Wireless Competition Act, Pub. L. No. 113–144, 128 Stat. 1751 (2014) (restoring the 2010 DMCA exemption that permitted mobile phone unlocking).

been granted, and then only for the most widespread and basic of computing devices. The Internet of Things represents a rapid and riotous blooming of many different types of technology. Exempting these devices one by one, in a process that only occurs once every three years and is hotly contested by device manufacturers, will not work. The overwhelming majority of the Internet of Things will remain locked up. Furthermore, the DMCA specifies that exceptions only last for three years,[40] and thus can subsequently be reversed. Relying on the DMCA 1201 exception mechanism provides only limited case-by-case relief for an overarching problem.

It is wonderful that there are individual breakthroughs in individual areas of law for specific devices. But we need something more permanent and wide-ranging. We need a system that recognizes and will apply ownership rights to the dominant devices of tomorrow. A few years from now, we may need to modify our smart houses, our autonomous cars, and our smartwatches (do you really want a device that monitors your heart rate and location to answer to a company rather than to you?). And that doesn't include the inventions we haven't even thought of yet. The right must be broader and more robust. We must be able to hack anything we own, to repair it, to modify it, to improve it, and to keep it secure from a manufacturer's forced updates or obsolescence.

Right 2: The Right to Sell

Imagine you buy a unit in a condominium. Only after you buy are you told that you are free to leave the community at any time, but you cannot sell your condo to anyone else. You can abandon it, but you cannot transfer it. What's more, nobody else can stay there. You can't have family visit on weekends or lease it out, either. You are stuck in that community; there is no way to get your money back out.

This is the situation with Audible, iTunes, or any of a number of other accounts tied to specific companies. Users buy and pay for Audible books, usually at the same price as a CD of the same recording. The difference between the two products is that users cannot sell or lend the digital version to someone else. In fact, a user cannot even access the recordings without going through an app that reports her reading or listening habits to Amazon. The power to sell is the power to get out of a given company's locked-in ecosystem, to either go somewhere else (say, from Amazon to iBooks) or just recoup some money and do something else entirely.

40 17 U.S.C. § 1201(a)(1)(D) (2012).

As discussed in earlier chapters, companies want to lock in their customers. Companies are not happy when a customer buys a used copy from another customer for a cheaper price. Companies want to make that second sale at full price. This happened to my students. Law books are expensive, often costing hundreds of dollars per new copy. I like to assign the same book that I have used in past years so that students who wish to buy a used copy can find one at a much lower price. (It also saves me some preparation time, of course.) Some students are so nostalgic for Torts and Contracts class that they keep their books – I just finally got rid of mine a few months ago. But I'm willing to bet I am the exception. Most students want to sell their books, not least because they need the money to buy the next round of textbooks. So it set off a minor scandal when a major law publisher, Aspen, tied its physical books to an online subscription and then demanded the books back at the end of the class.[41] In a pretty funny turn, law professor Josh Blackman, who raised the scandal, was especially appalled that the policy would be applied to a property law textbook. Confronted with strong opposition from both professors and students, Aspen backed down and permitted students to buy, own, and resell their copies, a painful lesson in the residual power of property to fire the public imagination.

Public relations stumbles aside, the purpose of the restriction was clear: to undermine any property interest in the books, and to prevent students from reselling what they purchased. Another publisher, West, made the same move, but without the bizarre demand that students return the physical copies. Instead, it simply made parts of the casebook available online through a one-time code attached to the book. This code grants the student a twelve-month license to access the online content, and West's license agreement explicitly states that access is limited to one student and non-transferable.[42] Resell the book, the code no longer works, and the new owner does not have access to the additional materials. The book is worth much less, perhaps so much so that school bookstores would not buy the used copies. When that happens, the company benefits, and both students – the would-be buyer and seller – are worse off.

---

[41] *See* Joe Patrice, *Casebook Publisher Has Aggressive New Plan to Rip Off Law Students*, Above the L. (May 8, 2014, 11:12 AM), http://abovethelaw.com/2014/05/casebook-publisher-has-aggressive-new-plan-to-rip-off-law-students/ ("Starting with their next editions, Aspen [planned to ban] resale of their books and [planned to] enforce the ban by making students return the books at the end of class.").

[42] *License Agreement*, West Acad. Publ'g, http://www.interactivecasebook.com/license/licenseagreement.htm (last visited July 26, 2016)(providing terms of use for the online portion of the casebook). West further retains the right to "terminate this Agreement immediately upon giving written notice of termination to Licensee." *Id.*

It is worth remembering what a revolution eBay was. The idea that you could now sell your old junk for new-to-you wonderful things was amazing and liberating. Need to clear out old clothes? eBay. Need to find out if those old vinyl records are worth anything to anyone? eBay. Need to buy *pretty much anything* without paying full price? eBay. There are lots of other secondhand sites now, but the point is, freeing up the secondhand market was incredibly liberating for sellers. It freed up both cash and closet space! (It was liberating for buyers too, but not so much for their closets.)

The current attack on ownership is essentially an attack on eBay. If ownership dies, eBay's model will have to change or wither. eBay would become just another retail website, competing with Amazon or Alibaba. The company does not want that, and neither should we. We should be aiming for a worldwide secondhand market, one that lets us get the most out of what we own, and lets someone else get good use out of it if we do not want it anymore. Property ownership carries with it a right to sell in order to ensure that value does not get uselessly chained in place.

eBay is right to be worried. Companies' attacks on individual ownership will not just remain within the digital realm. Aspen tied use of its physical book to its online website. It would have had a hard time arguing that the book was subject to end-of-semester recall because the text was merely "licensed,"[43] not sold, although more and more of these digital-type claims are being made about physical objects. Rather, Aspen aimed to rely on the "lifetime" digital access it offered students through its website when they purchased the book. Any time a student used the website while not following the license (which would require return of the physical book), she would be a copyright infringer. Online rules will not stay online. Unless we act, the bad rules that cover intellectual property will come to limit our rights in everyday physical property. That is what worries eBay. It should worry us too.

How can we fix this? One answer is straightforward, but pretty unlikely in the near term. We need to clarify that the first sale rules of the U.S. Copyright Act apply to digital copies. This wouldn't require an amendment of the law, since the words say pretty clearly that a publisher's or manufacturer's rights in a specific copy end when it sells that specific copy. But I do not want to oversell the point. Courts have generally followed the lead of companies when they say that they only licensed a copy and did not sell it (despite the "Buy now!" language companies use everywhere except in contracts as lengthy as

---

[43] Daniel Nazer, *Aspen to Students: Your Property Book Is Not Your Property*, Elec. Frontier Found. (May 8, 2014), https://www.eff.org/deeplinks/2014/05/aspen-students-your-property-book-not-your-property.

this chapter). A redrafted first sale right clarifying that, when I buy an Audible book, I own the copy in MP3 form just the way I would in CD form, would be effortless to draft, but hard to get past industry lobbyists.

A hybrid solution, at least for lawyers, is to convince courts otherwise. There is no shortage of cases listed in this book where courts stood up for consumer property rights. Usually they did so where the physical component of the product seemed to predominate over the software component. Lawyers continue to bring and sometimes win cases where the closest analogy is to traditional property ownership, not to intellectual property licensing. Although property rightsholders dominate the debate, there are a few soft spots in their defense walls. One of the easiest points to poke is that something isn't property or not-property just because the seller says it is. I can't sell you a car, then turn around and claim I didn't. And I also shouldn't be able to enter into a deal that has all the indications of a sale – I use the word "sell," you pay me once, you keep the thing forever, you can delete or destroy it if you want – and yet still claim that I didn't sell it to you. So it may be useful to keep hammering home this point to courts: the way they're interpreting copyright law is inconsistent with long-standing common-law tradition, with buyers' expectations, with buyers' ownership of the physical components of their smart property, and with the language ("Buy now!") sellers use to persuade consumers to buy.

Similarly, there should be a sustained attack on courts' broad construction that owners are actually "mere licensees" of their copies. The term "licensee" means something very different, and much narrower, in traditional property law than it does in intellectual property law. A true "mere licensee" applies in few property cases. For example, someone who purchases a ticket to watch a movie or a basketball game is a mere licensee. She is permitted to be there, but does not have any particular right to stay there. If she chats on her phone during the movie or cheers too raucously at the game, she can be removed. If those are the only rights consumers are getting when they click "Buy now!", they are being defrauded.

Challenging the "mere licensee" characterization will be a long road, but a fruitful one. Courts are accustomed to taking companies at their word when they use the magic words "licensed, not sold."[44] The lead case is *Vernor v. Autodesk*,[45] in which the Ninth Circuit Court of Appeals considered the ability of parties who had paid thousands of dollars for software to resell

[44] *See* Aaron Perzanowski & Jason Schultz, *Reconciling Intellectual and Personal Property*, 90 NOTRE DAME L. REV. 1211, 1219 (2015).
[45] 621 F.3d 1102 (9th Cir. 2010).

the physical disks on which the software resided once they were done with it. The *Vernor* court set out a three-part test: first, whether the rightsholder had characterized the transaction as a sale or a license; second, whether the rightsholder had placed limits on the consumer's right to transfer; and third, whether the rightsholder had placed limits on the consumer's right to use the software.[46]

The Ninth Circuit's reasoning was circular. Per the first sale doctrine (or just basic property law), if a copy is sold, the buyer has certain rights (including the right to sell) *no matter what* the copyright holder wants. So the *Vernor* test is empty. The first part, whether the rightsholder *says* the transaction is a license, begins where it intends to end up: that is of course what the rightsholder needs to demonstrate to the court. Just saying so does not make it so. The second part, whether the rightsholder limited the resale rights of the consumer, is the very purpose of the inquiry! If the transaction is a sale, then it does not matter what the rightsholder says. So asking whether the rightsholder did something it could not do if the transaction were a sale does not tell us anything about whether the transaction is a sale or a license. The third part, whether the rightsholder can control the use of the software per the End User License Agreement, is the same. Again, if the copy is sold, the rightsholder's ability to control most of the owner's uses of that copy is exhausted. Three rounds of circular thinking put us back where we began: without a practical way to tell if the item was sold or simply licensed.

Copyright law should abandon the current, naive approach to distinguishing licenses from sales. Just asking the copyright holder how *it* wants the transaction to be characterized is no solution. Nor do the other *Vernor* queries cast any light; they just beg the question. Copyright law might take notice of other, far more developed areas of law where this matter of whether or not something was truly sold has been considered for decades. One area of law is the Uniform Commercial Code, which already plays an important role in determining consumer protection regarding sales of products and in fact already governs physical sales of software CDs to consumers. The UCC faced a similar problem. Judges needed to be able to tell when a company sold something to a consumer, which transferred ownership, and when a company just leased it to the consumer.[47] Think about a car. There is a big difference between selling and leasing a car. In law, there are lots of reasons (mostly to

---

[46] *See id.* at 1111–12 (setting out the test).

[47] *See, e.g., In re* Bailey, 326 B.R. 156, 160 (W.D. Ark. 2005) (construing whether an agreement constituted "a sale or a lease"); Carlson v. Giachetti, 616 N.E.2d 810, 810 (Mass. App. 1993) (observing that the question of when "an equipment lease is to be treated as a 'true lease' or as a security agreement is an issue that has been litigated extensively for more than two decades").

do with tax law and bankruptcy) to characterize something that is actually a sale as a lease.

So judges and the drafters of the UCC got smart. They needed to know when something was a "true sale" even when it was characterized as a lease.[48] For example, assume I go bankrupt. If I own my car, my creditors can take it, even though I am still making monthly payments on it. But if I am renting my car, my creditors can't take it, because it does not belong to me. From cars we can extrapolate to important commercial assets sneakily recharacterized as leases when they were in fact sales. In all of those cases the parties characterized the transaction as a lease, with a document that said "LEASE AGREEMENT" in big bold letters, just as every End User License Agreement makes it clear that the rightsholder thinks it is just licensing the product, not selling it. So the first thing judges needed to do was ignore the characterization of the parties.

Courts then went to the truly relevant question: when do the facts of a transaction show that the parties conducted a true sale even though the contract between the parties said that it was a lease? Courts did this by taking a hard look at what they termed the "economic realities" of the transaction. Was the transaction a onetime deal, or did the supposed lessor actually expect anything of value to be returned at the end of the lease? If the good was destroyed or damaged, who bore the economic loss? If the good rose in value, who benefited from the economic gain? Questions like this helped courts pierce the characterization of the parties and the endless inventiveness of lawyers who wanted to disguise what was actually a sale as a lease.[49]

I am not suggesting that the UCC's statutory test for distinguishing leases from sales be applied directly by courts trying to distinguish licenses from sales. There are minor points of difference. But different areas of law borrow from one another all the time, and here the basic question is the same: did one party actually sell something to another under cover of legal trickery? The UCC takeaway is that judges in a mature discipline cannot and do not simply accept the characterization of the parties as to whether a transaction is a sale that transfers ownership. Doing so only reaffirms the position of the party with more power (when you signed up for iTunes, you didn't have the opportunity to cross out that word "license," did you?). We have long understood that preventing the hollowing out of property requires an inquiry into the economic realities of a transaction. Where a consumer makes a onetime payment and has a

---

[48] *See* U.C.C. § 1–203 and accompanying Official Comments.
[49] *Cf. Vernor*, 621 F.3d at 1114 (holding the "economic realities" not "dispositive" despite focusing on that factor in Bankruptcy cases).

perpetual right to the resource (that is, the supposed "licensor" never gets it back), or where the licensor may get it back but only after the economic value of the property is pretty much gone, then we can say with confidence that what happened was not a license but a sale, no matter what the copyright holder says. And that goes double when the rightsholder has used words like "Buy now!" or "sell" or "purchase" in describing the transaction to the consumer. Language tucked deep inside a EULA should not be able to change what the transaction actually was. It is high time copyright law graduated to a more mature test, one that examines the economic realities of supposed "license" transactions.

An additional line of attack to undo what Aaron Perzanowski, Jason Schultz, and Chris Jay Hoofnagle call the "'Buy Now' lie"[50] is through consumer protection law. The Federal Trade Commission in particular vets companies for unfair or deceptive trade practices. I just bought an Audible book for an upcoming trip. When I bought it, I hit a button that said "Buy now!" It did not say "rent now" or "license now" or anything like that. "Buy" is different from "rent" or "stream." There can be nothing more deceptive than selling someone something, then claiming you did not really sell it to them. It's open and shut. And if the FTC is slow to arrive at the party, state attorneys general can use existing consumer protection statutes to show it the way. If California – where many tech giants are headquartered – decided to investigate companies for the "buy now" lie, industry practices would change quickly indeed.

Finally, we can try to protect ourselves, as suggested by the old canard "Buyer beware." Of course, this is hard to do if companies are deceptive. Often consumers have no choice – every smartphone comes with an End User License Agreement. But there is some truth to it. Students should avoid textbooks with accompanying online programs. Consumers should understand that when an e-book sells for the same price as a physical copy, they are getting ripped off to the tune of however much could be obtained on resale – hundreds of dollars in the case of my students' textbooks. Consumer education and awareness will not fix the problem, but it will protect consumers somewhat and put pressure on companies, like Aspen, that try to extend their control over digital content by interfering with the traditional right to sell property.

---

50 AARON PERZANOWSKI & JASON SCHULTZ, THE END OF OWNERSHIP: PERSONAL PROPERTY IN THE DIGITAL ECONOMY 83 (MIT Press 2016); *see generally* Aaron Perzanowski & Chris Jay Hoofnagle, *What We Buy When We 'Buy Now'*, 165 U. PENN. L.REV. 315 (2017) (discussing consumers' perceptions of "buy now" and similar marketing language).

Right 3: The Right to Run

The right to run is the modern expression of the traditional right of a property owner to use and enjoy her own property. Certainly, we do not have absolute control over our property in daily life – we cannot drive the wrong way on the interstate. But we do not have to ask permission to start our car, take it to the car wash, drive to the grocery store, and buy potatoes. Once we buy those potatoes, we can cook them whenever and wherever and however we please. For the vast majority of property uses, we simply do not have to ask. We do what we want without permission, and no one steps in to tell us to stop.

By contrast, we cannot use our smart or digital property as we wish. Quite the opposite: owners must beg permission of device manufacturers to install software or even to use their devices. iPhone owners cannot install software that Apple does not like. Android owners cannot run certain programs that require administrative root access to the device. In extreme cases, the manufacturer or developer can hold a device hostage and prevent an owner from using her own property until she "agrees" to new legal terms. Nintendo released a new update for Wii U consoles that prevented access to games until the owner clicked "I Agree."[51] LG disabled important functionality in smart TVs when owners refused a license update that permitted LG to spy on the owner's viewing habits for advertising purposes.[52] In each case the manufacturer disabled the owner's property until the owner agreed to give up her legal rights. Imagine the same thing happening with a pacemaker, or with business-critical machinery. As in *2001: A Space Odyssey*, our smart devices have been programmed to respond to our requests with "I'm sorry Dave, I'm afraid I can't do that."

Under the current system of intellectual property, we are dependent on the good graces of licensors to use our software-enabled property. Recall the RAM copy doctrine, which holds that every use of a computer or other chip-embedded device is copyright infringement unless the user complies with every jot and tittle of the End User License Agreement. It is hard to overstate the strangeness that the RAM copy doctrine has introduced into the online relationship between owners and intellectual property licensors. Imagine buying a book at a bookstore and taking it home. The dust jacket, oddly, says that by purchasing the book, the purchaser has agreed not to criticize it publicly or

---

[51] *See* Kit Walsh, *Nintendo Updates Take Wii U Hostage Until You "Agree" to New Legal Terms*, ELEC. FRONTIER FOUND. (Oct. 13, 2014), https://www.eff.org/deeplinks/2014/10/nintendo-updates-take-wii-u-hostage-until-you-agree-new-legal-terms.

[52] *See* Jill Scharr, *LG TVs Demand Private Data in Exchange for 'Smart' Apps*, TOM'S GUIDE (Nov. 22, 2013), http://www.tomsguide.com/us/lg-smarttv-snooping-update,news-17902.html; *see also* Ryan W. Neal, *LG Admits to Smart TV Spying: Will Release Update Allowing Customers to Opt-Out of Data Collection*, INT'L BUS. TIMES (Nov. 25, 2013, 12:32 PM), http://www.ibtimes.com/lg-admits-smart-tv-spying-will-release-update-allowing-customers-opt-out-data-1484670.

sell it to anyone else. You read the book – and it is bad. You write an excoriating review, post it online, and sell the book to recoup your losses. You have not committed any kind of copyright infringement. You did not make a copy of the book while you were reading it. Copyright is simply not involved.

Now imagine the same book, but in e-book format. The e-book comes with the same restrictions, and your reaction is the same. Only now you *are* a copyright infringer, because you opened the book (technically making a copy from ROM into RAM) on your electronic device while not following the use restrictions of the rightsholder. Opening a book on your bookshelf does not involve copyright law. Opening a book on a Kindle does.

The degree of control that copyright holders maintain over particular copies thanks to the RAM copy doctrine has destroyed traditional property rights for consumers of digital goods. Recall how Amazon remotely deleted digital editions of 1984 and *Animal Farm* from people's Kindles in 2009 over a copyright dispute between the e-books' publisher and rightsholder. That would not have happened with physical property. No company has the right to forcibly reclaim physical property that has been fully paid for without consumers' permission or knowledge, and yet we permit the digital equivalent. One "purchaser" of 1984 "never imagined that Amazon actually had the right, the authority or even the ability to delete something that [he] had already purchased."[53] As cryptographer and computer security expert Bruce Schneier put it at the time: "As a Kindle owner, I'm frustrated. I can't lend people books and I can't sell books that I've already read, and now it turns out that I can't even count on still having my books tomorrow."[54]

Kindle owners cannot read or let others read their own books without following rules that Amazon has tacked on. iPhone owners cannot run software on their own device without Apple's permission. Business owners cannot rely on being able to run their equipment in the event of a dispute with the manufacturer. These examples, and hundreds more like them, demonstrate the need for a right to use, a right to run. The owner of digital or smart property must have the final say over what that property does, what functions it can perform, and what software it can run.

Right 4: The Right to Ban

The fourth right in the property ownership "bundle of sticks" is simultaneously the easiest case to make for digital property rights and the hardest to actually

[53] *See* Brad Stone, *Amazon Erases Orwell Books From Kindle*, N.Y. TIMES (July 17, 2009), http://www.nytimes.com/2009/07/18/technology/companies/18amazon.html?_r=0.

[54] *Id.*

enforce. Exclusion is the foundation of property. Some theorists believe it is the most important element of property.[55] An owner may not have the right to build whatever she wishes on her land (because of municipal, state, or federal land-use regulations) or the ability to use her property completely independent of the wishes of others (she might be blocked from building structures – usually fences – out of spite or ones that deprive neighbors of light or air, for example),[56] but she at the very least may exclude others from her land. One minimalist way to define ownership is to say that the owner is the one who cannot be excluded. Common law property rules, for example, define co-owners as people who cannot exclude each other from having full use and enjoyment of the property.[57] With digital and smart property, however, we are in serious danger of being treated as digital tenants on our own software-enhanced devices. As owners of our devices, we need to be doing the excluding, not the ones being excluded.

Property law has traditionally recognized the right to exclude as encompassing two parts: a right to engage in self-help to keep intruders out (think: locks, gates, and doors) and the backing of law to enforce rights against the most egregious intruders (think: a case in trespass or conversion against someone who damages your property). Likewise, the right of owners to ban intruders from their digital and smart property requires a combination of both self-help and the backing of law. Right now, without strong legal rights to exclude intrusive developers and advertisers from their devices, owners are left to fend for themselves.

One way to conceptualize the current state of affairs is to imagine what traditional property rights would look like if we required property owners to defend their property with technology alone, without the backing of the law. Locks exist, but they do not stop anyone with a brick. People could sneak onto land or into a house any time they could physically enter the space. Architects

[55] *See, e.g.*, Wendy J. Gordon, *An Inquiry into the Merits of Copyright: The Challenges of Consistency, Consent, and Encouragement Theory*, 41 Stan. L. Rev. 1343, 1356 (1989) ("The right to exclude is generally agreed to be the most important of the owner's entitlements.").
[56] *See, e.g.*, Prah v. Maretti, 108 Wis. 2d 223, 240, 321 N.W.2d 182, 191 (1982) (holding "that the private nuisance doctrine applies to obstruction of access to sunlight across adjoining land"); Sundowner, Inc. v. King, 95 Idaho 367, 368, 509 P.2d 785, 786 (1973) ("Under the modern American rule . . . one may not erect a structure for the sole purpose of annoying his neighbor. Many courts hold that a spite fence which serves no useful purpose may give rise to an action for both injunctive relief and damages.").
[57] *See* Thomas W. Merrill, *Property and the Right to Exclude*, 77 Neb. L. Rev. 730, 750 (1998) (noting that "cotenants in a tenancy in common or joint tenancy cannot exclude each other from full use and enjoyment of the property, but as to the rest of the world they manage the resource as private property").

would face no sanction for building secret rooms inside the houses they built, each with its own surveillance personnel, and for attempting to hide those rooms from the homebuyers. Worse yet, the homebuyer would expressly not be given the design schematics for her home, and there would be no way to determine if the house had been bugged. Only if she found one of the rooms more or less by accident could she evict the personnel. And even then she could not trust the eviction process, since the person called in to evict the spy could well be an employee of the snooping architect. With code, one can never be sure that some small snippet has not been left behind to regrow and re-infect a computer system after it has been cleaned.

As things stand, consumers are left to fend for themselves against the companies that coded and manufactured their property. Consumers cannot exclude intruders, and the intruders can exclude device owners from many functions of their own property. Exclusion of the cast of characters who invade our devices on a daily basis is simply not possible without the help of law. They are too many, and they are too deeply embedded in our devices to be rooted out by the consumer alone. But as a thought exercise, let us consider what it would take to actually exclude all these different actors from one of our devices. Such an exercise will introduce us to all the entities that must be subject to a true owner's right to ban them from her device.

A Thought Exercise in Digital Exclusion

Suppose that a hypothetical consumer were to try to exclude intruders from her smartphone. She must first secure the data on the device, so that intruders cannot read it. This would require her to encrypt the entire device, not just files or folders on it. She must ensure that the device does not regularly store information in a different unencrypted location, such as an unencrypted SD card. She must be certain that the device is not storing data in a cloud location that a company can read. For example, even though Google's services are well-encrypted, Google is the provider of that encryption, and therefore regularly reads users' data to glean advertising insights. As Vint Cerf, a Google executive and "founding father" of the internet, put it, "we [Google] couldn't run our system if everything in it were encrypted because then we wouldn't know which ads to show you."[58]

For many devices, cloud storage is enabled by default, and the user may not even be aware that the device is uploading her data to the company's servers

---

[58] Matt Rosoff, *Google's Business Model Is in Conflict With Your Privacy*, Bus. Insider (Nov. 2, 2011, 6:05 PM), http://www.businessinsider.com/googles-business-model-is-in-conflict-with-your-privacy-2011-11.

without her consent. Apple's devices, for one, enable cloud storage not only for data that the user wishes to store elsewhere, but also for every temporary or unsaved file on several widely used applications and even for local files residing on a user's encrypted hard drive. If an Apple user opens a word processor, types something to make a note, but never saves the file, the file may be stored on Apple servers unbeknownst to the user.

Even if our hypothetical user were to successfully encrypt her data, it is unlikely that she could truly keep intruders out. Encryption is only as secure as the password, and our user will have to pick a very long and random one to memorize and use. Advances in password-cracking technology have created a state of affairs in which programs such as Hashcat can guess every word in the English language, and indeed every sentence of many commonly known books (such as the Bible), within a matter of minutes. One successful Hashcat attempt cracked the password "Ph'nglui mglw'nafh Cthulhu R'lyeh wgah'nagl fhtagn1," an occult phrase from H. P. Lovecraft's short story *The Call of Cthulhu*.[59] (And yes, the password creator had put the 1 at the end for supposedly additional security.)

If our user can fully secure her data, she must still worry about those who have legitimate access to the device but may have allowed or inserted loopholes or quiet surveillance snippets into the code. App providers commonly take far more data than the app requires. There is no universally accepted way to staunch this flow of data from the apps on a device. Some versions of open source operating systems can prohibit an app from accessing some personal data, but this means hacking the device and replacing the operating system. Moreover, not all apps are apparent to the user. Just as a computer can run malicious code, smart property is capable of running silent apps, and apps may perform functions well beyond the expectation of the consumer who downloads them. Bruce Schneier notes that a frequently downloaded flashlight app for Android phones – Brightest Flashlight Free – started collecting its users' location information even before they clicked "accept" to agree to the license agreement.[60] This agreement also failed to acknowledge that the information could be sold to third parties. Surely most, if not all, of Brightest Flashlight Free's fifty million users would not expect an app that merely turns on a phone's flashlight to need, want, or be able to track their every move. Other seemingly innocuous apps, like Angry Birds, have been targeted by the NSA

---

[59] *See* Mark Ward, *The Gentle Art of Cracking Passwords*, BBC News (Dec. 2, 2013), http://www .bbc.com/news/technology-24519306.
[60] *See* Bruce Schneier, Data and Goliath 46–47 (W.W. Norton, Inc. 2015).

and GCHQ for the trove of user data they collect.[61] Overreach may not even be intentional. When Pokémon GO was initially released, the app mistakenly requested and received not just access to iPhone users' information, but full read-write-delete access to users' Google accounts.[62]

Sometimes the lax practices of legitimate guests invite unwanted intruders. Companies that place malware or spyware on consumers' computers often leave back doors "protected" by unsophisticated passwords. Cybersecurity expert Robert Graham was able to extract the certificate from Superfish – the spyware program discussed in the opening of this chapter – and crack the password that encrypted it in less than three hours.[63] Anyone who had that password (the lowercase name of the company!) could compromise the computer. The password was the same on all computers that had Superfish installed. Superfish was not only a threat itself; it also increased the chances that other unauthorized parties could successfully get in.

Once our hypothetical user has attempted to deal with direct attacks on data on the device, and with overreaching application providers, she must then turn her attention to the device's operating system. A device's operating system is usually designed to leak data about the user to its designer. Android, for one, requires a Google sign-in in order for most functions to operate, and the system regularly records the user's browsing and location activity for Google unless the user finds and changes obscure settings. Even then, the device still records a lot of information, but in a way not visible to the user. If you have a Google account and have not turned off your search history, it is an interesting experience to log in and see every single search you have made while logged into that account or into a browser or device linked to that account. Other operating systems are little better. Apple claims to make less use of its users' data for advertising purposes, but its devices are little better in terms of user tracking. Security analysts discovered that Apple devices stored

---

[61] *See* James Ball, *Angry Birds and 'Leaky' Phone Apps Targeted by NSA and GCHQ for User Data*, GUARDIAN (Jan. 28, 2014, 2:51 PM), http://www.theguardian.com/world/2014/jan/27/nsa-gchq-smartphone-app-angry-birds-personal-data ("Dozens of classified documents ... detail the NSA and GCHQ efforts to piggyback on this commercial data collection for their own purposes.").

[62] *See* Jason Cipriani, *Pokémon GO Can See Everything in Your Google Account. Here's How to Stop It*, CNET (July 11, 2016, 6:13 PM), https://www.cnet.com/how-to/Pokémon-go-google-account-access ("[I]f you use an iOS device and a Google account to sign up for Pokémon GO, the app is granted full access to your Google account. That means the developer of Pokémon GO, Niantic, may have access to your emails, Google Drive, calendar, contacts, photos, Chrome browsing history, search history, Maps data ... and, well, anything else linked to your Google account.").

[63] *See* Fox-Brewster, *supra* note 2 (reporting that "Graham has now extracted the key").

a user's location data in unencrypted format directly on the device.[64] And Microsoft has now switched to a new operating system format that gathers much of a user's information directly from her desktop or laptop.[65]

Open-source projects provide some alternatives, but a user must be enough of a computer expert to replace the operating system, and must bear serious interoperability costs – many programs are not written to work with open-source operating systems. Furthermore, some free open-source systems, like Ubuntu, have now begun funding operations by selling advertisers direct access to consumers, whether or not they wish it, right on their desktops. When a user searches for an application or file on her own computer, the search is sent to Ubuntu's servers, which is then forwarded to Amazon, as well as to other third parties, to display search results to the user.[66] If the user then clicks an Amazon link and buys anything, Ubuntu's developer gets a commission.[67] Since the advertisements are unencrypted, others sharing a wireless network with the user are able to get a good idea of her searches. Whether searching for a résumé to find a new job or for legal documents to file for divorce, the user cannot even look for these things on her own computer without broadcasting the searches to the world.

And even if our user were to install an operating system that could be trusted not to leak data to advertisers, the manufacturer is an ever-present threat. A hardware manufacturer can leave programs running in the software and firmware that runs the device, and re-route information to its benefit. In 2013, one analyst tracked down a strange stream of data emanating from his Motorola phone. He had not authorized the transmission of his social media information, passwords, and the like, to another device, yet every nine minutes his phone was contacting an unknown server and transmitting that data. Upon

[64] *See How Apple's iPhone and iPad Secretly Store a User's Location Data?*, INT'L BUS. TIMES (Apr. 21, 2011, 6:45 AM), http://www.ibtimes.com/how-apples-iphone-ipad-secretly-store-users-location-data-video-280801 ("[Researchers] discovered that the database of a user's locations are stored on the iPhone and also in any other device the iPhone is synced with.").
[65] Recall our discussion of Windows 10 earlier in this chapter.
[66] *See* Micah Lee, *Privacy in Ubuntu 12.10: Amazon Ads and Data Leaks*, EFF (Oct. 29, 2012), http://www.eff.org/deeplinks/2012/10/privacy-ubuntu-1210-amazon-ads-and-data-leaks ("[W]hen you search for something in Dash, your computer makes a secure HTTPS connection to productsearch.ubuntu.com, sending along your search query and your IP address. If it returns Amazon products to display, your computer then insecurely loads the product images from Amazon's server over HTTP.").
[67] *See* Scott Gilbertson, *Ay Caramba, Ubuntu 12.10: Get It Right on Amazon!*, REGISTER (Oct. 18, 2012, 3:00 PM), http://www.theregister.co.uk/2012/10/18/ubuntu_12_10_review (reporting that if Ubuntu users "end up buying something after clicking on one of the Amazon results, Canonical gets a small percentage of the sale").

further tracking the server, he determined that it was a server maintained by Motorola.[68]

Finally, even if our exclusion-minded user were able to secure her data on the device – and she cannot – her data are subject to even more surveillance when the device communicates with any other server. The information is of course received by the target server. The sender intends it to be. But those who have privileged access to user devices may use that access to intercept information in transit. The manufacturer of a computer may abuse its position to load a consumer's computer with malware (as we saw with Lenovo). That malware then not only leaks all the user's encrypted communications for the benefit of the manufacturer (who was paid to install the malware), but also leaves backdoors through which other intruders can intercept or falsify communications. Verizon, for instance, was sanctioned by the FCC for attaching a "supercookie" to all communications with its customers by adding a unique identifier to all communications to and from the device.[69] The identifier tracked all the consumers' movements across the internet. Consumers could not remove the identifier because it was added to their communications after they had been transmitted to Verizon. The FCC stepped in after other websites learned how to read the identifier and track consumers wherever they went online for advertising purposes.[70]

Ultimately, even if the consumer were to do her best to exclude others from taking her data, she would be hard-pressed to understand precisely what kinds of data smart devices gather. More and more consumers are beginning to realize that their web traffic and geolocations are being tracked. However, as discussed earlier, new interface modes, including voice and gesture controls, provide new means of monitoring. Combine ambient sound and accelerometer data with the vast network of data already being recorded by other smart devices, and users' every move can be monitored, tracked, and contextualized.

It is fruitless to try to use technology alone to protect citizens' smart devices from intruders, but the attempt, even if hypothetical, is revealing. Owners need help to exclude unwanted entities that access their devices, and to prevent

---

[68] Ben Lincoln, *Motorola is Listening*, BENEATH THE WAVES, www.beneaththewaves.net/Projects/Motorola_Is_Listening.html#Analysis1 (last updated July 28, 2013) (recounting the analyst's experience and providing steps to reproduce the issue).

[69] *See* Andrea Peterson, *FCC Cracks Down on Verizon Wireless for Using 'Supercookies'*, WASH. POST (Mar. 7, 2016), http://www.washingtonpost.com/news/the-switch/wp/2016/03/07/fcc-cracks-down-on-verizons-supercookies.

[70] *See id.* (reporting that "Verizon must pay a $1.35 million fine and will only be able to use the tracking mechanism when users connect to Verizon's corporate family of services unless the company gets customers' opt-in consent").

legitimate guests from letting intruders in. Smart property is designed to leak data. Much of the data that is collected is not necessary for the device to function. Much of the data that *is* necessary for the device to function is used by the gathering company in ways the user cannot predict. At the outset, therefore, a strictly technical solution is not possible. Educating consumers to use exclusion technologies falls far short of a true solution. Users need a legal right to ban.

Backing Up the Right to Ban

There are some simple ways to implement this right. The first, and easiest, is to make the default rule for devices one of trespass to property. If a guest snoops where it is not wanted, or a program intrudes without permission, fierce and effective legal sanctions must be at the owner's disposal. Trespass is a particularly useful way to conceptualize developer overreach. The usual response of an overreaching developer or advertiser is that although they may have intruded without the user's permission, they have done no harm. Trespass standards for harm are easier to establish. It does not matter if someone has not particularly harmed your land when they walked through it – they are still a trespasser and can be removed. Even if one uses the more lenient measure of Trespass to Chattels, which in the computer context is usually measured by consumption of bandwidth or other computing resources, the harm calculus is far simpler. Is the app or software bogging the processor down by soaking up valuable processor cycles, running the battery down, soaking up storage space, or clogging the user's bandwidth? These are all practical, down-to-earth questions that a court can answer, and that do not require the more complex calculus of privacy harms, to which courts have generally been hostile. Either of these trespass standards provides a clearer model of harm than routing the user's complaint through privacy law. After all, it is fairly easy to establish that a developer did overreach its permissions. Courts consider it much harder to determine whether the resulting invasion of privacy really hurt the user.

A second proposal is almost as simple. There is an emerging best practice that permits device users to refuse or revoke application permissions on a permission-by-permission, application-by-application, time-by-time basis. This permits the user to provide some information, to some applications, some of the time, and to revoke a permission for an application without revoking it for every application. This more developed permissions control is the essence of returning to owners control over their devices. Device operating systems should permit users to partially or completely ban a program from the device, and to limit the categories of information a program receives, even if the program is permitted. The option to ban should be clear and conspicuous, not hidden deep within the architecture of a device. Attempts to avoid or subvert an owner's ability to clearly identify who is accessing the device and to ban them if not desired should be treated as unfair and deceptive trade practices.

There has been serious, positive movement on this front. Apple, for all its strict control of the consumer experience, has been more responsive to consumer demand for granular control over permissions. iPhones have allowed users to control their applications on a per-permission basis for years. So if a flashlight app wants, preposterously, location data, call information, and identity, the consumer simply looking to illuminate a dark room can just say no, and expect her device to enforce that preference. Android is finally responding to consumers as well. The newest iteration of the Android operating system, Marshmallow, features app-by-app permission control in that apps ask the first time they need to seek a given resource (although that control still functions on the "ask once, collect forever" model preferred by advertisers). It is not perfect, but it is progress, and the progress indicates a clear direction.

In sum, a device should not be so designed as to answer to the manufacturer, or the app designer, or the carrier, or the operating system designer, or to anyone or any other entity above the commands of the owner. Devices should have easy-to-use mechanisms for rooting, along with any reasonable warning to the user of the consequences of doing so. Users should be able to revoke permissions for apps on a resource-by-resource basis. If a user believes that an app does not need access to all of her contacts, or to her calendar (which could contain sensitive work, medical, or other personal information), she should be able to refuse or remove that permission. And finally, as with people who enter land or use someone's personal property: permission to use the owner's property at one time point should not indicate permission to use the owner's property in perpetuity.

TASK 2: LIMIT THE REACH OF CONTRACTUAL LICENSES

As discussed throughout this book, intellectual property licenses now control consumer activity that has nothing to do with intellectual property. They also govern situations, such as simply turning on a computer or browsing a website, that have never before involved copyright law.

There are some practical moves necessary to limit the reach of these contractual licenses. To start, the single most important thing we can do is strengthen the concept of digital ownership. True ownership of property is the opposite of the limited licenses that companies claim consumers get when they buy digital and smart property. Everything in this book has been about how to strengthen digital ownership. So, in a way, everything has been about how to limit the contract-license approach. To that end, there are some specific things we can do to weaken the contract-license model: strengthen exhaustion, abolish RAM copies, separate contractual promises from IP license conditions, and finally, retool consent.

Strengthening Exhaustion

As Aaron Perzanowski and Jason Schultz have persuasively written, the first thing we must do is reinforce the idea that once a company has sold a product, its power to control what the user does with the product has definitively ended.[71] This is a hard line to sell under current court decisions and Copyright Office reports. (The latter have no force of law, but are influential with courts). Courts, and the Copyright Office, have traditionally accepted that there is no first sale right for completely digital property. I hope that courts can be convinced that exhaustion has played, and must continue to play, a critical role in balancing consumer and corporate interests. I hope that courts can be convinced that digital first sale is in fact the best interpretation of the Copyright Act. I hope that courts can be convinced that the Copyright Office is simply wrong when it claims no technology can create discrete and rivalrous digital resources. But, even under the best circumstances, that discussion will take time, and the outcome is by no means clear.[72]

In the meantime, though, courts can strengthen exhaustion by working backwards from physical property. Companies have yet to successfully claim that when they sell a smartphone, they have not sold anything to the consumer. That's simply wrong: they have at least sold the physical casing and components. So we can begin with the traditional understanding of property to argue that certain types of necessary, simple software are sold, not licensed. Consider sales of goods with embedded software – things like coffee makers, calculators, or your bluetooth-enabled toothbrush. Under the Uniform Commercial Code, such sales are simply considered goods, not software.[73] The software necessary to run the good is rolled into the good itself.

---

[71] See Perzanowski & Schultz, *supra* note 44, at 1216 (advocating "increased reliance on exhaustion to resolve a range of disputes over personal use by consumers that are typically analyzed through the lenses of fair use and implied license").

[72] See generally *id.* (discussing the various views regarding copyright law and digital property).

[73] See U.C.C. § 9–102(a)(44) ("Goods . . . . includes a computer program embedded in goods . . . if (i) the program is associated with the goods in such a manner that it customarily is considered part of the goods, or (ii) by becoming the owner of the goods, a person acquires a right to use the program in connection with the goods.")

In earlier chapters I explained that physicality is not a great proxy for what is and is not property. What is the difference between an MP3 on a hard disk and an MP3 on a compact disc? But if courts are going to continue to apply first sale exhaustion to CDs and not MP3s, then maybe it is time for some creative hacking of the legal system. For example, recall the silly federal court rule that said if buyers want to sell their MP3s, they have to sell their entire computer.[74] Well, okay, done. Physical storage mediums come pretty cheap and small these days (some for even pennies on Amazon – not including shipping, of course). If a cheap chip is all it takes to sell my MP3s on eBay, that is easy enough. Injecting a little bit of physicality into a digital system can help courts realize that customers do in fact own something after all, at least as far as the physical components are concerned.

Abolishing RAM Copies

A key part of reducing the power of copyright licenses is to put to rest the RAM copy doctrine of *MAI v. Peak Systems*.[75] We have examined the doctrine in depth elsewhere, but it bears repeating: the RAM copy doctrine holds that copyright is involved not just when a user makes a true, persistent, separate copy of the original that she can use or give independently to someone else, but also whenever the consumer makes use of her own purchase. Turning on a Kindle and reading a Dan Brown novel should not involve copyright law. A Kindle reader has not made a true copy by turning the computer on. She cannot sell an extra copy of the book; all she has done is pull up *The Da Vinci Code* on her screen. Her action does not affect the market of the bookseller. In fact, the opposite is true: if she could not pull the book up on her screen, what point would there be in her buying it in the first place?

Courts must stop treating the routine use of digital books, movies, music, and software as if the company has made some special concession by letting the buyer use what she purchased. The e-book was sold to be read, the MP3 to be heard, the digital movie to be watched. The user has not done anything involving copyright law when she reads the e-book, listens to the music, or hits "play" on her computer, just as an illegal copy is not made when she reads a book in print, listens to a record, or hits "play" on a DVD player. When a purchaser uses the property for the purpose for which it was intended, and in

---

[74] *See* Capitol Records, LLC v. ReDigi, Inc., 934 F. Supp. 2d 640, 656 (S.D.N.Y. 2013) (recognizing that the Copyright Act "still protects a lawful owner's sale of her 'particular' phonorecord, be it a computer hard disk, iPod, or other memory device onto which the file was originally downloaded").

[75] 991 F.2d 511 (1993).

doing so makes no permanent copy that leaves no trace on the seller's market, then copyright law should have absolutely nothing to do with the relationship between buyer and seller.[76]

Removing copyright law from the company–consumer relationship will go a long way toward correcting the imbalance of power between company and consumer. Copyright liability is intended to stop people who make copies to undermine the seller's market, which is why violations can cost a whopping $150,000 per song or movie pirated. But these are not damages that should be used to intimidate those who simply purchase books and read them. Basic non-copyright contract damages, meanwhile, are far less substantial. Usually, under a contract, the victim of the breach gets the value of the deal: the "benefit of the bargain." Think about a company who claims that a user, by loading her song onto a different MP3 player, has broken a contract. So what? The company already got the sale, it got the benefit of the bargain. It lost nothing by letting the consumer listen to the music on whatever device she wishes. Confiscating the nail-studded club of copyright infringement will greatly reduce companies' incentive to insert into their copyright license agreements silly terms that have absolutely nothing to do with copyright law.

Separating Contractual Promises from IP License Conditions

Imagine the purchaser of a new video game. Let's call her Gamer. The game has rules that players must follow, and that Gamer promises to follow in the EULA. Some of those rules have to do with copyright law – such as prohibiting the making or distribution of illegal copies of the software. But some of the rules have absolutely nothing to do with software or copyright at all. One of the rules is that players must be nice to other players of the game. One day, Gamer becomes angry at another player and curses into her headset. She has broken the game's rules, and her promise in the EULA. But is she a copyright infringer? Should her curse cost her $150,000?

This was more or less the case before the Ninth Circuit Court of Appeals in *MDY v. Blizzard Entertainment*.[77] Blizzard made the popular video game World of Warcraft (as mentioned earlier, the game that Blizzard lauded for its inherent lock-in effect). When players signed up to play World of Warcraft, they agreed not to cheat. But MDY offered a program that let players cheat by

---

[76] *See* Aaron Perzanowski, *Fixing RAM Copies*, 104 Nw. U.L. Rev. 1067, 1108 (2010) ("The foundation of *Peak's* RAM copy doctrine – the current dominant approach among courts – is at best unsteady.... [C]opyright law must develop a reliable and predictable standard to finally replace *Peak*.").

[77] 629 F.3d 928 (9th Cir. 2010).

automating gameplay through the use of a "bot."[78] Blizzard argued that MDY was liable not only for the players' cheating, but also for the players' copyright infringement. By now, you can probably guess Blizzard's theory: when the players cheated, they loaded their copy of World of Warcraft from ROM into RAM, making a RAM copy. And when they made that "copy" (actually, just double-clicked to start the game) while thinking bad thoughts about cheating, they were in violation of the terms of the software license. Hence, they were copyright infringers.

MDY may not have been the most sympathetic defendant; it did help players cheat. But MDY made a great point: Blizzard should not be able to control the actual everyday lives of its users through its license and the RAM copy doctrine. Imagine a few other rules Blizzard could have put in its EULA: playing the game while wearing beige clothing could be copyright infringement. Playing the game while intending to vote Democratic (or Republican) in the next election could be copyright infringement. Playing the game while not standing on your head could be copyright infringement. And because companies can – and do – change their EULAs at any time, those rules could change day by day. Those who do not follow those rules could be struck by the $150,000 club of copyright infringement.

The Ninth Circuit agreed that rules about cheating had nothing to do with copyright law.[79] World of Warcraft players were not copyright infringers when they broke a promise that had nothing to do with copyright. In turn, MDY was not liable for the players' infringement. MDY did lose on another ground, which was that it had helped consumers break their ordinary non-copyright contractual promises not to cheat.[80] We can live with that. The damages for breach of contract for Blizzard against a player who has paid for the game are, again, nil. And MDY should not have helped people cheat. But the path Blizzard took to punish MDY would have had the side effect of turning millions of Blizzard's customers into copyright infringers. That is not quite a best business practice.

MDY is just one case, and it was hardly clear-cut. Part of the Ninth Circuit holding relied on the fact that Blizzard had not put all its rules for gameplay directly into its license agreement. Blizzard put them in a different document called a Code of Conduct. As a result of the ruling, game companies now put

---

[78] *See MDY*, 629 F.3d at 935 ("[The program] . . . moves the mouse around and pushes keys on the keyboard. You tell it about your character, where you want to kill things, and when you want to kill. Then it kills for you, automatically.")

[79] *See id.* at 952–55 (holding MDY not liable for copyright infringement).

[80] *See id.* at 958 (remanding "Blizzard's claim for tortious interference with contract").

their rules for all kinds of things directly into their license agreements. And if that is all that *MDY* stands for, then it is a pretty boring case.

But if *MDY* stands for something different – that companies should not be able to make consumers jump through circus hoops under the whip of copyright infringement – then it is quite an interesting case. That avenue is well worth exploring. Not every promise from a consumer to a company has to do with making copies of copyrighted materials. Sometimes a promise to play nicely is just a promise to play nicely. Note that weakening the RAM copy doctrine would have a big influence here – if companies were unable to assert that consumers are making a copy when using the product as intended, it would be hard to for them to argue that their strange behavior controls have anything at all to do with copyright.

Retooling Consent

The rights to hack, sell, run, and ban will mean nothing if we give them up when we click "I agree" to a contract that we must click to access a device. It is not enough to hide the right to access someone's property deep in an unreadable electronic legal document that no one understands. There must be a higher standard for consent to access property. We would not allow a company physical access to someone's bedroom on the basis of an obscure and incomprehensible clause in a contract. We certainly would not allow an appliance distributor unlimited access to our home merely because we agreed that a repair person could enter a single time to fix our refrigerator. Yet this is how things stand online.

We need to retool consent. No one understands what they are agreeing to when they click "I Agree." Even Chief Justice Roberts has admitted he does not read online contracts, because the important provisions become "lost in the legalese."[81] He noted that "we sit there and say that this person should have known, he should have been warned that this is what might happen," but "when you get too much of that, you have nothing."[82] Roberts concluded: "There has to be a more effective way of alerting people to what they really should know."[83]

Roberts is correct – requiring users to read and understand complex legal documents that strip away their right to property and privacy will not fix the inequities that arise in online contracting. Instead, contracts should conform

[81] Canisius College, *Part 2 of Q&A with Chief Justice of the United States John G. Roberts Jr.*, YouTube (Oct. 24, 2010), http://www.YouTube.com/watch?v=ypX2iLdKQI4.
[82] *Id.*   [83] *Id.*

to user expectations. We need to minimize the distance between what people expect when they click "I Agree" and what they get. There are two ways to do this. The first idea, which has already been attempted, was to force consumers to read ever-longer contracts on ever-smaller screens. That system – as Chief Justice Roberts noted – has failed. The second and more promising approach is to construe and limit contracts in light of consumers' expectations of what they and others may do with their property. People expect and desire to control their own property, to have it answer to them and not to a faraway technology company. Limiting online contracts to basic user expectations about property and privacy would have the salutary effect of channeling online contracting practice in a new direction, one much more closely aligned with consumer protection.

It should take more than a simple "I Agree" for a company to get unlimited access to your home, car, and personal health and biometric data (among many other things) through its control of your Internet of Things devices. There is at least some escape from a computer. You can leave it on the desk. But there is no escape from mobile computing, which citizens carry with them or is already embedded in the infrastructure everywhere they go. In such a context, consent implies the ability to say yes to a use of data as a consequence of the right to say no. In today's digitized world, it is not possible, practically speaking, to refuse corporate data gathering. Facebook runs a shadow version of its social network, in which it collects and connects information about people who do not use Facebook.[84] If a person walks into a room with an Xbox One or a Samsung Smart Television, she has no choice as to whether the device is listening and watching. For consent to work there needs to be some ability to opt out. At minimum, that ability should attach to objects which the user herself owns.

TASK 3: MAKE MINIMUM NECESSARY CHANGES TO STATUTORY LAW

There must also be some minimum changes to statutory law in order for consumers to exercise traditionally recognized property rights over their digital assets. Congress is admittedly a hard place to seek solutions. Yet there is some hope. People care about control over their iPhones, Android tablets, smart

---

[84] *See* Christopher Zara, *Facebook Privacy Lawsuit Alleges Social Network Created 'Shadow Profiles' of Non-Users*, INT'L BUS. TIMES (Apr. 24, 2015, 11:36 AM), http://www.ibtimes.com/facebook-privacy-lawsuit-alleges-social-network-created-shadow-profiles-non-users-1895840 ("Facebook has even collected such data on nonusers . . . by scanning photos and creating 'shadow profiles' of people whose photos are uploaded to the site but do not have Facebook accounts.").

watches, and new cars. They understand that their entire lives are recorded through these devices. They resent the limits on their use and control of their own property. There has been enough political foment around these issues that both sides of the congressional aisle have some strong incentive for change.

The Digital Millennium Copyright Act's anti-circumvention rules must be scaled back to permit owners to modify and use their devices. Perhaps the easiest way to accomplish this change is by requesting that the Librarian of Congress exercise the statutory authority under the DMCA to exempt certain categories of goods from the Act's provisions. But this would leave the basic structure of the law in place – any device not specifically exempted will raise the problem again. Since DMCA exemptions only last for three years, the fight between groups such as the Electronic Frontier Foundation and manufacturers such as John Deere could continue indefinitely. And finally, since DMCA exemptions do not extend to third-party coders, the exemptions generally mean nothing unless the owner herself has the coding chops to make the modifications.

The best move is to scrap DMCA Section 1201 entirely. It does little good, and a lot of harm. It has failed to stop the arms race between code crackers and digital rights management, and instead has served to let companies lock consumers out of their own devices. A partial reform, which has the sole virtue of being better than the current state of affairs, would be to apply Librarian of Congress exemptions to creators of software or other products that would permit owners to exercise their rights under the exemptions. So if the Librarian of Congress were to permit users to tinker with their own smartphones, coders would be permitted to design software to help the non-experts among us to do that. If the Librarian of Congress were to permit car owners to tinker with their car software, mechanics could design computerized tools to help owners do that.

Beyond that limited reform, the core of DMCA Section 1201 is irredeemable. We might try to tie the breaking of DRM more closely to making an illegal copy – that is pirating movies, music, or other files – but so long as most courts still follow the RAM copy doctrine, every use of a computer counts as making a copy. Reforming the DMCA to trigger only upon the making of a true illegal copy would work only if *MAI* were universally repudiated by the Courts of Appeals (or the Supreme Court), and that will not happen in the near term. To be clear, both reform of DMCA 1201 and the RAM copy doctrine are badly needed, but the likelihood of them happening simultaneously and along the same lines is low.

The Federal Arbitration Act also warrants revision to ensure that consumers can assert their claims in court, and that courts can develop precedent governing ownership of online and digital resources. Almost all modern contracts for online and digital goods or services, including the End User License Agreements and Terms of Use that govern software licenses for software embedded in physical objects, require that consumers agree to go to arbitration to enforce their claims rather than go to court. This may seem insignificant, as arbitral panels may do a decent job. But arbitral decisions do not become precedent, which slowly bends the path of the common law. Cases covering new technologies must be considered by courts so that the balance between company and consumer, between prior and emerging stakeholders, can be maintained. The strength of a common law system for technological societies is that law may develop rapidly and organically, with rules that iterate societal expectations and improve as multiple courts weigh in. However, since all cases must go to arbitration, new law cannot develop, new rules cannot grow, new precedent cannot be set, and the law of digital property cannot evolve.

The Federal Arbitration Act has served to reroute consumer cases out of courts and therefore out of the consideration of the common law. This was the opposite of the act's original intention, which was to permit large corporate entities to opt out of complex and costly litigation. It is not without irony that one notes that the FAA today is generally not used against corporations, which have the market power to refuse arbitration clauses, but against ordinary citizens. A change to the Federal Arbitration Act to exclude consumer arbitration would permit courts to return to work on digital consumer cases.

Reform in these three areas – basic property law, contract law, and related statutory law – will provide the basis for jailbreaking ownership. Such reform is doable, and much-needed reforms are already underway. People understand what is at stake when they no longer control their own property. People broadly ignore the rules that prevent them from modifying their gaming consoles and phones, and the same companies that cheerfully sued their customers for copying music do not yet dare to press the issue. But the first lawsuits against other companies that, for example, help you fix your software-controlled car, have already begun. A crisis is brewing. Companies will only continue to argue that ownership is an outdated notion that did not survive with smart and digital property. Owners, lawmakers, and policymakers must be ready to push back.

TASK 4: FOSTER TECHNOLOGICAL SHIFTS TO JAILBREAK OWNERSHIP

In addition to changes in the law, the rights to hack, sell, run, and ban also require technological shifts. This is not to say that technological self-help and the market will carry the day unassisted. They will not. But consumers cannot win when the technological deck is stacked against them. Better tools are needed, as well as their inclusion as a matter of best practices and regulatory enforcement. Tools permitting users to digitally sequester applications that take more data than they need to run, tools that permit users to provide null data sets or, better yet, false data sets to overreaching programs, and tools that actually secure devices, without backdoors or built-in security flaws, are needed to permit users to protect their personal privacy. Tools permitting users to root their devices and take control, in the same way that a user of a PC can choose to run her computer in administrative mode, are necessary to permit users to run the code they need to run without asking permission of the manufacturer. Most importantly, coders need tools to crack open commercial software so that they can write simple, useable tools that consumers can use to do all of these things.

Third-Party Technologies

Companies have little incentive to build tools for consumers that would prevent companies themselves from accessing potentially valuable data. That task needs to be tackled by hackers, coding groups, consumer advocate groups, and private companies that want to move into building a market for pro-consumer technologies. The existing technological structure needs to have certain features to enable these groups to build tools for owners to use on their devices. The basic challenge is interoperability: how to build code that can effectively interface with other code.

Open-source
The gold standard for code is open-source. This means that the source code can be read by anyone. It does not mean that the code can be used by anyone. Traditional copyright protections (for the actual expression of the code) and patent protection (to the extent patent protection remains available after *Alice Corp. v. CLS Bank Int'l*[85]) still prevent competitors from reusing code directly. But the value in using open-source code is that others can build smoothly interoperable code. Consider the Android Open Source Project (AOSP), which propelled Android past Apple as the most widely adopted smartphone operating system. AOSP's open-source code made it attractive for manufacturers, who could modify versions of AOSP to suit what they thought customers

[85] Alice Corp. Pty. Ltd. v. CLS Bank Int'l, 134 S. Ct. 2347, 2352 (2014) (holding a "computerized scheme for mitigating 'settlement risk'" ineligible for patent protection). The ruling focused on the principle in patent law that abstract ideas or concepts alone cannot be patented. The "generic" computer program lacked the necessary originality for a patent because it embodied a fundamental concept of economics. *Id.*

wanted, a process called "skinning." Independent groups developed code that made a version of the AOSP free for anyone who could install it (I began using Cyanogen myself after researchers discovered Motorola was redirecting social media information to its own servers). Individuals contributed bits of code that made the system better. And other people were able to develop applications that interacted with AOSP. They did not need Google's approval. They were simply able to develop code that met owners' needs.

Root Access

While open-source code makes it easier to develop code that interoperates with a given device, root access permits a range of apps to be installed on a device, and to function at full capacity. Root access is the power one usually exercises as an owner of a computer – the power to run whatever code the user with root access wishes. But many smart devices ship without root access, meaning that the manufacturer has the power to run certain code on the device, but the buyer of the device cannot tell it to run similar code. Companies limit root access because malicious code can damage the machine or compromise the user's data, and giving malicious code root access is particularly dangerous.

But the same argument could be made for computers. Root access is just the equivalent of running a program in "administrator" mode. Users often hear that it is best to browse the internet from a guest or non-administrator account, and use an administrator account only when necessary. Most versions of Windows require a special just-in-time permission to grant a program administrator access. True, giving that kind of power to the owner of the computer can be dangerous. But letting a sixteen-year-old get behind the wheel of the rolling tons of destruction we call cars is dangerous too. At some point, denying people administrator access to their own property crosses over into raw paternalism.

Root access is critical for an owner to be able to act as final arbiter of what code runs on her device. But few owners write their own code. Most of the code that a root user runs is designed by third parties. So root access is also critically important for users to be able to use other people's code to get their property running the way they wish. Just like the right to fix your own car is useless without the right to go to a mechanic, so the right to modify your own smart property is useless without the right to root the device and run and install third-party software. This is not hard to do: denying root access to a consumer requires extra code and work for a company (especially since consumers keep finding exploits to use to root their devices, requiring companies to run over-the-air updates to remove the root access again). So, an important technological building block to permitting users to control their own devices is to permit them root access in the device as shipped, and to stop removing root access via over-the-air updates.

Modularity: Removability and Interoperability

The flipside to the power to install and run code is the power to remove it. Code must be easy to remove. To achieve that, regulatory agencies should consider whether code is designed to be modular. In an earlier chapter I discussed the merits of modular objects: they contain and encapsulate complexity. Well-written code is modular. Each bit of code is an object with restricted inputs and outputs. A well-written code object can be swapped with a different code object without compromising the whole system. If I make a Lego statue of Darth Vader, I can take one brick out and replace it with another. If the feet look bad, I can take the feet off, make new ones out of Lego blocks, and plug them back in. If I made the statue out of marble, I could not do that. Taking off the feet could shatter the marble.

Modularity is key to the right to ban. Apps need to be built modularly so they can be selectively restricted or removed by consumers. When apps are intentionally built into the operating system at such a deep level that removing them causes the system to fail, then users cannot ban the app from their system. This is not only bad code; it is intentional. Operating system designers and manufacturers get a lot of money from companies eager to ensure that their apps get on your phone – and stay there. I'm sure you have had this experience: you get a new phone, but its free memory is already limited – half of the phone is taken up with apps you do not like and will not use. Worst of all, there is no way to delete them (without root access, that is). The operating system manufacturer has taken money from the app developers to ensure that these invaders stay on your property, even when you, the owner, say "Get out."

Companies offer the excuse that the app is somehow so deeply entangled with the operating system that removing it would impair the functioning of the whole system. Apple CEO Tim Cook responded to consumer demand for the ability to remove bloatware by stating: "This is a more complex issue than it first appears . . . . There are some apps that are linked to something else on the iPhone. If they were to be removed they might cause issues elsewhere on the phone. There are other apps that aren't like that. So over time, I think with the ones that aren't like that, we'll figure out a way . . . ."[86]

[86] Lily Hay Newman, *Tim Cook Says You Might Be Able to Remove Apple's Un-Deletable Apps. At Some Point. Maybe.*, SLATE (Sept. 15, 2015), http://www.slate.com/blogs/future_tense/2015/09/15/tim_cook_says_you_might_be_able_to_remove_apple_s_un_deletable_apps.html.

But there is a way: let users delete bloatware apps that do not connect to the operating system, and stop hijacking users' digital real estate to inflate the bottom line. "It's not that we want to suck up your real estate," Cook said "We're not motivated to do that."[87] This is hardly believable. Bloatware does not magically appear on a device tightly controlled by Apple, Samsung, or Google. The manufacturer put it there because companies pay them to do that. And while there is clear value to the company in having the consumer encounter the software already on her phone, defying the consumer's desire to remove an unwanted app in the hope that she will eventually love it is like repeatedly asking out someone you've just met at a bar. After the first polite refusal, it's just harassment.

Further, applications that are so deeply built into the operating system as to be irremovable should not be designed that way. Apple does not hire bad programmers. Those programmers understand modularity and object-oriented programming. If an app is indeed so deeply integrated with the operating system that removing it would cause damage, that is purposefully bad coding, a self-inflicted wound to keep the user from deleting bloatware or switching to a better product.

One big way to enforce the right to ban is for regulatory agencies, primarily the FTC, to understand modularity and object-oriented programming. The FTC has not hesitated in other areas to use its Section 5 authority to sanction unfair business practices against companies that do not use best practices, most recently in the arena of data security and encryption.[88] It is no stretch at all to say that the intentional abandonment of core principles of software design to increase profits and force users to continue to accept invasive programs on their machines is a textbook definition of unfair. Imagine if a car dealer filled the trunk of her cars with dirty laundry and soldered the lock so unsuspecting buyers could not ditch the stuff. It would be an unacceptable invasion of your property. Bloatware is no different.

Requiring programmers to follow basic principles of good software design would reap significant advantages. Once apps are properly modular, consumers can engage in self-help to practice their right to ban. Even if a company does not let you uninstall a program – and it should be required to – individual coders and coding groups can come to the rescue. There are many

---

[87] *Id.*

[88] *See, e.g.,* Fed. Trade Comm'n v. Lifelock Inc., No. CV-10-00530-PHX-JJT, 2016 WL 692048, at *2 (D. Ariz. Jan. 4, 2016) (ordering a $100,000,000 judgment against a company for misleading consumers about its data security practices). For an overview of, among other things, the FTC's data security cases, see generally *Privacy & Security Update (2015)*, FTC (Jan. 2016), https://www.ftc.gov/reports/privacy-data-security-update-2015.

ways to root your phone, and once rooted, there are apps that permit you to remove or freeze bloatware. For the enormous majority, there is a significant positive effect, not a negative one, on the operating system. I do not want to offend football fans, but for an e-sports fan like myself, there is no reason for me to have NFL Mobile on my phone. Removing that bloatware app does not remotely affect my operating system. In fact, it gives me more space and makes my system run faster. I should not have to jump through technological hoops just to use my own property efficiently and as I desire.

For third-party developers to bother to write applications that let us clean up our devices, however, code objects must not only be modular, but interoperable. Systems should be designed so that modules can be replaced, not just removed. To swap out modules, a module's inputs and outputs – the places where the module's code interfaces with the rest of the system – must accept standardized inputs and outputs. At the very least, the inputs and outputs must be discoverable by creators of other modules.

To discover the necessary inputs and outputs, third-party developers must often reverse-engineer code (often the system code) to find out what inputs and outputs it needs. Because interoperability is so important for networks to function, even the most restrictive statutes include exceptions for reverse-engineering code to create interoperability. Section 1201 of the Digital Millennium Copyright Act is a great example. Although it's generally not permitted to hack someone else's code to break into copyrighted content, it is permissible to do that if your goal is to build a product that does not copy, but instead works alongside – interoperates – with that code. But this permission is thwarted by court rulings that if even one employee of a third-party company agrees to the EULA, the entire company gives up the right to reverse-engineer as a matter of contract law.[89] A company seeking to create interoperable code must either require its employees to hack around the product EULA every time, or give up the company's rights to create code that works with the code of the target product.

This seems to be a fixable situation. First, courts could accept that clicking "I Agree" upon installation is a move without legal implications designed to permit the installer to reverse-engineer the code. Remember, under the DMCA, developers are permitted to hack intrusion countermeasures, including a EULA, for purposes of seeing how someone else's code works and to ensure interoperability. Clicking "I Agree" need not be an act with legal significance. It might be a purely technological act, just a way of getting into the software.

[89] *See Jung*, 422 F.3d at 639; *Bowers*, 320 F.3d at 1327.

Second, courts could take a broader look at the effect of locking third-party developers out of interoperable software. Preventing interoperability is one of the prime tools of companies seeking to lock in consumers. If a company wants to force users to use its word processing program, it could make its operating system incompatible with any other word processor. It's a transparent move to block consumers from going elsewhere. Once courts realize the anticompetitive effects of forcing developers to give up their right to create interoperable code, courts may take an approach more sophisticated than holding that when any employee clicks "I Agree," the entire company loses the right to develop interoperable – and competitive – code.

How to Get First-Party Developers to Help

It would be wonderful if the big designers and developers – the Googles, Apples, and Samsungs – did more to develop the state of the art for privacy-enhancing technologies. Thus far, efforts to get them to help have largely proven ineffective. Currently, one regulatory push in Washington, D.C., is toward asking developers to give consumers more information so that they can make informed choices. But consumers are already snowed under with information. Right now, "informed consent" is about as effective for consumers as pouring a teacup of water over the head of a drowning swimmer. A second regulatory push is for product manufacturers to design privacy directly into their products, a trend called "privacy-by-design." This could work – but only if regulatory agencies put teeth into it. A company that makes money from customers' data may have little incentive to give its customers tools to protect their data from the company itself. And even those companies that don't monetize consumer data directly have little incentive to pay to code safety measures into their products. In other words, the fox is marching around the henhouse.

How can we get companies to include basic safety technologies, like default encryption of devices or connections, in their products? The solution, I suspect, is to do it the same way we got companies to install seatbelts in cars, protective rails on walkways, and handguards on chainsaws. The basic formula was set out by the famous judge Billings Learned Hand in a case called *United States v. Carroll Towing*.[90] If the precaution costs less than the harm it would prevent, the company should use the precaution. Although consumers cannot use this standard directly against companies (because of arbitration agreements), a

----

[90] 159 F.2d 169 (2d Cir. 1947).

Carroll Towing- inspired analysis can help regulatory agencies develop a best-practices jurisprudence, so that wise protective measures and design decisions can spread from one context to another. This is consistent with the use of settlements by the FTC (and now FCC), in a manner similar to that of common law courts, to spread best practices from one part of the information economy to another.[91] The beauty of the standard is in its simplicity: if the protection measure is already on the market, then a company must use it. But, more than that, a *Carroll Towing*– style standard does not look solely to current industry practice to determine whether a given protection should be used. If a new precaution would be less costly than, say, a massive data breach, the new precaution should be used as well. *Carroll Towing* is a lasting case not merely because it establishes a clear baseline formula for adopting technological precautions, but because it uses the law to establish an always evolving and improving standard of precautions as the technology develops. That is why a 1947 case from a court of appeals remains famous.

Application of a cost-benefit safety analysis to design concerns is already part of the FTC's privacy jurisprudence. Consider the series of FTC settlements that developed and spread the obligation to protect consumers' data with encryption, pretty much the most basic best practice there is. Initially, the FTC said that it was "deceptive" under Section 5 of the Federal Trade Commission Act when a company promised to secure data, but didn't. Once those cases were a matter of course, the FTC changed tactics, asserting that it was "unfair" under Section 5 of the Act for companies not to use encryption for certain types of data.[92] In this way, the industry standard for encryption spread from premium practice to industry minimum, from something only a few careful companies did to something every responsible company needed to do. Interestingly, "unfairness" analysis under Section 5 is very much like *Carroll Towing*, just adapted for the regulatory context. The current FTC understanding of an "unfair" act or practice is one that causes injury that is (1) substantial; (2) not offset by greater benefits; and (3) unavoidable by consumers. There is plenty of daylight between the two standards, but the similarities are startling. If consumers can't avoid the problem, then the company is the cheapest cost

---

[91] *See* CHRIS JAY HOOFNAGLE, FEDERAL TRADE COMMISSION PRIVACY LAW AND POLICY (Cambridge 2016); Daniel Solove & Woodrow Hartzog, *The FTC and the New Common Law of Privacy*, 114 COLUM. L. REV. 583 (2014) (explaining "the mechanics of these settlement agreements and describe how and why they have come to function as a de facto body of common law").

[92] *See Privacy & Data Security Update, supra* note 91 ("In Wyndham Hotels and Resorts, the Third Circuit affirmed the FTC's authority to challenge unfair data security practices using its Section 5 authority.")

avoider and thus should bear the regulatory burden of determining whether to adopt a precaution. And then the technology is subject to the standard test: if the practice causes greater injury than offsetting benefits, it is unfair. If the cost-benefit balance goes the other way, it is not. It therefore seems likely that regulatory agencies will follow courts of earlier eras in adopting rules that help promote the spread of best practices, including development and deployment of data safety features, throughout data ecosystems.

Obviousness

In particular, some best practices already stand out as critical basic concepts for enabling consumers to control what they buy: (1) the operation of technology must be open and obvious to the user; (2) technological protection measures must be simple to use; and (3) the default rules matter. Consider open-ness and obviousness. Carrier IQ, Superfish, and Verizon supercookies have one thing in common. They were hidden deep in the system. Verizon claims it informed customers that it was attaching the digital equivalent of a tracking collar to them, but consumers in fact had no idea. This is but one of many examples of the practice of procuring political and legal cover by "disclosing" invasive activity buried deep in a long, vague, intentionally complicated, mandatory, and unavoidable privacy policy. The practice has got to stop.

In real life, we operate with an expectation of clear notice and appropriate context. Think about a FedEx delivery person, or political canvassers going door-to-door. The delivery person drives a clearly labeled vehicle (plus, we're the one who ordered the package). Perhaps the political canvassers are not particularly welcome, but we do not have the same reaction to them as we would to someone who snuck in our back door in the middle of the night. Even if, improbably, this early-morning guest were to have slipped a notice in the mailbox alongside the junk mail a day before, visitors dressed in black who sneak in at three o'clock in the morning do not receive a warm reception. That is the real-life equivalent of Verizon's and others' underhanded intrusion methods.

Best practices are emerging to make intrusive technology more obvious. A great example is smartphone geolocation capabilities. GPS is a killer app for smartphones – I can't live (or at least navigate!) without Google Maps – and a great value to the consumer. But it's also incredibly invasive. There are times I do not want my phone reporting my location to a bunch of advertisers. Few of us would be pleased to be inundated with advertisements for marriage advice books after visiting a therapist, for example.

That is why smartphone geolocation has become much more well-engineered from the user interface perspective. On most smartphones it is now easy to turn geolocation on and off. Websites and cell phones work together to offer geolocation in "just in time" fashion. A website on a browser will not simply take your geolocation information. The site asks for it as you enter the site, and you get the chance to say no.

Better yet, some geolocation implementations have an icon along the top of the phone indicating when geolocation is on. This is a user-friendly reminder that the device is currently gathering location data and passing it along to a large number of entities with a digital presence on the phone. This notice can be helpful – a user thinks, "Oh, GPS is on. I don't want that right now," and turns it off. It would be even better if GPS could learn over time, with a few well-placed just-in-time questions, when and where you would like it to operate. For example, I could do quite nicely with GPS turned off unless requested, or when on a long trip. Digital technology is capable of learning my mother's birthday even though neither she nor my father has ever stored that date in their phones (this happened just yesterday). Compared to that, designing GPS and other applications to be more perceptive of and responsive to owner inclinations should not be all that hard for a system to learn.

Simplicity

Concurrent with obviousness is the expectation that privacy-protective technologies be simple to use. This does not mean they have to be unsophisticated. True simplicity encapsulates and manages complexity, rather than avoiding it. Consider the difference between a well-designed graph and a long, unreadable table of numbers. Think about the polished interface of an iPhone. A tremendous amount of effort went into smoothing the interface between computer and human. That interface is capable of complicated interactions precisely because they have been made graphically simple.

Simplicity is poorly regulated because it is ostensibly hard to define. Court attempts to make certain disclosures more prominent or clear in privacy policies have just led to paragraphs of disclosures in all capital letters on the back page of some privacy policy: not a resounding success. We are learning a lot about simplicity, however. One way to define simplicity is a lack of intentional transaction costs. A more expansive definition might define simplicity as the lack of resistance to achieving a desired result. We might measure the intellectual resistance of privacy-enhancing technologies: how hard it is for a consumer to achieve her desired result. This is not particularly hard to determine. Regulatory agencies could test technology on consumers, determine the consumers' preferences, and then test the amount of time and energy it takes to achieve that result using different structures. That time and energy would be a reasonable measure of the resistance of the system. Under such a definition, simplicity – again, the lack of resistance to achieving desired results – is easy and relatively inexpensive to measure. This approach would permit regulatory agencies to foster simplicity best practices throughout the data economy.

Default

Representatives from Mozilla, the creator of the Firefox browser, spoke at a congressional hearing about adoption rates for privacy-enhancing technologies. Their subject was the Do Not Track flag, a way for consumers to express their desire to not have their web activity tracked. Do Not Track sets a simple flag in a user's outgoing web traffic that is easily read by the receiving server. If the Do Not Track flag equals 0, companies may track. If it equals 1, the customer has requested not to be tracked. (Companies claim users do not know what "do not track" means, and so ignore the signal.[93] If the FTC were to begin cracking down on this disregard for user preference, as I hope it will, it seems likely that companies would quickly grasp the meaning of this phrase.)

Mozilla found something interesting. If it enabled Do Not Track by default, nearly 90 percent of its customers used the flag. If it required users to find the setting and set it manually in their browser, less than 20 percent used it. When Microsoft released a new version of Explorer that set the flag by default during installation, ad companies went berserk, eventually reneging on their public promises to respect the flag. Some opponents of Microsoft's move went so far as to propose reprogramming the Apache servers that run a lot of web traffic to automatically refuse traffic from the new Microsoft browser, a pretty transparent attempt to punish Microsoft for making the do-not-track flag simple to use.

Whether or not you think companies should respect consumer requests not to be tracked, the Mozilla discussion of default rules was particularly powerful. Companies were not opposed to consumers having tools that let them manage their own data flow, but they were against making it easy for customers to use those tools. Ease of use, in this instance, was cultivated by programming the option as a default. Companies have long managed transaction costs for the tools they build so that they can appear to be in compliance with best practices while still getting the data. Consider Facebook, which offers many privacy protecting tools, but also makes them nearly impossible to understand or use.

[93] *See* Elise Ackerman, *Google and Facebook Ignore "Do Not Track" Requests, Claim They Confuse Consumers*, FORBES (Feb. 27, 2013, 7:58 PM), http://www.forbes.com/sites/eliseackerman/2013/02/27/big-internet-companies-struggle-over-proper-response-to-consumers-do-not-track-requests/#ac1139168596; Joshua A.T. Fairfield, *Do-Not-Track as Default*, 11 NW. J. TECH. & INTELL. PROP. 575, 614 (2013).

Consumers should be able to buy products that protect them as a default
setting. After Edward Snowden, rightly or wrongly, disclosed the degree to
which the U.S. intelligence community had compromised basic encryption
standards and had cut deals with service providers, manufacturers, and developers, many consumers started looking for a smartphone that would not leak
all of their data by design.[94] A number of companies rose to the challenge,
including the makers of the Blackphone.[95] Blackphone 2 offers chip-level
security, default settings that protect the consumer, and is preloaded with an
operating system and applications designed to protect consumer privacy.[96]
No one seriously argues that consumers should not be able to buy computing devices that protect data by default. Yet advertising companies are eager
to impose sanctions on companies that include privacy-protective settings by
default. This approach has terrible consequences for consumer protection.
Regulators should protect consumer rights by taking a close look at attempts to
lock privacy-protective measures out of the market. There is no need to man-
date default installation or use of protective technologies – all that is needed
is to ensure data-addicted companies cannot freeze these technologies out.

BREAKING FREE

Property rights should not be the sole province of large companies. The little
guys should own their small part too. To save ownership, we need to not only
limit the reach of intellectual property licenses and online contracts, but also
build a positive strong legal institution of digital and smart property ownership
for consumers. Companies should no longer be able to lie, to claim that they
are "selling" consumers digital assets when they are in fact just offering the
digital equivalent of renting. When consumers do buy, they need basic rights
to hack, sell, run, and ban. They need the right to hack in order to make
their property answer to them, not to the manufacturer. Owners need the
right to sell in order to free themselves from digital ecosystems, to take their
iBooks with them to a different reading application, or to cash out of one
system so that they can buy into another. Owners need the right to run in

---

[94] *See* Martyn Williams, *Encrypted Android Phone Is Only the Beginning for Blackphone and
Silent Circle*, PC WORLD (Feb. 24, 2014, 8:29 AM), http://www.pcworld.com/article/2101000/
blackphone-plans-more-secure-devices-bouyed-by-snowden-leaks.html ("[The founder] said
he's seen a recent uptick in interest in Silent Circle's products. He attributes that to the series
of leaks from former government security contractor Edward Snowden.").

[95] *See id.*

[96] *See* Michael Calore, *Review: Silent Circle Blackphone 2*, WIRED (Sept. 28, 2015, 1:00 AM),
http://www.wired.com/2015/09/review-blackphone-2/ (explaining the phone's advanced security features).

order to get the promised value out of their property. Not only should they be able to run the code they need on their device, but owners should also be able to stop manufacturers from forcing obsolescence and retroactively changing an owner's value proposition by limiting or restricting what the owner may do after the time of purchase. And finally, owners need both legal and technological help to ban the host of intruders on their own devices. Exclusion is the cornerstone of property law, and it should tell us something that of the traditional property rights, exclusion is the power consumers have least of in regard to their digital and smart property.

9

Owners or Owned?

When I explained the premise of this book to a colleague, he remarked: "Property is the oldest area of law there is. You can have property without contracts. But you can't have contracts without property." His view, and I think it is the right one, is that contracts (and licenses) represent arrangements to convey resources – houses, land, labor, bits, and bytes – from one party to another, but that those contracts have to have something to move: property. I responded that this was precisely the problem I was working on. Online, we have a world of contractual licenses, but no ownership interests changing hands. Online, we have contracts without property, obligation without possessions, a world where we owe but do not own.

Fixing property rights is a pragmatic necessity. We need them for markets to function – without property, markets have nothing to move. Despite the insistence of some economic theorists, markets alone cannot solve the property problem. The market is no magical fix. The invisible hand sometimes gropes blindly. In the case of digital and smart property, markets have failed for two related reasons. For one, property rights must be clear. The fuzzier the object of a market transaction, the costlier it becomes to move that resource through the market. Imagine buying a sweater, but the seller clings to one of the yarn ends so that the sweater unravels as you walk away. In the end, you have purchased nothing at all. The retention of trailing strings of rights complicates digital resource deals to the point that parties cannot know with confidence what is being bought or sold. These complications drive up transaction costs, since parties must spend time and frustration finding out what they can do if they buy an asset. This is related to the second reason that digital and smart property markets have failed. Markets rely on honest information about the nature of the rights conveyed. When companies are free to use dishonest language about buying and selling – when they are in fact selling nothing at all, or far less than the buyer expects – the market cannot function.

Digital rights are inextricably intertwined with ordinary property. Online and offline are no longer discrete spheres, and can no longer be governed effectively under radically different systems. One of many examples is found in the release of the augmented reality game Pokémon GO. The game assigns physical locations to Pokémon – cute and absurd digital animals – which players collect by going to the assigned spots. People are drawn to real places to collect imaginary animals, and their actions have very real and physical consequences. The game was hugely popular. Almost overnight, college kids, senior citizens, teenagers, and parents (and the occasional law professor, plus daughters) were walking through parks, along streets, hanging out at monuments, and trespassing through backyards. Traffic patterns were disrupted. Enterprising muggers started using the game to draw players to dark alleys. One failing ice cream store saw its business saved because it was located near several Pokéstops – locations where players can collect the items they need to catch internet critters.

Because the digital game impacts physical land, landowners have banded together in a class-action lawsuit, suing, among others, the creator of Pokémon GO, Niantic, for encouraging trespass onto their lands. The thrust of the lawsuit was that Niantic had ostensibly profited from the owners' lands. People pay to play the game; the purpose of the game is to catch animals; and the animals are located, via GPS, on the owners' properties. This is not to say Niantic should be liable: from its perspective, none of this is real. The game is an augmented layer of reality laid on top of the real one. The company itself has not trespassed on anyone's land, and has told players to be careful in about as many ways as it can.

What drew Niantic and property owners into conflict is a collision of digital and real worlds. Those worlds are no longer separate. The embedding of software into objects means software pervades everyday life. And the connection of digital databases to the real world – such as the one that says where that elusive Scyther is – means that we cannot afford to keep these systems separate. The world is no longer like oil and water, with the depths of property separated from a thin oil of software and contract rights. Rather, it has become more like milk in your coffee: mixed, indistinguishable, inseparable. Imagine Starbucks selling you a cup of coffee, but retaining ownership over the cream in it. It's just not a feasible model of property. We need to collapse these rights into a single thing – ownership – that bounds complexity, makes things simple, and gets us our morning caffeine fix without all this headache.

FREEDOM AND FEUDALISM

Property reform is not only a pragmatic necessity, but a political one. I have avoided political discussion in this book, primarily because property as a subject is so emotionally charged, and I want very much to draw in people across the political spectrum. But I believe property reform to be necessary in order to help ameliorate – not solve! – certain deep and growing problems. In particular, property is under attack from those at the top of the economic ladder who wish to use intellectual property law to concentrate all ownership in the hands of a few. This causes centralization and inequality. Conversely, at the bottom of the ladder are those (and their advocates) who – entirely justifiably – notice that property systems haven't done them much good, and therefore think we can dispense with the institution altogether. What good is property, they wonder, if the end result of that storied institution is that many people have nothing?

I do not pretend that digital property reform – or resurgence – will fix the problem of the haves and have-nots. At best, it is an adjustment between those who have bought digital and smart property and those who would like to sell it for full price but transfer few or no ownership rights. But within those constraints, I do think that property reform, particularly in the shape of taking disorganized, obscure, conflicting, and voluminous contractual rights and turning them into clear, defined property rights that consumers can buy and courts will recognize and enforce, will help move the power of ownership from the center to the edges, from manufacturers and software designers to individuals, families, and small businesses.

Property reform will have these positive effects because, I believe, traditional property rights still matter. Property helps us build our identity by exerting influence over our contexts. It permits us to act free of the restraint of others. And it enables society to maximize human welfare, in a sort of limited fashion, by permitting the free flow of resources between members of society with minimum friction. These are the identity, liberty, and welfare views of property that I have discussed throughout this book.

I have stated earlier, we can unify these three principles in service of a higher goal. Property rules must be measured with a human yardstick. The guiding principle, as expressed by Amartya Sen (in economics broadly) and Jedediah Purdy (with respect to property theory in particular), is that property rules should enable humans to do more. Property rules should expand the human range of options. When they don't, they should be reformed. Purdy terms this range of human options freedom. Sen calls it capability. What ultimately matters is whether a given ruleset expands or contracts the range of what humans can actually do.

Here we have a choice. Property rules can increase human potential, or reduce it. They can increase the number of viable options a human has, or cut off some potential paths.[1] My primary concern throughout this book has been that intellectual property and contract law, as they are currently used, serve to reduce the range of human options. I believe a resurgence of traditional property rules applied to digital and smart property could help increase the range of human possibilities by putting more power into ordinary owners' hands. I have tried to identify some rules that I think will increase human potential by pushing power over smart and digital property out of the centralized hands of intellectual property rightsholders and into the hands of consumers and individual owners.

We can draw a straight line – although it is not one often drawn – from Adam Smith, who sought property reform to free humans from economic slavery both literal and figurative, through Hernando de Soto, who attempted to bring marginalized property interests (and the property interests of the marginalized) into the mainstream, through Amartya Sen and Jedediah Purdy, who sought to maximize human potentiality, to Thomas Piketty, who is worried about wealth inequality. I want to plot the next point on that line. Digital wealth in our society is colossally centralized. Individual people own very little digital wealth. Individual owners' range of viable options with their smart and digital property is increasingly restricted. That has got to change. By naming digital and smart property for what they are, I want to transfer rights in those resources from the massive intellectual property rightsholding companies out to the periphery, to individual owners of individual devices. I want to increase each individual owner's range of viable options.

Shifting ownership from the center to the edges increases the range of human potentiality in two clear ways. First, it lets owners do things *to* their property: modify it, repair it, control it. Second, it lets owners do more *with* their smart or digital property: move it, store it permanently, back it up, use it on another device, sell it. An owner not locked to a specific e-book service can take her books with her on whatever device she wishes. An owner with an unlocked smartphone can go to the cheapest carrier. She may run the newest app on her phone regardless of whether the app provider has paid off the device manufacturer with a piece of the action.

A capabilities view of smart and digital property is a natural – indeed, inevitable – fit. Smart and digital property are our tools. Like all tools, their

---

[1] Jedediah Purdy, *A Freedom-Promoting Approach to Property: A Renewed Tradition for New Debates*, 72 U. Chi. L. Rev. 1237, 1243–44 (2005).

purpose is to extend human capacity to accomplish things. Our tools let us do more. How do I get to the wedding on time? Google Maps. How do I write a book, coordinating with research assistants and editors in multiple countries, while traveling to academic conferences and the odd family vacation? Google Docs. These tools increase the range of human potential. Controls on these tools reduce the range of human potential. Securing our interests in our tools is a direct means to expanding the range of human potentiality.

Enabling us to do more *to* and *with* our property is worth quite a bit of efficiency loss. If property interests are slightly more chaotic in the hands of individuals than they are in the hands of intellectual property industries, so be it. I would rather have productive chaos than sterile efficiency. If the price of letting individuals hack and experiment with the devices they use to help run their lives is some extra coordination and standard-setting to handle the flowering of many different formats and device configurations, good. That is healthy diversity, and a sign of a growing technological ecosystem. Pushing property out from a sterile center to a fertile fringe will place legal rights where they will do the most good, and enable people to make the most of their resources and tools.[2]

Pushing property from the center out to the edges, where it can do the most good for the most people, will require challenging the feudal model of property ownership. We should systematically choose freedom instead of feudalism. We should choose to measure property with the yardstick of potentiality. And perhaps most importantly, we should reject the idea of freedom as an abstract principle, and recognize that freedoms need resources and tools to become possibilities. I am not free to travel if I have no car. I am not free to speak if I have no internet connection. The freedom to starve is no freedom at all, but coercion of the deepest sort.

RESTORING INTELLECTUAL PROPERTY

What about intellectual property rightsholders? I believe a revival of traditional property will be good for them, too. Here we need to distinguish between motives. Many companies do not *want* to monitor their customers' every move, to build and maintain expensive defensive DRM systems, and to incur the negative publicity of suing their customer base. They do it because they feel they have to do so to stop piracy. That's a legitimate concern, even if they are using the wrong tools to do it. There are other companies, though, that have misused

---

[2] JONATHAN ZITTRAIN, THE FUTURE OF THE INTERNET AND HOW TO STOP IT (Yale University Press 2008).

the anti-piracy powers they have under copyright law to lock consumers out of their property, to lock them into buying only from the company, and to seize control of aftermarkets and secondary markets, such as the market for used goods. The distinction between these two motives is important, because ownership rights are entirely consistent with – even complementary to – the interests of legitimate rightsholders. Honest purchasers are, by definition, not pirates. Indeed, piracy hurts owners' interests as much as it does that of rightsholders. By bringing intellectual property back into alignment with traditional property, we can restore the natural alliance between property owners and intellectual property rightsholders.

Restricting ownership has very little to do with stopping illegal copying. In fact, much of what is now called piracy and hacking is driven not by a desire to get illegal copies for free, but by the desire to exercise control over one's own purchases. For example, during the DRM music wars when music was locked to one player, my friends would purchase a song legally, then download it illegally so they could play it on any device. They felt a moral obligation to pay for music, and a deep indignation that they could not do what they wished with what they purchased. By depriving owners of any stake in a product, rightsholders have set themselves at odds with purchasers.

Rather than make enemies of owners, rightsholders could make them allies. True owners care about what happens to their property. One way you can damage property is by diluting its value, by making more copies. The owner of a dollar naturally opposes counterfeiting. The owner of a rare baseball card opposes technology that could make a million fake copies. The owner of a special item in a massively multiplayer game would oppose cheats and hacks that give everyone a copy of the now not-so-special item. An owner of a bitcoin opposes hacking the blockchain – in fact, as I have discussed, a major reason the blockchain is so secure is that only a person with majority ownership of the assets on the chain (51 percent, for example) could falsify and therefore destroy it. On the other hand, consumers with no ownership stake have no reason to oppose dupes, hacks, cracks, rips, or other methods of illegally duplicating intellectual property. On the contrary, they have every reason to develop, spread, and use such methods, since they own nothing anyway.

More broadly, intellectual property law has drifted from its moorings. Its intended purpose was to promote innovation and productivity. Intellectual property rights were supposed to permit creators to create freely, to permit others to build on cultural and scientific accomplishments. And property was one of the systems that permitted intellectual property creators to secure the benefits of their inventions and creations without limiting the creative power of others. I can buy a painting, the painter receives reward for her work, and

I can place the painting where I wish. Today, intellectual property rules may well still spur some creativity, but mostly they consist of what people *cannot* do with what they buy, rather than what they *can* do. Our neo-feudal system of property centralization and control is enabled primarily through copyright license restrictions.

Intellectual property and traditional property rights have long been complementary. Take things at the simplest level. An artist's rights in her painting are important. But to eat, she must sell the painting to someone else, and that person wants a property interest in it. Imagine, though, that she lived in a society with intellectual property rights but no traditional property rights. No one would buy the painting. They might pay a few cents to look at it, but that would restrict art to museums or galleries. Much of what people do with art – use it to shape a room or home, to enrich their living context – would vanish. Creators need good property rights to sell, as well as intellectual property rights to license. Taking property rights out of the picture for the digital artist or band that distributes its MP3s online reduces the artists' inventory. Ultimately, intellectual property is lost without its partner, traditional property.

Thus, by freeing traditional property we strengthen intellectual property as well. We return it to its rightful place as an engine of innovation and creativity. Rights in intellectual property are not the enemy. I do not propose that "information wants to be free," or that intellectual property rights should be disestablished. Rather, I think that the failure – so far – to develop good digital property rules has caused intellectual property to devour itself from within. Let's fix that.

As for the illegitimate use of intellectual property powers to seize aftermarkets and lock in consumers, there I have less sympathy. Companies have been able to have their cake and eat it too. They are still permitted to use language of "buy" and "sell" in consumer transactions, even though their license agreements state that they aren't selling anything. This dishonesty permits them to charge the same prices for e-books that they do for physical books, while actually conveying far fewer rights to the buyer. As long as dishonest language is permitted in online sales, we should not expect companies to care about offering true property rights to consumers. But I am hopeful that if we held companies to their representations, at least some of them would switch to selling things straight up.

There have been many failed attempts to prune back intellectual property. Part of the problem is industry lobbying. But another big part is conceptual. It is hard to stop a legal system from spreading into nearby empty conceptual space. If we have no traditional property rights online, then intellectual property will spread to fill the gap. Law, like nature, abhors a vacuum. A court asked to resolve a novel question of technology law will grope for the nearest tool.

The solution is not just to move the tool of intellectual property further away from the judge's groping hand, but to nudge the tool of traditional property closer. The solution is not just to pare back intellectual property overreach, but to foster growth of theories of actual old-fashioned ownership interests in intangible property of all sorts. And it is not enough just to remark that law has always had categories of intangible property. We need to develop a freestanding theory of information-based property. It should be made as easy as possible for judges and policymakers to realize that one can own a bit-coin as well as a dollar, an e-book as well as a textbook, an internet domain name as well as a plot of land. We can do that by adding increasingly compli-cated tweaks to current property theory, or by trying to kick off a true shift in how we view all property. In the long run, I think the latter will do the most good.

CONCLUDING WORDS

Property is a looking glass. We look into it and we see ourselves, our vision for what it means to cooperate, to achieve, and to share and apportion resources. One danger, though, is that we might see in others' views of property a dark reflection, a caricature. This person is a right-wing economist, that one a copyleft libertarian, the third a progressive free-market socialist.

My hope is that we use the idea of property to unite, rather than divide. Most people feel instinctively connected to the resources that they command, whether the purpose of that command is to secure a life for themselves, to help others, to create distance between themselves and others, or to draw others closer in cooperative endeavor. Property represents our power to control our environment. The extension of property principles to digital assets is therefore inevitable, as long as we seek to control our environments. It doesn't matter whether our environments are physical, virtual, or an augmented reality hybrid. As long as individual self-determination remains a human demand, the idea of property will exert a powerful draw on the human imagination.

That is not to say we can't make our lives complicated. We can make property complex and costly by attempting to make a sort of pseudo-property out of networks of online contracts, kind of like the way you both own and don't own your e-books and Google Play purchases. I don't see much value in doing that, though. It introduces complexity for complexity's sake. The primary effect of those innovations is to make buyers insecure in their purchases, and to undermine the value of digital assets.

I have painted a scary picture of potential futures, but let me end on a note of optimism. There will be protests, but I firmly believe we will win. Industry lobbyists will complain and buy lawmakers, and they may do a lot of damage along the way, but they will eventually lose. I believe that the idea, the emotion, the story of private property is too strong for the companies to resist. Where humans care deeply, the law must follow, or lose legitimacy. So I predict confidently that the laws that corrode property interests will fall, across the broad warp and weft of the law. The Stored Communications Act, which permits snooping on email that has been "abandoned" by storage in the cloud, will be rewritten. DMCA 1201, which lets companies lock owners out of their own property, will be reworked. Cell phones will be unlocked. Car enthusiasts will be free to tinker. Farmers will have the right to repair their tractors. The FTC will bring actions against abusive manufacturers of Internet of Things devices. Courts will recognize that stealing Bitcoin is theft.

If the law doesn't give us the right to do what we wish with what is ours, we will take it back. What is legally right isn't necessarily morally right. If our smartphones lock us out, we have every moral right to hack them and take control back. If our smart homes are spying on us, we have every moral right to do whatever needs to be done to stop the spying. If our e-books are locked to a service that might just go away, we have every moral right to hack them and put them in a format we can keep. Look at the music wars: companies locked their music up with DRM, sued their customers, sought damaging legislation in Congress. They won every battle, but they lost the war. People wanted to do as they wished with their own music, to be able to play it on any device, to take it wherever they wished. They modified their computers to make that happen, and the music industry realized it had to change or wither. That fight was just a microcosm of the coming fights about a vast range of digital resources. And the outcomes will be the same. It is just a matter of time.

Index